KT-470-143

DUBLIN
and Surroundings

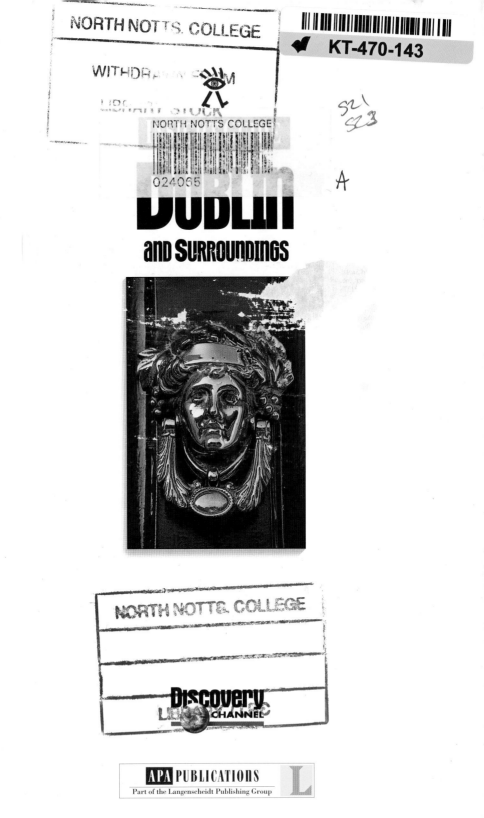

Discovery CHANNEL

APA PUBLICATIONS
Part of the Langenscheidt Publishing Group

ABOUT THIS BOOK

Editorial

Project Editor
Brian Bell
Contributing Editor
Liam McAuley
Updated by
Donna Dailey

Distribution

UK & Ireland
GeoCenter International Ltd
The Viables Centre, Harrow Way
Basingstoke, Hants RG22 4BJ
Fax: (44) 1256-817988

United States
Langenscheidt Publishers, Inc.
46-35 54th Road, Maspeth, NY 11378
Fax: (718) 784-0640

Canada
Prologue Inc.
1650 Lionel Bertrand Blvd., Boisbriand
Québec, Canada J7H 1N7
Tel: (450) 434-0306. Fax: (450) 434-2627

Worldwide
Apa Publications GmbH & Co.
Verlag KG (Singapore branch)
38 Joo Koon Road, Singapore 628990
Tel: (65) 6865-1600. Fax: (65) 6861-6438

Printing

Insight Print Services (Pte) Ltd
38 Joo Koon Road, Singapore 628990
Tel: (65) 6865-1600. Fax: (65) 6861-6438

©2002 Apa Publications GmbH & Co.
Verlag KG (Singapore branch)
All Rights Reserved

First Edition 1989
Second Edition 1999
Updated 2002

This guidebook combines the
interests and enthusiasms of
two of the world's best known
information providers: Insight
Guides, whose titles have set the
standard for visual travel guides
since 1970, and Discovery Channel, the world's premier source of
nonfiction television programming.

Insight Guides' editors provide
practical advice and general
understanding about a place's history, culture, institutions and people. Discovery Channel and its
web site, www. discovery.com,
help millions of viewers
explore their world from
the comfort of home
and encourage them
to explore it firsthand.

How to use this book
This book is carefully structured
both to convey an understanding
of the city and its culture, and to
guide readers efficiently through
its sights and activities:

◆ To understand Dublin today,
you need to know something of
its past. The first part of the
book covers the city's history
and culture in lively essays written by specialists.

◆ The main Places section provides a full run-down of all the
attractions worth seeing.

◆ The Travel Tips listings
are a convenient point
of reference for infor-
mation on travel,
hotels, restaurants,

THE
IRISH
WHISKEY
CORNER

sion, so much the better since Ireland is the world's leading manufacturer of illusions.

But the information in this book is far from illusory, having been provided by people who live and work in Dublin. The principal writer, **Liam McAuley**, who produced the Places section, is an editor with the *Irish Times*. and the fact-filled Travel Tips section was written by **Anna Coogan**, who works for the *Evening Herald*. The food chapter came from **Liz Ryan**, restaurant critic of the *Evening Herald* and a novelist. The chapter on pubs drew on years of research by **Eugene McEldowney**, a senior editor with the *Irish Times* and also a novelist. The "Birth of the Celtic Tiger" chapter, analysing the issues confronting the city today came from **Frank McDonald**, a respected journalist and author who has campaigned effectively on crucial environmental issues. The chapter on contemporary music was written by **Brian Boyd**, one of Dublin's top music journalists, and the insightful review of Dublin's writers was penned by **Charles Hunter**. The chapter on Glasnevin Cemetery was written by **Gavin McEldowney**.

The history chapters build on the authoritative work in the first edition of this book by **Peter Somerville-Large**, a Dubliner of Anglo-Irish stock whose book *Dublin* is a standard reference work. Text by **Deirdre Purcell**, **Noel McFarlane**, **Lorna Siggins** and **Seamus Martin** has also migrated to this edition.

Most of the pictures are by **Tom Kelly**, a leading Dublin photographer, and **Geray Sweeney**, who is based in Belfast.

shops and festivals. Information may be located quickly by using the index on the back cover flap – and the flaps also serve as handy bookmarks.

◆ Photographs are chosen not only to illustrate geography and buildings but also to convey the many moods of the city and the everyday lives of its people.

The contributors

This edition has been edited by Insight Guides' editorial director, **Brian Bell**. Having grown up in Northern Ireland, he believes that he can combine his partisan affection for the Republic's capital with an outsider's dispassionate eye. If that is an illu-

Map Legend

▬ ▪ ▬	International Boundary
▬ ▬ ▬	County Boundary
⊖	Border Crossing
▬ ▬ ▬	Ferry Route
✈ ✈	Airport: International/ Regional
🚌	Bus Station
P	Parking
❶	Tourist Information
✉	Post Office
╪ † ╪	Church / Ruins
†	Monastery
☾	Mosque
✡	Synagogue
◢ ⌂	Castle / Ruins
∴	Archaeological Site
∩	Cave
⚊	Statue/Monument
★	Place of Interest

The main places of interest in the Places section are co-ordinated by number with a full-colour map (e.g. ❶), and a symbol at the top of every right-hand page tells you where to find the map.

CONTENTS

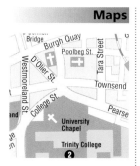

Celebrating
Bloomsday
(see page 86)

Travel Tips

Information panels

Insight on ...

Places

THE ALLURE OF DUBLIN

Ireland's capital is back in fashion, having revived its old role as a European city. But just what is its appeal?

There is a wonderfully comic moment in Sean O'Casey's play *Juno and the Paycock* when Captain Boyle, a one-time canal bargee who likes to pretend he was actually a sea-going skipper, talks about sitting on the deck of his (imaginary) ship in some far-flung corner of the oceans and gazing in awe and wonder at the heavens: "What *is* the stars?", he ponders. "What *is* the stars?" It is with something of the same dazed bafflement that Dubliners contemplate their native city. For what *is* Dublin? What indeed?

Of course, as any gazetteer will tell you, Dublin is the capital city of Ireland, a town of more than a million people, a seaport at the mouth of the river Liffey, a centre of government, commerce and industry, a place of great cultural and historical interest. Guidebooks will describe its superb natural setting on a wide plain overlooked by hills and headlands and facing a broad, sweeping bay. They will tell of its fine 18th-century architecture, its quizzical, loquacious, resilient people.

But are you really much the wiser? Admittedly, you could say the same of any city on earth, but the damnable thing about Dublin is that you could live there all your life and still be unable satisfactorily to sum up the city (though if you became anything of a Dubliner in the process you'd expend plenty of words in the attempt).

Singing pubs

Many great men have tried. As the birthplace of Jonathan Swift, Oscar Wilde, W. B. Yeats, James Joyce, George Bernard Shaw, Samuel Beckett and many other great writers, Dublin has been written about more than any city of its size in the world. Often its writers have disparaged their birthplace. "My sentimental regard for Ireland does not include the capital," said Shaw, with characteristic *hauteur.*

Joyce, too, was often less than complimentary, yet Dublin provided him with the setting for all his books, even though he spent nearly his entire adult life abroad. He once claimed that, if the city were destroyed, it could be rebuilt brick by brick from his description in *Ulysses.* But in his last book, *Finnegans Wake,* he found the English language could not contain the place, so he invented a language of his own, calling the city by more than 200 different names: *Dobbelin, Durlbin, Dambaling, Doubtlynn, Drooplin, troublin, Annapolis, riverpool, bubblin, Durblana, Hurdleberry Fenn, Publin...* (You can understand at least that last one.) Who knows what he would have done had he lived to write another book?

Visitors come to Dublin with many different expectations and most of them find these hopes fulfilled. Americans expect to be charmed by the chat and the blarney, and they are. Germans expect a city of nat-

PRECEDING PAGES: detail from the O'Connell Monument, O'Connell Street; the Parnell Monument, also in O'Connell Street; St Patrick's Day parade outside the Bank of Ireland; classic Georgian doorways. **LEFT:** perfectly poured pints of Guinness.

ural non-conformists, a happy contrast to the order and ultra-efficiency of home, and they are not disappointed. Scandinavians expect "singing pubs", and some pubs sing. The English sometimes seem bemused that they are not in charge any more, but they are reassured by signs of fecklessness and amused to find pre-World War I British pillarboxes still in use (though now painted green).

You may see the city as a shrine of Irish nationalism; as the world capital of talk; as the gateway to the lovely Irish landscape; as a city full of churches, priests and nuns; as a (somewhat despoiled) monument to 18th-century architecture; as the setting for the great works of Joyce; as the home of the Abbey Theatre; or as a great place for a pub crawl. As the writer Ulick O'Connor remarked: "Dublin to an alcoholic is like a girls' gymnasium to a sex maniac. Its atmosphere generates a drinking mood."

Yes, Dublin is all these things and more, and every visitor should try to find his or her own Dublin. But it is not a place that you should take too seriously, for it finds it hard to be entirely serious about itself. An example of this trait was the decision to celebrate the city's "millennium" in 1988, even though the Viking settlement of *Dyflin* was established not in 988, but in 841. The excuse for the event was that in 988, according to a reliable medieval annalist, the Irish King Mael Sechnaill II captured the Viking town and imposed a tax on its population. As the annalist puts it, "he captures the town and makes it Irish". So far, so good – or at least not so bad. But then a present-day annalist pointed out that his medieval counterpart had given dates incorrectly (by one year) up to 1014, so that the events given for 988 actually happened in 989. To all of this, the general Dublin response was: "Who cares? Okay, we might be 147 years late in celebrating our millennium, but why not have the party now?"

Blighted capital

Not that the approval was universal. One critic dismissed the millennium as an *ad hoc* anniversary "invented to give the Dubs something to shout about, an anniversary prompted more by rivalry with Cork, which recently celebrated its 800th birthday, than by any fact of history; a celebration. designed to raise the spirits of the inhabitants of a blighted capital whose problems won't be solved by a lick or two of paint."

If this remark had been delivered in suitably caustic tones to a gathering in one of the city's hostelries (as, indeed, it may have been before being committed to print), its author would have raised a cheer from like-minded listeners. Equally, he would have drawn from his opponents the charge of "begrudgery" (ungenerous carping, jealousy). This is a word you will hear often in Dublin if you stay long enough, as begrudgery is a time-honoured Dublin habit. So, too, is cheering in pubs.

Within this book you will discover many other aspects of Dublin: its history, its writers, its eccentrics, its street life, its talk, its pubs, its religion, its music, its great buildings, its sights and sounds. But you will not discover your own Dublin; that you will have to find for yourself.

You may succeed or fail, but you should enjoy the attempt. And when it is time to leave, you can ask yourself the question: "What *is* Dublin?" Answers on a postcard, please. ❏

RIGHT: Dublin is a haven for antiques hunters.

AN UNTIDY ELEGANCE

Much of the city's Georgian grandeur was destroyed by developers, but big efforts are now being made to restore the remaining masterpieces

The Civics Institute of Ireland lovingly set out the capital's potential in an exhaustive *Dublin Civic Survey*, published in 1925: "Dublin is a city of magnificent possibilities – not even inferior to Paris – placed astride a fine river, geographically well situated, and generally of great beauty and interest. It is in the centre of one of the finest bays in Europe, giving its inhabitants ready access to the sea, hemmed in by vast stretches of fertile land and picturesque hills."

It was a beguiling picture, but the survey's authors readily admitted that the magnificent possibilities had not been realised: "In the past Dublin has been compared to an apple that has bloomed, then withered, and finally decayed at the core. Dublin of today presents to the visitor a lamentable picture! It has assumed during the last half century an artificial centre in the Sackville (O'Connell) Street area, too far eastward, and too near the dock district, causing an abandonment of the true geographical centre... There is no segregation of buildings of one class into certain suitable areas, or what is called 'zoning'. There is no control over the frontage design of buildings, except in a small portion of the city, known as the 'destroyed area' since the political troubles of 1916 and 1922... Street advertisements run riot in Dublin, and destroy the appearance both of streets and buildings... The housing of the working classes for the most part is provided by the use of old Georgian mansions, which have not been properly converted to such use."

The search for civic spirit

The catalogue of dismaying inadequacies continued, followed by a prescient comment about what the future might hold: "The importance of a civic ideal – whereby all units essential to city life may co-operate and advance in an orderly manner – is not yet realised by the mass of our citizens. Within the past few years, the population of the capital has been augmented by a dis-

proportionately large rural element. This accretion cannot be expected to possess advanced civic ideals, for its notions are naturally primitive. Furthermore, it can think only in a narrow commercial sphere; with the lure of city life it becomes undisciplined. Critics of progress maintain that Dublin must ever lack the seething

population that other capitals possess; that it must ever lack extensive trade and industry; and that its people will always lack the civic spirit."

The ruthless property development of the 1960s and '70s, which destroyed more of Dublin's architectural heritage than the Easter Rising and the civil war combined, was one sign of this triumph of commercialism over civic pride. Some blamed the country's lack of a strong visual sense – it's easier to name 20 Irish writers than five Irish painters – but others put it down to simple greed. In recent years, though, the city's prosperity has funded the cleaning up of many shabby corners and the restoration of some of its Georgian splendour.

LEFT: classic Georgian frontages in Fitzwilliam Square.
RIGHT: James Gandon's great Custom House.

The making of a city

Dublin is essentially an 18th-century creation. The city's Viking founders built only in wood and no structures remain from that period. From the Anglo-Norman era there are two splendid relics – the cathedrals of Christ Church and St Patrick, both heavily restored over the centuries – and a few fragments, such as St Audoen's Church and sections of Dublin Castle. Stone was imported from Britain to build churches, which were designed in Early English Gothic style instead of Irish Romanesque.

Little building was done in the 15th and 16th centuries, and the one great remnant of the 17th

The city's architectural fabric expanded at an astonishing rate, with elegant streets and squares sprouting up on both sides of the Liffey – to the north around Mountjoy and Rutland (now Parnell) squares, and Sackville (now O'Connell) Street; to the south around St Stephen's Green, Merrion and Fitzwilliam squares. Many of the houses in these grand terraces boasted opulent interiors, with lavishly decorated ceilings. Enlightened town planning ensured that they were given space to breathe: the Wide Streets Commissioners were established in 1756 to supervise "Making Wide and Convenient Streets".

But Dublin's real distinction among Georgian

century is the classically foursquare Royal Hospital at Kilmainham, to the west of the city.

The medieval town only really became a city after the 1690 victory of the Protestant William III over the Catholic James II at the Battle of the Boyne. This struggle was part of a much wider European power-play, but in Dublin it had the effect of bringing a new security and confidence to the Anglo-Irish Ascendancy, the descendants of the English settlers who had been given Irish land by the English Crown (see pages 36–37).

In the next century, the city's population, which had been 60,000 in 1700, trebled to 180,000, making Dublin the second largest city of the British Empire.

WHAT IS GEORGIAN ARCHITECTURE?

The term is a loose one, encompassing various styles prevalent in Britain between the accession of George I in 1714 and the death of George IV in 1830. Georgian taste, reacting against the ornately baroque, favoured a return to the classical styles of Greece and Rome.

The Anglo-Irish (see pages 36–37) brought Georgian architecture to Dublin, creating whole squares of uniform, symmetrical townhouses, with classical pillars, pedimented doors and windows, and graceful mouldings. The harmoniously proportioned rooms were perfect for Thomas Chippendale's elegant furniture and Thomas Gainsborough's formal paintings.

cities is that its 18th-century terraces are complemented by splendid public buildings of the same period: the Custom House, Four Courts and King's Inns (all designed by the era's greatest architect, James Gandon, 1743–1820), City Hall, the Bank of Ireland, Leinster House, and most of Trinity College.

The north–south split

Dublin is divided by the River Liffey and the rivalry that exists between Northsiders and Southsiders goes back centuries. Dublin Castle, the centre of British power, was on the south side, as were the two cathedrals (both

economic decline; many of the prosperous Anglo-Irish moved to England and over the next century many of their fine houses, especially north of the Liffey, became crowded slum tenements for the city's teeming poor. The middle classes fled, establishing Victorian suburbs.

Severe damage to the city centre's fabric was inflicted by the conflicts of the 1916 Rising and the civil war of 1921–22 (*see pages 46–47*). Conservation was a minor issue in subsequent decades as the new Republic sought to establish itself economically, and there was in any case a lack of political willpower to spend scarce resources on preserving the symbols of colo-

Protestant despite the Catholic affiliation of most Dubliners. But the building of the grandest Georgian houses on the north side began to shift the balance of fashion in the 18th century. The trend was reversed by the Earl of Kildare, who built a palace (now Leinster House, home of Ireland's parliament) in Molesworth fields on the south side. Asked why he had chosen the wrong end of town, he supposedly replied: "Wherever I go, fashion will follow me."

The 1800 Act of Union which abolished Ireland's parliament doomed the country to a long

ABOVE: a panorama of Dublin in 1890 shows how dominant churches were in the low-rise city.

nialism. By the time the country finally enjoyed a measure of prosperity in the 1960s and 1970s, uncontrolled property development led to entire streetscapes being replaced with office blocks.

In more recent times, however, the state-sponsored regeneration of Temple Bar, the refurbishment of North Great George's Street by enthusiastic residents, and the restoration of great showpieces such as the Royal Hospital Kilmainham and the Custom House tell a different tale. To some extent, the increasing importance of tourism has given a spur to the new preservationists, but a more compelling motivation is a genuine new-found pride among Dubliners in their city's great architectural heritage. ❑

Decisive Dates

250 BC Celtic people – who first arrived in Ireland sometime in the previous century – settle at the mouth of the River Liffey. Their village later becomes known as *Ath Cliath* (The Ford of the Hurdles).

450 AD St Patrick, who arrived in Ireland in 432 to convert it to Christianity, visits Dublin, according to legend, and baptises people in St Patrick's Well (now in the grounds of St Patrick's Cathedral).

837 The first Viking fleet sails up the Liffey.

841 The Vikings establish a fortified raiding base which grows into a port and trading post. For almost

11 centuries, Dublin will be under foreign control.

1014 Brian Ború, High King of Ireland, defeats the Norsemen at Clontarf, north of Dublin, ending Viking expansion in Ireland. He is killed in the battle.

1170 A force of Anglo-Normans, who invaded the previous year at Waterford, captures Dublin.

1172 England's King Henry II visits the city and grants it to "my men of Bristol". Christ Church Cathedral is built on the site of an earlier Viking-Irish church.

1191 St Patrick's Cathedral is founded.

1204 Building of Dublin Castle begins. It will be the stronghold of English rule until Independence.

1347 The Black Death kills perhaps 4,000 Dubliners, about one in three.

1537 King Henry VIII, now self-appointed head of the Church of England, orders the dissolution of the Irish monasteries. In 1541 he takes the title "King of Ireland".

1592 Queen Elizabeth I founds Trinity College on the site of the Priory of All Hallows.

1607 Hugh O'Neill, Earl of Tyrone, and Rory O'Donnell, Earl of Tyrconnell, whose attempt to stop the English conquest of Ulster ended with their defeat in 1601 at the Battle of Kinsale, escape to the Continent along with many other Gaelic chieftains. This is known as the Flight of the Earls. Their lands are handed over to English and Scottish settlers.

1649–52 Oliver Cromwell suppresses Ireland's Catholics, who supported King Charles I in the English Civil War. Vast tracts of land are seized – their owners being told to get "to Hell or to Connacht" – and given to Cromwellian troops in lieu of pay.

1685 James II, a Catholic, succeeds his brother, Charles II, on the English throne.

1688 William of Orange, a Dutch Protestant prince, seizes the English throne. James II lands in Ireland and rallies his Catholic supporters.

1690 King James flees through Dublin after William defeats him at the Battle of the Boyne. When he accuses his "cowardly Irish soldiers" of running away, Lady Tyrconnell retorts: "It appears that Your Majesty has won the race."

1692 The Irish Parliament excludes Catholics and passes harsh anti-Catholic measures (Penal Laws).

1710 The Mansion House, still the official residence of Dublin's Lord Mayor, is built.

1713 Jonathan Swift becomes dean of St Patrick's Cathedral.

1734 A woman called Molly Malone is buried in St John's Churchyard; she is believed to be the fishmonger celebrated in Dublin's most famous song ("Alive, alive-oh...")..

1742 Handel's *Messiah* oratorio receives its first performance in the Musick Hall, Fishamble Street.

1759 Arthur Guinness opens his brewery at St James's Gate.

1781 Building of the Custom House begins. James Gandon's other masterpiece, the Four Courts, is begun in 1785.

1782 Ireland is granted legislative independence in "Grattan's Parliament". The composer John Field, creator of the nocturne, is born.

1798 The United Irishmen's rebellion is nipped in the bud in Dublin by the arrest of Lord Edward Fitz-Gerald, who dies of wounds received. The rebel leader Wolfe Tone is captured and taken to Dublin, where he escapes execution by committing suicide.

1800 By the Act of Union, the Irish Parliament, persuaded by bribery, dissolves itself and the United Kingdom of Great Britain and Ireland is formed.
1803 Robert Emmet, a Protestant doctor's son, attempts a rebellion. He is hanged after delivering a ringing speech from the dock.
1823 The barrister Daniel O'Connell founds the Catholic Association to campaign for the right of Catholics to become Members of Parliament.
1829 Britain grants O'Connell's demands.
1841 O'Connell, 66, becomes Dublin's Lord Mayor.
1843 O'Connell calls "monster meetings" to demand repeal of the Act of Union.
1847 With the Great Famine at its height, soup kitchens are set up around Dublin.
1867 Members of the Irish Republican Brotherhood (Fenians) attempt rebellion in five counties, including Dublin.
1875 Charles Stewart Parnell is elected as MP for Meath; he becomes leader of the Home Rule movement and "uncrowned king of Ireland".
1886 First Irish Home Rule Bill is rejected by Britain.
1889 Captain William O'Shea files for divorce from his wife Kitty, citing Parnell as co-respondent. Parnell is ruined by the scandal; he dies a year later.
1893 Second Home Rule Bill is defeated.
1904 The Abbey Theatre is founded.
1912 Third Home Rule Bill is passed by Britain. Ulster Protestants, led by Edward Carson, threaten armed revolt if they are governed from Dublin.
1916 The Easter Rising. Activists seize public buildings in Dublin and proclaim a republic, but are defeated after a week of fierce fighting. The city centre is ruined by British artillery. The Rising is initially unpopular, but the execution of 15 rebel leaders arouses public sympathy and support.
1919 The first Dáil Eireann (Irish Republican Parliament) meets in Dublin's Mansion House, adopts a provisional constitution and elects Eamon de Valera as its president.
1919–21 The Irish Volunteers, now known as the Irish Republican Army (IRA), wage guerrilla war against the British army.
1920 The Government of Ireland Act provides for separate parliaments in the North and South.
1921 In the Anglo-Irish Treaty, signed in London, 26 counties become a Free State with dominion status within the British Commonwealth, but six counties in the North remain part of the United Kingdom.
1922 The Dáil approves the Treaty, but a minority of

Republicans, led by de Valera, reject it. As the Four Courts is occupied by the IRA and bombarded by troops of the new Free State, Ireland's official public records go up in smoke. The civil war lasts for two years. James Joyce's masterpiece *Ulysses*, about a day in the life of Dublin, is published in Paris.
1923 W. B. Yeats wins the Nobel Prize for Literature.
1925 George Bernard Shaw wins it too.
1927 Eamon de Valera enters the Dáil as leader of a new party, Fianna Fáil ("Soldiers of Destiny").
1932 Fianna Fáil wins general election and de Valera becomes *Taoiseach* (prime minister), a position he is to hold for 16 years.
1937 Under the terms of a new constitution, the

Irish Free State officially becomes "Eire".
1939–45 Eire remains neutral in World War II.
1949 The Republic of Ireland is established.
1973 Ireland becomes a member of the EEC.
1974 Ulster loyalist terrorists set off bombs in central Dublin, killing 25 people.
1988 Dublin celebrates its millennium – historically dubious but a boost to the city's self-confidence.
1995 The introduction of divorce in Ireland is narrowly approved in a referendum.
2000 A new Millennium pedestrian bridge is built across the Liffey.
2002 Ireland adopts the euro as its currency. The Spire of Dublin is erected on O'Connell Street, and work starts on a new plaza in front of the GPO. ❏

PRECEDING PAGES: mural at the Setanta Centre.
LEFT: ancient dagger hilt. **RIGHT:** Dublin's crest.

BEGINNINGS

The Vikings created the town but were subjugated by the Normans.
Then Henry VIII declared himself King of Ireland and a new subjugation began

Dublin Bay was settled by humans more than 5,000 years ago, first by Mesolithic shore dwellers, then by Neolithic communities. After Christianity came to Ireland, churches, hermit cells and monastic foundations were soon scattered across the land.

But it wasn't until the coming of the Vikings that Dublin had its start as a town: in 841, a group of Norwegian seafarers brought their flat-bottomed longships up onto a sandy beach in one of the few sheltered harbours in the east coast. Then, as now, the promontory of Howth to the north and the Wicklow hills to the south curved round an area made marshy by the shallow tidal river, Liffey, and its tributaries.

The meaning of Dublin

Near the mouth of the river Poddle was a pre-Viking structure built on piles of stones named *Ath Cliath* (the Hurdle Ford). At the point where the Poddle met the Liffey, a black pool (or *dubh-linn*) emerged. Here, beside a number of well-established Gaelic churches and monastic settlements, the newcomers built a stockade along a ridge covered with hazelwood. They were forced to flee for a time, but other Norse groups reinvaded until, on a cold Wednesday in December 919, victory at the Battle of Dublin resulted in the permanent presence of the "blond demons" in eastern Ireland. Despite persistent opposition from the Irish and defeat at the decisive Battle of Clontarf in 1014, they stayed.

After the normal pattern of Viking expansion, the Norsemen created a flourishing trading colony once they gained a permanent foothold. The rich agricultural territory was exploited, contact with other Norse colonies was maintained, and the men of Dublin became merchants and craftsmen, while continuing to be raiders.

Excavations have produced evidence of their skills at shipbuilding, tanning, weaving, comb-making and bronze work. As they brought few women from Scandinavia, they married Irish

women over the years. These intermarriages encouraged the fusion of Gaelic and Norse culture – the Norse language took on a mainly Irish syntax, while in the years following the baptism of King Sitric in 925, the Vikings abandoned the old Norse gods and became Christian.

In 1170, the prosperous little Hiberno-Norse

town was overwhelmed by an aggressive and resourceful force of Norman warriors led by Strongbow, who had come to Ireland at the invitation of Dermot MacMurrough, King of Leinster. Their conquest was legitimised the following year through a charter granted by Henry II of England. This opened the way for many new immigrants from all over the southwest of England and Wales. Most of the immigrants, however, came from Bristol.

The newcomers were great builders: amid friction and rivalry, the two cathedrals of Christ Church and St Patrick rose within a few years, together with other churches in tiny crowded parishes like St Audoen's. Dublin Castle – part

LEFT: an intricately carved Celtic cross.
RIGHT: Tara brooch from the 8th century.

garrison, part administrative office, part prison – dominated the scene, its brooding walls a reminder to the Irish of the conqueror's presence.

The walled town, guarded on the southern side by the Liffey – the water-highway to England and the Continent – expanded its administration by introducing bailiffs, a sheriff's court, a mint and a "loyal and discrete Mayor". The powerful Merchant's Guild, together with the 10 encircling religious houses, controlled the wealth.

At the height of the Anglo-Norman development there were around 8,000 people in Dublin. According to the bones and garbage excavated from their middens, they lived well, eating shell-

fish, salt beef, mutton and large quantities of pork. They imported luxuries like spices, figs, raisins, walnuts and a good deal of wine.

The town strove to keep Gaelic Irishmen out of civic life, banning them from the guilds and excluding them from civil or clerical office. But the outsiders continued to trickle in, seeking sanctuary from famine, war and servitude, and the population, especially the poor, became mixed, much as it had been in Viking times.

The decline of Norman rule began with the havoc of Edward Bruce's invasion of 1317, when most of the suburbs were burned. Dublin was constantly threatened by unfriendly Wicklow septs, safe in their forest-covered hills, while the territory of the conquerors was reduced to a wavering ribbon of land along the east coast known as the Pale. The Black Death had a particularly destructive effect on the little empire where numbers were important. While elsewhere in Ireland the Normans had become almost totally Hibernicised, in Dublin a sense of isolation increased as officialdom clung to English ways and the English language.

Further subjugation

Unrest in the late Middle Ages culminated in Silken Thomas's rebellion in 1534. Its brutal suppression began a new era of conquest. Henry VIII's self-proclamation as King of Ireland as well as of England in 1536 brought the Reformation to Dublin: there, the dissolution of the monasteries was briskly implemented as their lands were sold or acquired by Henry's supporters. The campaign of subjugation of Gaelic Ireland gave the town renewed importance as it became the main base for English operations. A new wave of immigrants flowed in – soldiers, adventurers, administrators, lawyers and men of learning like Edmund Spenser who brought in a cultural awareness of the Renaissance.

The founding of Trinity College on the confiscated land which had belonged to the Priory of All Hallows, given by King Henry to the citizens of Dublin as a reward for their loyalty, marked the climax of the Reformation programme. At its outset, the ultimately futile aim of this "counterblast to Popery" was to convert the Irish to Protestantism. ❏

THE EARLY IRISH CHARACTER

Although the Romans did not try to conquer Ireland – the road system might be better if they had – Roman historian, Diodorus Siculus, described in the 1st century BC one of the races which settled in Ireland: "Physically the Celts are terrifying in appearance, with deep-sounding and very harsh voices. In conversation they use few words and speak in riddles, for the most part hinting at things and leaving a great deal to be understood. They frequently exaggerate with the aim of extolling themselves and diminishing the status of others. They are boasters and threateners and given to bombastic self-dramatisation and yet they are quick of mind and with good natural ability for learning."

LEFT: monument to the ancient warrior Strongbow in Christ Church Cathedral. **RIGHT:** a page from the 9th-century *Book of Kells*, preserved in Trinity College.

RULE FROM LONDON

Swift wrote, Handel composed, and Gandon designed his noble buildings.

It was Dublin's golden age – unless, that is, you were Catholic

The dissent and turmoil that developed during the first part of the 17th century arose from the grievances of different sections of society. The old Irish, the bulk of the population, were in disarray following the defeat of the Irish chieftains by the army of Elizabeth I at the Battle of Kinsale in 1601. As well as continuing the work of her father, Henry VIII, in trying to impose the Reformation on the country, Elizabeth also wanted to protect England's right flank against an invasion from her main opponent, Spain.

The Anglo-Irish families who had been part of Irish life for centuries, now known as *Sean-Ghaill* or Old English, in general clung to Catholicism, especially as the Counter-Reformation gained strength. Since they found themselves unable to accept the Act of Supremacy, which placed power firmly in London, all important legal and official appointments went to the *Nua-Ghaill* or New English, who had poured into Ireland to benefit from the conquests.

Period of crisis

A general atmosphere of intolerance, highlighted by the reluctance of Charles I, who reigned from 1625 to 1649, to implement the "Graces" – concessions that dropped recusancy fines and eased barriers to inheritance and office holding – welded this stratum of society with the native Irish. The stage was set for strife.

In 1633, Thomas Wentworth, later Earl of Strafford, became Lord Deputy. He devoted much of his seven-year autocratic term of office to reform and tried to make Dublin a beautiful and fashionable capital. It was during this time that the city had its first theatre. But Strafford's rule coincided with a period of crisis: his efforts were destroyed by war and his life ended on the scaffold.

During the conflict between King Charles and his parliament, Ireland was used as a pawn. In Dublin, as elsewhere in Ireland, old English and native Irish united in revolt against injustices, confiscations, favour shown to newcomers and exclusion from civil rights. In varying confrontations between Parliamentarians, Royalists, Government, Confederate and Irish forces, Dublin was largely wrecked by the long war whose financial burden it bore.

In the early years of conflict, the city was swollen with numerous Protestant refugees fleeing the uprising of 1641 when Catholics in Ulster, hoping to recover their confiscated lands, rebelled at Portadown and massacred large numbers of Protestants. Later, although it was the only major town in Ireland to escape capture, Dublin suffered immense damage and became miserably depopulated, the decrease in numbers speeded by an outbreak of plague which was said to have

---

LEFT: James, Duke of Ormond, whose support for England's Charles II won him lands in Ireland.
RIGHT: ancient stocks in Christ Church Cathedral.

claimed 1,300 lives a week. At least half the houses were pulled down or fell into ruin.

During the years of the Commonwealth, the period from 1649 to 1660 when England's monarchy was replaced by the Protectorate presided over by Oliver Cromwell, Dublin made a remarkably swift recovery from the devastation of the war. But it needed the Restoration of the monarchy for its flowering as a capital city. The Duke of Ormonde, his varied military career behind him, arrived in July 1662, and

CURSE OF CROMWELL

Oliver Cromwell's 20,000 Ironside troops suppressed rebellion by devastating the Irish countryside. By 1652 a third of the Catholic Irish had been slaughtered.

elsewhere in the city, attracting the first of Dublin's notoriously rowdy audiences.

When King James II succeeded his brother, Charles II, in 1685, Ormonde was recalled to be replaced by the Catholic Earl of Tyrconnell. The cause of religion was to bring the renewed rumble of war. James II, himself a Catholic, raised hopes by introducing an Act of Parliament that would have ousted the Protestant settlers in Ireland. But, before it could be put into practice, the English Establishment called in a Dutch

was greeted with universal rejoicing. During his long rule as Lord Deputy, he brought into fruition Strafford's ideas and set in motion an ambitious planning and building programme. While much of the old city wall was pulled down, a new network of streets made a setting for handsome public buildings like the Royal Hospital and the Blew Coat School.

Trade, particularly in linen and wool, was encouraged and there was an atmosphere of sustained prosperity. Literary and cultural life gained impetus as booksellers and newspapers sought readers, the Dublin Philosophical Society was founded, and the theatre, extinguished by the war, returned to Smock Alley and then

prince, the Protestant William of Orange who was married to James's daughter Mary, to put a stop to James's "Popish ways".

Persecution intensifies

James came to Dublin, where the citizens welcomed him with the usual bells and bonfires. But a long summer's day brought another twist in history. On the evening of 12 July 1690, Dubliners watched their city filling up with exhausted soldiers fleeing the Battle of the Boyne (*see page 228*), at which William decisively defeated James.

From that day, Roman Catholics became a persecuted majority in Ireland. The Treaty of

Limerick put an end to the ideas of toleration that Ormonde had fostered. In College Green, a pretty equestrian statue of King William III which over the years would be perpetually daubed, defaced or decorated with orange lilies, proved a potent symbol of oppression as Catholics were prohibited from entering Parliament, and the Penal Laws, modelled on laws enacted against Huguenots in France, were grimly observed.

As the Protestant historian W. E. H. Lecky put it: "many who would never have sought ascendancy if it had not been established, wished the preserve the privileges they had inherited, and

One of the most delightful buildings of this period is Marsh's Library (*see page 165*), commissioned by Archbishop Narcissus Marsh and designed by William Robinson, architect of the Royal Hospital. The library faces the brick walls of the Deanery where Marsh's enemy, Jonathan Swift, endured "wretched Dublin in miserable Ireland".

Swift and Handel

Dublin-born Swift returned reluctantly from England in 1713 to his appointment as Dean of St Patrick's and gradually came to terms with his native city, where his passionate partisan-

the most worthless Protestant, if he had nothing else to boast of, at least found it pleasing to think that he was a member of a dominant race." By the middle of the 18th century, only 7 percent of land was in Catholic hands.

With the disruption of war and subsequent blows to the economy, Dublin's development faltered, although there were some changes. Now familiar landmarks appeared: the Mansion House and the Custom House on the quays, and Parliament House on College Green.

ship of the ragged poor who surrounded his cathedral made him loved by his fellow citizens (*see page 162*). His intellect, his bitter humour, his massive literary output and his magnificent attacks on the wrongs of Ireland are reasons for considering him the greatest Dubliner of them all – but the city's destitute knew him best for his charities, both practical and personal. The author of *Gulliver's Travels* and the *Drapier Letters* went about with his pockets full of coins for the needy:

Power was never in his thought
And wealth he valued not a groat.

Swift was in the late stages of his terrible illness when Handel arrived. On 13 April

FAR LEFT: Jonathan Swift, who became dean of St Patrick's in 1713. **LEFT:** detail from the pulpit of St Werburgh's Church. **ABOVE:** Marsh's Library.

1742, the composer conducted to great acclaim the most important musical event in the city's history. The melodious shouts of "Halleluia!" ringing through the white and gold Music Hall in Fishamble Street heralded Dublin's golden era. The Age of Reason, when order and rationality were on the ascendant, was reflected in the capital by an exhilarating period of development.

A golden age

During the years of elegant expansion, architects touched with genius – Richard Cassels, Thomas Ivory, James Gandon and many others – enriched the city with noble buildings like the Royal Exchange, the Four Courts and the west front of Trinity. Powerful noblemen commissioned town houses such as Charlemont House, Belvedere House, Leinster House and Powerscourt House, all iced with the beautiful plasterwork that proclaimed the wealth and ostentation of their owners. The fashionable worshipped in classical churches, while hospitals were built, such as Swift's hospital for the mad and Bartholomew Mosse's lovely lying-in hospital topped with a golden cradle, whose graceful proportions may have had the purpose of hastening the healing process.

WOLFE TONE AND THE UNITED IRISHMEN

The guiding spirit behind the Society of United Irishmen was a Dublin Protestant, Theobald Wolfe Tone (1763–98), a graduate of Trinity College who sought to apply the French Revolution's ideals of liberty, equality and fraternity to Ireland's persecuted Catholics. In his twenties, he proposed to Britain's prime minister, William Pitt, a plan to establish a British colony in the South Seas. Pitt ignored it and Tone turned his energies to law and politics.

Something of an idealist, Tone believed that only if Protestants and Catholics united could Ireland prosper, and he made a special effort to preach that message in Belfast. The United Irishmen began as a debating group to further the cause, but soon contemplated armed rebellion. Tone,

who had been thinking of settling down in Pennsylvania as a farmer, was persuaded to sail instead to France and rally support against Britain. But a French battle fleet of 43 ships was lashed by a storm off the coast of Ireland in December 1796 and the invasion was aborted.

Pitt banned the United Irishmen and many of its leaders were arrested. This lack of leadership fatally weakened the Great Rebellion of May 1798. In six weeks of fighting, perhaps 50,000 died. Soliciting further support from Napoleon Bonaparte, Tone landed in Donegal with another party later that year, but was captured. He died in prison after an attempted suicide, but his martyrdom was assured. His grave in Bodenstown, near Dublin, is a place of pilgrimage.

Craftsmen did their work under patronage, and Irish furniture, silver and glass achieved a superb quality. It was the extra age of bucks, dandies, duellers, rakes, spendthrifts and scholars. The Parliament of Henry Grattan contributed an independent and liberal oratory.

The Anglo-Irish society that for the most part created and benefited from this golden age formed only part of the community. Although a Catholic middle class was developing and many Catho-

MASSIVE CORRUPTION

A rhyme summed up how many saw the vote for union with Britain:
How did they pass the Union?
By perjury and fraud;
By slaves who sold their land for gold
As Judas sold his God.

Dublin's experience of the events of 1798 was largely a reflection of the failure of revolution. The suppression of insurrection provoked the British prime minister, William Pitt, into proposing full union between Britain and Ireland, which would mean abolishing Ireland's 300-seat Parliament in Dublin and creating 100 seats for Irish representatives in the Imperial Parliament in London. The citizens rioted as the Bill made its progress through Parliament House on College

lics prospered, there was an increasing threat of violent response to injustice as their aspirations continued to be denied.

The groundwork for conflict been laid by the failure of the Irish Volunteers movement to bring about parliamentary reform and allow Catholics political franchise. The United Irishmen, inspired by the idealist patriot Wolfe Tone, brought together those seeking reform (*see panel on facing page*), but in 1794, the government outlawed the movement, driving it underground. By 1797, revolt was inevitable.

Green. But there were those, promised Catholic Emancipation, who saw it as a hopeful development. Others were persuaded.

Parliament abolishes itself

Irish leaders who wavered found themselves offered peerages, offices of state, and generous bribes. It worked: an initial majority of five against the union was turned into a majority of 46 voting for it. On 1 January 1801, the Act of Union became law and the Union Jack flew above Bedford Tower in Dublin Castle. Pitt called it a "voluntary association" within the Empire. In reality it was an ill-judged marriage that was to cause untold suffering. ❑

LEFT: Capel Street in 1800, painted by James Malton.
ABOVE: the Custom House, also by Malton (1766–1803).

The Anglo-Irish

The term "Anglo-Irish" often causes confusion. It can refer to Irish literature in the English language, or to political relations between Britain and Ireland (as in the Anglo-Irish Agreement). But it also describes the people who once dominated Dublin society and who left the city much of its most impressive architecture.

They were and are the descendants of waves of immigrants – Elizabethan adventurers, Cromwellian soldiers, Huguenot refugees,

associates of rich colonists pledged to settle vast tracts of land, or tradesmen like the Yorkshire linen merchant Jervis Yeats, one of whose descendants became Ireland's greatest poet. It often comes as a surprise to people outside Ireland to discover that they were not all landed gentry, but included small farmers, shopkeepers and businessmen as well, whose automatic sense of superiority was based on one simple fact: they were not Roman Catholic. There is a germ of truth in the playwright Brendan Behan's jibe that an Anglo-Irishman was "a Protestant on a horse".

Oddly enough, the idea of Ireland as a single, independent nation first took root among the Anglo-Irish, whose power grew from the dispossession of an earlier wave of settlers from Britain, the "Old English". These were the descendants of the early Norman invaders, who married the natives and adopted Gaelic ways, becoming, in a famous phrase, "more Irish than the Irish themselves".

Those who remained distinct from the Gaels because of their continued allegiance to the English crown were destroyed by the Reformation – they found they could not cling to their Catholic faith and remain loyal subjects of the sovereign. Like the Gaelic Irish, they were dispossessed and defeated as Protestantism became the factor determining power and wealth. Through confiscation and plantation under Queen Elizabeth I, King James I and Oliver Cromwell, the Protestants seized and retained power until one Lord Chief Justice felt able to declare that "the law does not presume any such person to exist as an Irish Roman Catholic."

Status and style

The victory of the Protestant King William over the Catholic James II at the Battle of the Boyne in 1690 confirmed their position of strength. In the century that followed, these "New English" reached a peak of prosperity as new methods of agriculture made their large farms more productive. As a result, the city of Dublin became second only to London within the British Isles in terms of wealth, status and style. In its 18th-century "golden age", its Protestant Ascendancy enjoyed a social life that was both decorous and dissipated, oblivious of the putrid, overcrowded slums and the sufferings of the poor. Great public buildings and private houses were built; theatres, concert halls and gambling dens were thriving; drinking, dandyism and duelling were rife.

Since Reformation days, the "New English" had seen themselves as Irish. When their sun was at its highest in the short-lived Irish Parliament (1782–1800) – legislatively independent but subject to the English Crown – Henry Grattan and his contemporaries strove to create an Irish nation, albeit a Protestant one. Another Protestant patriot, Wolfe Tone, thought differently: inspired by the ideals of the French Revolution, he formed the United Irishmen to try to win full independence from Britain, with equality for all Irishmen, regardless of class or religion. Instead, his failed revolt prompted the English to abolish Ireland's parliament.

The tenant as serf

In the 19th century, politics centred on the land question. Elsewhere in Europe, too, land was in the possession of a small, privileged group. But in Ireland, memories of conquest together with the religious divide widened the gulf between wealthy Anglo-Irish landlords and their miserably poor tenant farmers, whose every penny went on paying exorbitant rents to middlemen in a pathetic and often doomed attempt to stave off eviction and starvation.

that agrarian agitation against the sins of property owners should become linked with the drive for an independent nation. And it was an Anglo-Irishman, Charles Stewart Parnell, who led the great campaign.

The landlord has been transformed into an ogre and has vanished into legend. At least he had vitality. Today the role of the Anglo-Irishman is merely ornamental. He is a relic of a picturesque past; he can recite great Anglo-Irish names like a mantra: Berkeley the philosopher; Swift and Goldsmith the writers; Grattan and Burke, the parliamentarians... His people are vanishing, much as the "Old English" faded

As the century wore on and power began to ebb away from the landlords, there were those who continued to treat their tenants like serfs, such as Sir Charles Domville, who prided himself on running his huge estate as "a tight ship": "I require every labourer to keep his Clothes clean and well-mended and to wear Laced Boots with Gaiters to his knee. His whole time being mine, he is not to leave home without permission." It was inevitable

LEFT: Adam Loftus, a Yorkshireman, was first provost of Trinity College, and helped lay the foundations of the Ascendancy. **ABOVE:** Powerscourt, in County Wicklow, was one of the grandest English-built mansions.

away, but there are enough of them left for politicians to point to as proof of society's tolerance. They have eschewed politics and take no part in the ruling process, but they still find comfortable niches in business, law and medicine. Their final surge of distinction, the turn-of-the-century literary renaissance led by the poet William Butler Yeats and Lady Gregory, is well in the past. Apart from the playwright Samuel Beckett, who chose to live in Paris, the Anglo-Irish have contributed little to literature since Yeats was buried under Ben Bulben.

We are not a petty people, wrote Yeats. But, as history unfolds, it seems that the Anglo-Irish have finally become one. ❑

THE FIGHT FOR FREEDOM

It took more than a century to put an end to the Union, but the first consequence
of independence was a civil war that left the centre of Dublin in ruins

The Union changed Dublin, almost overnight, from a vibrant capital to a dismal provincial city. The economic effects of the wholesale exodus of a wealthy society were all too obvious as trade stagnated, crafts declined to the point of extinction, and the empty houses of departed aristocrats became schools and lodging houses.

As the slump took effect, Dublin was shaken by an abortive rebellion led by Robert Emmet, who attempted to seize Dublin Castle in July 1803. Emmet, son of a Protestant doctor, may have been an incompetent revolutionary, but his passionate speech at the trial that condemned him to death earned him a permanent niche in the patriotic pantheon: "Let no man write my epitaph... When my country takes her place among the nations of the earth, then, and not till then, let my epitaph be written."

New landmarks

By 1820, Dublin's economic decline had been aggravated further by the ending of the Napoleonic wars. However, there were signs of progress as the century advanced. The middle classes began to move from the centre of the city out to locations north and south of the canals. Gas lighting was introduced and in 1832, the railway between Dublin and Kingstown opened the way to new suburbs. New landmarks appeared such as the General Post Office which a century later would become a national shrine. Nearly opposite it, loyal citizens erected the Nelson Pillar, a monument to an English hero who had nothing whatsoever to do with Ireland.

In 1815, St Mary's Pro-Cathedral was built in an unworthy setting in Marlborough Street, pushed out of sight by Protestant opposition. By 1829 – the year of Catholic Emancipation which secured the right of

Catholics to sit as MPs in the English House of Commons without having to take the Oath of Supremacy – Catholics formed over 70 percent of Dublin's population. Emancipation owed much to the efforts of Daniel O'Connell, the first Catholic MP of modern times (*see page 40*). Ten years later, following

the Municipal Corporation Act of 1840 which ensured for the first time that municipal officials were elected by ratepayers, he became Dublin's first Catholic Lord Mayor.

Slums and squalor

Overcrowded squalid slums had long been a feature of Dublin and during the 19th century the misery increased. Fever hospitals opened to take in the victims of frequent typhus epidemics. There was no plumbing or regular water supply. Drunkenness was encouraged by scores of distilleries and breweries, and Donnybrook Fair, an annual festival established by Royal Charter in 1204,

---

LEFT: Sackville Street (now O'Connell Street) in the 18th century; Nelson's pillar was destroyed in 1966.
RIGHT: Daniel O'Connell, known as "the Liberator".

had become a ragged frenzy of debauchery. It was ended in 1855, but not before the English language acquired the word "donnybrook", meaning an uproar or free-for-all. Beggars swarmed: one visitor reported being stopped 87 times between Baggot Street and Dorset Street. Another observer wrote that Dublin was a place of "lamentable contrasts", with the well-to-do living near "a picture of ruin, disease, poverty, filth and wretchedness."

In 1838, workhouses were introduced under the Irish Poor Relief Act with the intention of filling them with clean, adequately fed, grateful paupers. These unpopular institutions were generally filled well below capacity. But in the winter of 1846, after the potato crop failed, thousands of destitute country people crowded into the city. Soon the workhouses were overflowing and had to close their doors to the starving, who resorted to outdoor relief and the notorious soup kitchens. Typhus and cholera brought further devastation.

Poor solution

In 1848 – while the famine still raged – there was the sputtering of a Young Irelanders' rebellion in Kilkenny, easily suppressed, fol-

WHY DANIEL O'CONNELL'S NAME LIVES ON

O'Connell Street, the O'Connell Bridge, the O'Connell Monument… in the centre of Dublin there's no escaping the name of the man once dubbed "the uncrowned king of Ireland".

Daniel O'Connell (1775–1847) was a Catholic lawyer from a well-off Kerry family. Like many of his contemporaries, he had been educated in France and the ideals of the French Revolution had entered his thinking. He wanted no revolution in Ireland, though, not even a separation from the British Crown. What he campaigned for, with powerful oratory, was the right of Catholics to become Members of Parliament. Soon landlords were alarmed by the success of O'Connell's Catholic Association, particularly when its leader, standing for parliament in 1828 as a "Man of the People", won overwhelmingly. A Catholic Emancipation Bill was passed and O'Connell was dubbed "The Liberator".

O'Connell began to rally support for a repeal of the union. When his appeals struck few chords in parliament, he held monster rallies all over Ireland. In 1844 he was jailed for three months on a charge of seditious conspiracy.

In 1845 the Great Famine intervened. A million people died, more than a million emigrated, and a third of the land changed hands. The new landlords, many Catholic, proved as harsh as the old ones and O'Connell's non-violent nationalism was eclipsed by young radicals prepared to threaten the use of violence. O'Connell, his dreams and his health shattered, died in Sardinia at the age of 71.

lowed by a visit by Queen Victoria which, contrary to expectations, was a success. The Nelson Pillar was illuminated with electric light and crowds cheered wherever she went. The contrast between rebellion and loyalty and the presence of great numbers of British soldiers in what continued to be a garrison were characteristic of 19th-century Dublin.

In 1868, the Irish Republican Brotherhood, allied to the Fenians (formed 10 years previously in Dublin and New York), planned

WORDS, NOT ACTION

A patriot, seeing another revolt fail, declared: "God knows, if eloquence could free or save a people, we ought to be the freest and safest people on the face of the globe."

of a Protestant Wicklow landowner, he entered Parliament at the age of 29 as Member for Meath. His success in bringing cohesion to the obstructionist methods of supporters of Home Rule was followed by his campaign as president of the Land League. This aimed to prevent poor farmers from being rack-rented and evicted, and ultimately to win them ownership of their farms. The slogan "the land of Ireland for the people of Ireland" welded nationalist opinion. Later the thrust of his

another rebellion. Though another failure, it roused the conscience of William Gladstone, the British prime minister, who thereafter strove to bring about Home Rule for Ireland.

Parnell's power

In O'Connell Street, Charles Stewart Parnell is commemorated by a bronze statue standing before an obelisk stamped with a golden harp and a rousing message. The son

LEFT: sampling hops at the Guinness brewery in 1905.
ABOVE: influential politician Charles Stewart Parnell.
ABOVE RIGHT: a satirical view of the influences being brought to bear on the poet and politician W. B. Yeats.

politics switched from agrarian disruption to constitutionalism.

Parnell had inspired the tactic of ostracising anyone who took over an evicted farmer's land. It was used to such effect against a notorious Captain Boycott in Co. Mayo that his surname entered the English language – "moral Coventry", Parnell called it. Ironically, it was an uproar over the morality of his own life that destroyed his career, after he had survived a term of imprisonment and an attempt to implicate him in the Phoenix Park murders of 1882. When his long-standing liaison with a married woman, Kitty O'Shea, became public knowledge, his party split bitterly, and Parnell was rejected as leader. He died soon after in 1891, aged 45. A crowd of about 200,000 people packed Dublin for his funeral.

The poet W. B. Yeats claimed that disillusion in Irish politics following Parnell's downfall stimulated "the modern literature of Ireland and indeed all that stir of thought which prepared for the Anglo-Irish war". Certainly, the political malaise following the failure of the Home Rule Bill in 1892 coincided with a remarkable literary renaissance spearheaded by Yeats; its roll-call of dazzling talent also included George Moore,

A cultural nationalism

After the example of the Gaelic Athletic Association founded in 1885 by Michael Cusack (the model for the chauvinist citizen in *Ulysses),* Douglas Hyde, a Gaelic scholar who would become Ireland's first president, co-founded the Gaelic League to help preserve Irish as a spoken language. A great success, the League had 600 branches by 1908.

The collective expression of cultural nationalism known as "Irish-Ireland" supported the campaigns of different groups seeking political independence. Sinn Féin – meaning "Ourselves" – inspired by Arthur

George Russell, James Stephens, Lady Gregory and John Millington Synge. The Abbey Theatre, founded in 1904, helped to revitalise the national consciousness with the reworking of old legends and the highlighting of a heroic peasantry. These astonishing achievements in literature and theatre were accomplished by Yeats and his associates in little more than a decade.

Another literary colossus, James Joyce, who concentrated his genius on describing a summer's day in Dublin in *Ulysses*, rejected any political creed, scorned the exuberance of the Gaelic revival and, like Wilde and Shaw, spent his adult life abroad.

Griffith, a young printer, proposed that Irish members should boycott Parliament in London and aim at a return to the old constitutional position of Grattan's parliament. The revival of the Irish Republican Brotherhood (IRB) was due largely to the inspiration of Thomas Clarke, a militant Fenian imprisoned for his activities; he returned from exile in America to open a tobacco shop in Parnell Street which became a centre for republican activity. In 1913, two adherents of the IRB, Bulmer Hobson and Sean MacDermott, established the Irish Volunteers, which became the Irish Republican Army in 1916.

Meanwhile the socialist, James Larkin,

reorganised casual labour and founded the Irish Transport and General Workers Union. His opposition to capital exploitation culminated in a full-scale lock-out in 1913; the resultant riots, rallies and baton charges had one far-reaching result in the formation of the Irish Citizen's Army as a worker's defence force by Larkin and a Scottish-born socialist named James Connolly.

Patrick Pearse, a founder member of the Irish Volunteers, was inducted into the IRB soon after. The son of a Londoner who had a monumental stone works in what is now known as Pearse Street, he was "an unsmiling

The Easter Rising, plotted by a Secret Military Council of the Irish Republican Brotherhood and intended for Easter Sunday, 1916, was deferred for a day because of a series of mishaps which confined the fighting to Dublin. On Monday 24 April, 1,558 Volunteers led by Pearse, and 224 men of Connolly's Citizen's Army seized 14 key Dublin buildings, including the Four Courts, a mill and a biscuit factory. The General Post Office, its windows stuffed with mailbags, became the rebel headquarters; from its steps Pearse read out a historic proclamation: "Irishmen and Irishwomen; In the name of

enthusiast with mesmeric eyes", according to one observer. Pearse's mystical belief in the purifying shedding of blood was shared by many at the beginning of the European war.

The Easter Rising

In 1914, John Redmond, leader of the Irish Parliamentary Party at Westminster, secured the promise of Home Rule in return for Irish support in the war against Germany. However, militant republicans had other plans.

God and of the dead generations from which she receives her old tradition of nationhood, Ireland, through us, summons her children to her flag and strikes for her freedom."

It took 20,000 British troops, devastating artillery bombardments, and six days' bitter fighting, before the rebels surrendered. The death toll was 64 rebels, 134 police and soldiers, and more than 220 civilians. The city centre was ruined.

At this point, popular feeling was against the rebels for the devastation they had caused, but then the British obligingly fulfilled Pearse's desire for martyrdom: only by a blood sacrifice, he believed, could the spirit

LEFT: two architects of the 1916 Easter Rising, James Connolly (far left) and Patrick Pearse.
ABOVE: troops hold a Dublin street against the rebels.

of the nation be stirred to triumphant revolt. Between 3 and 12 May, to mounting public sympathy and outrage, 15 rebel leaders were shot by firing squad. As one Anglo-Irish lady said, it was like "watching a stream of blood coming from beneath a closed door."

Reaction to the executions, together with the threat of conscription, encouraged the revival of Sinn Féin in 1917 and its overwhelming electoral success the following year when more than half its candidates were in jail. The first Dáil Eireann was convened in January 1919 at the same time that violence broke out with the killing of two police constables in Tipperary by Irish Volunteers.

Guerrilla warfare was fanned by the authorities' policy of reprisals, which encouraged popular support for the republicans. Dublin's share in this war of attrition included the events of "Bloody Sunday", 21 November 1921, when the killing of 11 British intelligence agents by Michael Collins's Special Intelligence Unit provoked revenge at a Gaelic football match at Croke Park: soldiers fired into the crowd, killing 12.

Pressure from English and world opinion led to a truce on 1 July 1921. Eamon de Valera, who had defended Boland's Mills during the Easter Rising and was now President of Dáil Eireann, turned down Lloyd George's proposals, but accredited five members of his government, led by Arthur Griffith and Michael Collins, to negotiate a treaty in London. The result was an agreement to create an Irish Free State with the constitutional status in the British Empire of a dominion, such as Canada. But crucially, six counties in the northeast of Ireland, where Unionists were in a majority and had armed themselves heavily to resist becoming part of a united Ireland, were to be retained within the United Kingdom.

Civil war breaks out

In a bitter debate at the Dáil, the Treaty was carried by 64 votes to 57. But intransigent republicans, led by de Valera, rejected compromise and called for complete independence. Civil war broke out in June 1922 – even before the formal transfer to power to the new state at Dublin Castle – and lasted 11 months, subjecting the centre of Dublin to further bombardments. In one, a fire at the Four Courts destroyed the Public Record Office and historic documents, deeds and titles dating back to Henry II were lost.

The Free State government, in its first six months, executed 77 republicans. Its first prime minister, Arthur Griffith, collapsed and died, worn out by the struggle. The Free State forces eventually won the war, but the fighting and executions left a legacy of bitterness that lasted for decades. ❑

MICHAEL COLLINS

When Irish film director Neil Jordan needed a hero for his 1996 Hollywood epic of Irish independence, it was an easy choice. The movie's title: *Michael Collins.* Born in County Cork in 1890, Collins spent 10 years as a clerk in London from the age of 16. He joined republican groups and took part in the Easter Rising of 1916.

From 1919 to 1921 he masterminded the guerrilla warfare that helped persuade Britain to sue for peace. As a delegate who put his name to the Anglo-Irish Treaty, he wrote: "Early this morning I signed my death warrant." He was right: as head of the pro-Treaty forces in Ireland's subsequent civil war, he was shot dead in an ambush in his native County Cork on 22 August 1922.

LEFT: troops shoot it out with Sinn Féin outside the Courts of Justice during the civil war in 1922.
RIGHT: Michael Collins, head of the pro-Treaty forces.

FIRST A REVOLUTION, THEN A CIVIL WAR

Bullets and shellfire ripped the heart out of the city centre between the Easter Rising of 1916 and the end of the Free State's civil war in August 1923

Few ordinary Dubliners supported the small band of unrepresentative middle-class intellectuals and their 150 supporters who, armed with a variety of venerable rifles and agricultural implements, took over the city's General Post Office on the sunny spring holiday morning of 24 April 1916 and solemnly read out, to the apathy of bystanders, the proclamation of the new Irish Republic. Many, indeed, saw the action as treacherous: World War I was at a critical point and many Irishmen were serving – and dying – in British regiments.

It was only when Britain, having crushed the revolt, began to execute the rebels, a few at a time, that derision for the upstarts turned to sympathy, then unqualified support.

The way to post-war independence was now clear, but the compromise that led to Britain retaining six northeastern counties as Northern Ireland divided the nation and led to a bitter civil war in the new Free State in 1922. O'Connell Street was in flames again, with 60 dying in the first eight days of savage fighting. Between 1916 and 1922, three-quarters of the street was demolished; it would never regain its former elegance.

◁ DE VALERA
Eamon de Valera defended Boland's Mill during the 1916 Rising. His rejection of the treaty with Britain led to civil war.

△ CIVIL WAR STRIFE
This 1922 battle caused a fire at the Four Courts which destroyed historic deeds and documents dating back to the 12th century.

◁ **THE SHELLED CITY**
The 1916 Rising ended when a British gunboat on the Liffey shelled rebel strongholds, burning out the revolutionaries.

△ **THE DOOMED LEADER**
Michael Collins, head of the provisional government, leaves Dublin Castle in January 1922. He would be shot dead 19 months later.

△ **CONSTANCE MARKIEVICZ**
An Irish Protestant who had married a Polish count, she was a 1916 rebel. Later she was the first woman elected to the London parliament.

△ **THE AFTERMATH**
Church Street after the 1916 Rising. The death toll was 64 rebels, 134 police and soldiers and 220 civilians. Martial law was imposed and 4,000 were arrested.

◁ **BACK TO THE WALL**
Suspects are frisked by troops in 1920. Many troops, recently returned from World War I, were not best suited to civilian duties.

DE VALERA: THE GREAT SURVIVOR

In 1916, Eamon de Valera, a 33-year-old mathematics teacher who would one day be Ireland's president, liberated a bakery against the wishes of its workers, who felt that even in a republic people had to eat. Because he had been born in New York, of an Irish mother and a Spanish father, he was the only Easter Rising commandant not to be executed.

Although president of Dáil Eireann in 1921, de Valera sent others to London to negotiate an independence treaty. That left him free to oppose their compromise, setting him against them in the civil war that followed.

The war ended in 1923 with de Valera's effective surrender and he did not achieve power until he headed the Fianna Fáil government in 1932. This ushered in an era of pious respectability as he vowed to revive the Gaelic language and culture. The economy stagnated, but he built Fianna Fáil into a formidable populist party and kept Ireland neutral during World War II.

He served two terms as Irish president (1959–73) and died in 1975, aged 92.

A FREE STATE

Eamon de Valera promoted traditional rural values. The Church promoted traditional Catholic values. Soon the strains began to show

The first step in the building of the new state was the rebuilding of much of Dublin. Costly and extensive restoration work began on the General Post Office (whose pillared portico, thanks to bad British marksmanship, was largely undamaged), the Custom House and the Four Courts. While tenements round about were ignored, the facades along O'Connell Street were built up. One legacy of the 1916 battle still visible is the bullet hole in the breast of the winged figure of Victory at the foot of Daniel O'Connell's statue.

The question of where the new parliament should conduct its deliberations had been settled during the Civil War, when the Royal Dublin Society received £68,000 compensation for vacating Leinster House so that the buildings could house the Dáil. It is said Leinster House was chosen rather than the old Parliament House on College Green (now the Bank of Ireland) because its high railings made it easier to defend in case of trouble.

New parties, old rivalries

Trouble seemed inevitable. The civil war was to dominate every aspect of political life in the Free State for the next half-century and the new parliament reflected the civil war battle lines. The opponents of the Treaty who, for the time being, did not sit in the Dáil, kept the name Sinn Féin until 1926, when Eamon de Valera, the most prominent survivor of the Easter Rising, founded Fianna Fáil, the "Soldiers of Destiny". Following the deaths of Michael Collins and Arthur Griffith, the governing Cumann na nGael, which merged with other parties in 1933 into Fine Gael, the "Tribe of the Gaels", was led by W. T. Cosgrave.

Those two political parties, Fianna Fáil and Fine Gael, still shape Irish politics today.

LEFT: the Free State's flag flies on top of the General Post Office, centre of the fighting in 1916.
RIGHT: a farewell to empire as Queen Victoria's statue is removed from outside the parliament building.

Fianna Fáil has traditionally drawn support from small farmers, the urban working class and the newly moneyed. Fine Gael's heartland has been among larger farmers and the professional classes. The Labour Party, which pre-dated partition, found it hard to build support: the trade unions, while nominally

pro-Labour, often did deals with Fianna Fáil, and the Church's anti-communist propaganda encouraged a fear of the Left.

In 1927, de Valera entered parliament (the Dáil) at the head of Fianna Fáil. He came to power in the 1932 election, ushering in a new era of pious respectability and vowing to reinstate the ancient Gaelic language and culture. "No longer," declared Dev, as he became affectionately known, "shall our children, like our cattle, be brought up for export."

Serious political and economic troubles had to be tackled in the new Free State. Many more Irishmen had lost their lives in the civil war than during the resistance to British rule.

Material damage, which included the systematic destruction of the railways by anti-Treaty forces, was formidable. The army, threatening further action if moves were not made towards full independence, was subdued only with enforced demobilisation and cuts in pay. Partition was a fact of life and the six counties in the northeast remaining under British rule were regarded as a festering sore.

While republican aspirations had been tarnished by conflict, the reputation of the

IRELAND'S DIASPORA

Economic hardship ensured that emigration did not decrease. In the early 1920s, an astonishing 43 percent of Irish-born men and women were living abroad.

1937 Constitution and held sway until the liberalising legislation of the 1990s.

In 1923, the Censorship of Films Act ensured that nothing immodest, impure or unchristian should be shown to film audiences. The scrutiny of literature followed: the zeal of the Censorship Board, established in 1930, in finding evil currents in the work of writers of international stature, invited constant derision. Education was reinforced as a religious power base. Presciently, the poet W. B. Yeats,

Catholic Church remained unblemished as the sternest fundamentals of faith fused with ideals of nationalism. While the foreigner had dominated, the bishops had been equivocal about siding with the ruling power, but now they could ally themselves wholeheartedly with a Catholic and Irish government.

With gusto, they formed a coalition of piety to ensure that the church's authority was consulted on policies relating to health, education and marriage. Divorce, which had hitherto been a privilege of the well-to-do, was declared to be "altogether unworthy of an Irish legislative body to sanction", an opinion which was endorsed in de Valera's

a member of the Irish Senate, warned de Valera that these policies might destroy aspirations for a united Ireland. "If you show that this country, Southern Ireland, is going to be governed by Catholic ideas and by Catholic ideas alone, you will never get the North," said Yeats. "You will put a wedge into the midst of this nation."

Like religion, the Irish language was a unifying factor in a society divided by the civil war and, with the Church's approval, dominated the curriculum of national schools. However, the efforts to impose Irish as the spoken and written language of the state proved an expensive failure.

Breaking with Britain

Determined to loosen the links with England by constitutional means, de Valera immediately put through legislation to abolish the oath of allegiance to the British Crown and began his onslaught on the office of Governor General, which ceased after the 1937 Constitution provided for a President. Far more serious consequences arose from the refusal in 1932 to repay land annuities to Britain, which retaliated with a 20 percent duty on Irish imports. Tariff barriers fostered de Valera's favourite policies of self-sufficiency, but trade, particularly in livestock,

firmed with the reference to the "special position" of Catholicism as the religion of the "great majority of citizens" (a clause deleted by referendum in 1972).

Independence had not eased the social evils associated with poverty. In the genteel Georgian squares of Dublin, maidservants put out dustbins in which hordes of cinder pickers and scavengers searched for gleanings. Despite improvements in hospital care funded by the proceeds of a horse-race sweepstake, tuberculosis – the "white plague" – continued to be an unrelenting killer. In an overcrowded city without industry, unemployment

suffered drastically. Industry and commerce made some progress under the guidance of an energetic minister, Sean Lemass, who encouraged the growth of state-sponsored bodies like the Irish Sugar Company and the national airline, Aer Lingus.

In 1937, de Valera introduced the Constitution which effectively brought to a climax his campaign to sever the association with Britain. The *de facto* situation by which Church and State ran in tandem was con-

was despairingly high. The teeming, filthy tenements with their hordes of barefoot children persisted.

The absence of war

During World War II – known in the Free State as "the Emergency" – de Valera maintained a policy of neutrality (made practicable in 1938 when the British prime minister, Neville Chamberlain, surrendered three ports retained by Britain under the terms of the Treaty). Neutrality was generally supported by the people – though 50,000 southern Irishmen volunteered to fight in the British Army against Germany – and the day after Ger-

LEFT: terraced houses like these were all that many could afford in the new Free State.
ABOVE: looking for a penny on the Ha'penny Bridge.

many invaded Poland, the Dáil declared for it without division. In the face of pressure from the Allies the policy was observed scrupulously – too scrupulously, some would say, as, for example, when de Valera called at the German Embassy to sign the book of condolences after Hitler's death was announced.

One notable exception to the rule occurred in 1941 when the Dublin Fire Brigade rushed to Belfast to help in the aftermath of a bombing raid. The *Daily Telegraph* of London reported that this action had formed "a bond of sympathy between North and South Ireland which no British or Irish statesmen has been able to establish in a generation." In the same year, the refusal of British shipping to continue bringing food to Ireland led to the creation of a small merchant shipping service which ferried supplies across U-Boat-infested seas to ease the rationing.

In Dublin, after private motoring virtually ceased because of the lack of fuel, a few freakish cars moved around powered by gas or charcoal. Since there were no coal supplies, stacks of turf were piled in Phoenix Park. "Glimmer men" called at houses to check cookers for the warmth that indicated that people had exceeded their meagre gas ration. Those who could afford it bought plenty of meat, since livestock could not be exported. Clothing and bread were rationed in 1943. At the worst time, weekly rations included 8 ounces (230 gm) of sugar, 6 ounces (170 gm) of butter, and – the greatest hardship – half an ounce (14 gm) of tea. Wages were frozen, the keeping of pigeons – potential message carriers – was prohibited, and a second form of censorship was imposed so that few items of hard news filtered into newspapers. The bleak city was alive with rumours. Occasionally, stray bombs were dropped by the Germans; on the night of 30 May 1941, 28 people died when a 500-lb (230-kg) bomb fell on the North Strand.

The debate over neutrality

It has been maintained that neutrality, made easier by the buffer of England, kept Ireland from participating in a morally dubious conflict. These arguments equate the fire-storms of Hamburg and the bombing of Dresden

THE TRAVELLING PEOPLE

Before beggars became a familiar sight on the streets of London in the 1980s and '90s, visitors to Dublin were visibly taken aback to find so many bedraggled women and children begging. The Dublin beggars, however, were less often the homeless victims of unemployment or drug-taking than members of Ireland's travelling community.

Although Ireland's 30,000 Travellers share similar traditions to the 500,000 Gypsies in France and Spain and the 3 million in Romania, they are completely Irish in their ethnic origins; the true Romanies, like the Romans, never reached Ireland. They used to be called "tinkers", a word deriving from the days before the discovery of aluminium when they fulfilled a valuable economic role in a society that was still mainly rural: mending utensils, making baskets and sieves, peddling knick-knacks, dealing in horses and selling scrap. That term gave way to "itinerants", which is intended to be more polite but smacks of condescension. "Travellers" is the word they prefer.

Until the early 1960s, almost all travellers lived in brightly painted horse-drawn caravans or in tents. They dressed differently from other people – especially the women, with plaid shawls wrapped around their head and shoulders. Then, as demand for their trade diminished, they began drifting into urban areas such as Dublin.

with the excesses of the Third Reich and ignore the fact that, had Britain been invaded, so too would Ireland. Indeed, the Germans had been planning an invasion of Ireland, "Operation Green", as a vital springboard to an assault on Britain. In a handbook designed to brief their battalions, they noted that "the Irishman supports a community founded upon equality for all, but associates with this an extraordinary personal need for independence which easily leads to indiscipline and pugnacity."

WARTIME VOLUNTEERS

Although the Free State remained neutral during World War II, 50,000 southern Irishmen voluntarily joined the British forces.

demonstrate republican loyalties. The new government quivered when the Church, nervous that its authority might be weakened, opposed a mild welfare programme that threatened to offer women "gynaecological care not in accordance with Catholic principles". The author of the "Mother and Child" scheme was the Minister for Health, Dr Noel Browne, who had earlier organised the campaign to eradicate tuberculosis with striking success. But he lost the battle with the Church, and had to resign.

At Emergency's end, there was some satisfaction. Independence had been tried and tested, and in the next decade neutrality would continue to be Ireland's policy with its refusal to join NATO, largely as a gesture of opposition to the partition of Ireland.

Church and State

In 1949, the Republic of Ireland came into being as the last paper links with England were cut – ironically, not by Fianna Fáil, but by an inter-party government anxious to

LEFT: the Church loomed large in the new Ireland.
ABOVE: too many children, not enough houses.

The 1950s brought a number of changes of government, all overseeing a dismal decade marked by economic stagnation and high emigration. Nevertheless the period is remembered with nostalgia as the years when Dublin still retained the atmosphere of a great, big, shabby village where traffic was sparse, trams still ran, and sheep and cattle were driven to market through the streets. In 1953, an unsuccessful attempt to lift the gloom with a national festival called *An Tostal* ("pageant") left one legacy, the Dublin Theatre Festival, which has survived good times and bad times ever since.

But the Ireland of the 1950s was still a

repressed place. In 1954 a record 1,034 books were banned, and cinemagoers, if they wished to follow the plots of many films, had to cross the border to Belfast to see the unscissored versions. London's more lurid Sunday newspapers published tamer Dublin editions. The Catholic Church's prohibition on its adherents entering Trinity College continued and denunciations of the university by the steadfastly conservative Archbishop of Dublin, Dr McQuaid, became a familiar Lenten ritual.

But the traditional exuberance of the Irish couldn't be entirely suppressed. The last great literary Dubliners, for example, trav- elled from pub to pub, holding court. They included the playwright Brendan Behan (1923–64), author of *Borstal Boy* and *The Quare Fellow*; Brian O'Nolan (1911–66), who, as Flann O'Brien, wrote inventive novels such as *At-Swim-Two-Birds* and *The Third Policeman*; and the journalist and poet Patrick Kavanagh (1905–67).

The 1960s

Kavanagh derived much of his inspiration from his upbringing on a County Monaghan farm but now represented an increasing trend: the drift from country to town; by the mid-

THE FIGHT FOR OLD DUBLIN

Ireland's neutrality during World War II ensured that Dublin escaped major bombing. The destruction, when it came, was self-inflicted by uncontrolled property speculation.

In the early 1960s tracts of Georgian Dublin began falling to the demolition hammers of the developers. Whole streetscapes were razed and replaced by often unsympathetic office buildings. Not only did the authorities fail to prevent the destruction, they abetted it by collaborating eagerly with offshore financial interests.

In one of the worst examples, 26 houses in Fitzwilliam Street, the city's longest and best-preserved Georgian street, were flattened to make way for a new

Electricity Supply Board Headquarters. Citizens' protests were unavailing against the four horsemen of progress, prejudice, profit and vandalism.

Nor were protesters more successful a decade later in their attempts to prevent the re-interment of remnants of the Viking and medieval city at Wood Quay, near Christ Church Cathedral, which had been excavated for the erection of new council offices.

The climate today has improved – if nothing else, "heritage" is seen as a way of attracting tourist dollars. But the symmetry and graciousness of 18th-century Dublin, one of the ornaments of Europe, is long gone.

1950s a third of Dublin's citizens came from outside County Dublin. Eamon de Valera retired as Taoiseach in 1959 to become president, a largely symbolic office. For a few brief years, his successor, Sean Lemass, created an economic climate of stability and growth and raised the general standard of living. Protective tariffs with England were lifted, foreign investment was encouraged and agriculture was expanded in anticipation of Ireland's entry into the European Economic Community.

TELEVISION ARRIVES

Radio Telefís Éireann began transmitting in 1961, but the height of Dubliners' TV aerials betrayed a liking for the programmes broadcast from Belfast and England.

headway after the sweeping changes in attitudes following the Second Vatican Council.

After overwhelming approval of the move in a referendum, the Republic entered the EEC in 1972 on a wave of optimism. Sean Lemass set out vigorously to create new jobs by opening up the economy to foreign investment, attracting light engineering, pharmaceutical and electronics companies. At last, emigration appeared to be stemmed. Prosperity brought fundamental changes to the city fabric as the

As the quality of life improved, attitudes became more liberal. Television offered outside cultural influences, both from Britain and via the state's own new television service, Telefís Eireann, which began transmissions in 1961. In 1967, an amendment relaxed the powers of the Censorship Act. A comprehensive system of secondary education was introduced together with free school transport, and the ban on Catholics entering Trinity was lifted in 1970. Ecumenism made

population swelled by 30 percent; suburbs spread over green fields and supermarkets and shopping centres sprang up. Unfortunately, the bleak tower blocks of the working-class suburb of Ballymun, on the city's northern edge, repeated Britain's mistaken experiments in high-rise public housing.

The dream of Eamon de Valera faded fast. Interest in Gaelic language and culture waned and the voice of management consultants was heard in the land. The Irish, embracing consumerism with relish, seemed destined to become indistinguishable from the English. But cultural traditions were to prove more resilient than many suspected. ❑

LEFT: the state's founding father, Eamon de Valera and his pipe-smoking successor, Sean Lemass.
ABOVE: high-rise housing was tried out at Ballymun.

MODERN DUBLIN

As the economic power of the young increased and the political power of the
Church waned, family and social values were dramatically transformed

Dublin in the 1960s was blessedly free of political violence. True, the Nelson Pillar in O'Connell Street was blown up by republicans in 1966 to mark the 50th anniversary of the Easter Rising, but that act of destruction was regarded as symbolic. After its pre-war bombing campaign in England, its draconian suppression by de Valera in the 1940s and its unpopular and ineffective "border campaign" of the late 1950s, the IRA was no longer considered a serious threat by the governments in Dublin and Belfast.

But all was not well in Northern Ireland. Instead of gradually coming together, as the British had expected them to do after partition, the Catholic South and the Protestant-dominated North had ignored each other for 50 years. The Republic's prime minister, Sean Lemass, made an attempt to change the sterile rhetoric of partition with his cross-border meetings with the liberal Northern premier, Terence O'Neill, but their efforts bore no fruit.

Trouble in the North

In the face of continued discrimination against Roman Catholics in the North over jobs and housing, civil rights demonstrations began in the late 1960s. They met violent reaction from Protestants (broadly known as "loyalists" because of their allegiance to the British monarch) and repression, rather than reform, from the Northern state. After intercommunal violence broke out, the British army was called in to keep peace, but soon found itself caught up in a savage guerrilla war with a reborn IRA.

In 1970, two senior ministers of the Southern government were charged with importing arms for use in Northern Ireland. At the end of a sensational trial, they were acquitted. It was the last time there was any suggestion of

Dublin sorting out Northern problems by military means. Since then, the Republic has employed painful, patient diplomacy.

Dubliners have reacted at different times with rage, sympathy, horror and revulsion to the weary cycle of violence in the six counties of Northern Ireland – violence that has

sometimes spilled over south of the border. In 1969, after Protestant mobs of arsonists invaded Catholic ghettoes in Belfast and the first deaths of "the Troubles" occurred, angry crowds demonstrated outside the British Embassy in Dublin. After "Bloody Sunday" in January 1972, when British paratroopers in Derry shot dead 13 people, Jack Lynch, who was then Taoiseach, declared a day of national mourning. During it, more than 20,000 people jostled into Merrion Square to besiege the British Embassy, which was eventually burnt with petrol bombs.

In 1974, Dublin had its own unforgettable taste of horror when three car bombs placed

LEFT: rising... a statue of James Joyce was erected at Earl Street North. **RIGHT:** falling... the illegal demolition in 1966 of Nelson's pillar in O'Connell Street was timed to mark the Easter Rising's 50th anniversary.

by Northern Protestant extremists killed 25 people. Thirteen years later an IRA bombing of a war remembrance service in Enniskillen, County Fermanagh, just north of the border, in which nine people died, moved thousands of Dubliners to queue for hours at the Mansion House to sign a book of condolence.

In spite of their emotional ties with co-religionists in Northern Ireland, few Dubliners felt that a stable United Ireland could be achieved through bloodshed. A popular opinion in Dublin was

WEATHER REPORT

As foreign investment poured into the Republic in the 1970s, one euphoric trade minister, perhaps unwisely, dared to describe the country as "the sunbelt of Europe."

royalties. Some well-known names, such as thriller writer Frederick Forsyth, moved to the Dublin area to take advantage of the concession. One or two more provocative authors found it peculiar that, while one arm of the government was allowing them to live free of income tax, another was banning their books.

Feminism reached Dublin, flourishing richly in a climate long hostile to female initiative. In one celebrated protest against the ban on importing contraceptives

that Northerners, whatever their religion, were nothing but trouble and would be a destabilising influence in a united Ireland.

Anyway, what would Northerners have brought to the party? While the North was in crisis, the South in the 1970s was doing rather well. Financial subsidies from the European Community descended, as seemingly inexhaustible as Ireland's rain. Former farm labourers, to their delight, were earning good money assembling electronics components.

Culturally, too, the climate was brightening. Writers and artists, once forced to emigrate in search of intellectual freedom, were exempted from paying income tax on their

into the Republic, groups of women staged well-publicised shopping trips by train to Belfast. On returning to Dublin, they made a point of declaring their unlawful purchases to Customs officers and, on being asked to hand them over, informed the embarrassed young men that they were wearing them.

The soaring birthrate

Dublin's exploding birthrate had made it the youngest capital in Europe. But the 1980s were unkind to the youth of a city where more than a third of the population was classed as living in poverty. Rising juvenile crime and drug abuse were symptoms of their deprivation. Even the fates seemed to be against them: in 1981, 48 teenagers died in a fire at a disco; it was the city's worst civil disaster since medieval times.

The "brain drain" became visible in the queues of youngsters outside the US Embassy seeking visas; thousands of others went to the US to work illegally. Others tried their luck in Australia or Europe. Some of the brightest benefited from the boom in London's financial centres; many of the less fortunate, like the emigrants of the 1950s, drifted into dead-end jobs in the UK, or joined its half-forgotten population of drop-outs.

asms. Others detected idealism and maturity in a post-punk world, in the earnest lyrics that protest against modern ills.

The Haughey era

In 1979, Jack Lynch, who had followed Sean Lemass as Fianna Fáil leader, resigned as Taoiseach, to be succeeded after a bruising party contest by Charles Haughey. The early years of the "Haughey era" were marked by extraordinary political in-fighting. At one stage in 1981–82, there were three elections within 18 months. The country's complex electoral system of proportional representa-

But among the young who remained there was a sense of community, often expressed through the pop culture which Dublin so passionately absorbed, and to which it contributed mightily with its native sons Bob Geldof, pop singer turned famine-relief campaigner, and U2. Some social commentators were sceptical of the role of groups like U2, believing they acted as lightning conductors, diffusing youthful energy into safe enthusi-

LEFT: sales of newspapers are phenomenally high in Dublin – but they're not always taken too seriously.
ABOVE: joy-riding and vandalising cars became a big problem on the populous housing estates.

tion meant that Fianna Fáil minority administrations alternated with Fine Gael-Labour coalitions led by Garret FitzGerald, whose genial, absent-minded manner concealed a sharp political brain.

It was a Haughey administration that eventually introduced fiscal measures brutal enough to halt the Republic's economic deterioration. Public services were cut and unemployment soared, but the ground was laid for better times in the 1990s. That decade was ushered in by the election as Ireland's president of the left-wing Mary Robinson, a leading lawyer and feminist who stood for liberal and pluralist values. In her seven-year term, she was to transform the presidency from being a dumping ground for retired politicians to a force for social change.

Suspicions grew about Charles Haughey's financial probity and in 1992 he was forced from office, replaced by Albert Reynolds, a homelier, less charismatic figure. Five years later Haughey was investigated for receiving while in office more than £1m of undeclared funds from supermarket tycoon Ben Dunne.

An election in 1992 confirmed the desire for change that had swept Mary Robinson into the presidency two years earlier. The two big "civil war" parties, Fianna Fáil and Fine Gael, lost support, while the Labour Party more than doubled its parliamentary strength to assume a pivotal role in the country's politics. At last, a more modern politics seemed to be gaining ground. But Reynolds managed to scrape back as prime minister in early 1993 by piecing together a coalition.

The abortion debate

The 1992 election was extraordinary for another reason: the voters also had to adjudicate by referendum on a bizarre debate about abortion. The controversy had erupted just after Albert Reynolds first took office,

CHARLES HAUGHEY: CHARISMA AND CONTROVERSY

Charles J. Haughey's personality would dominate and divide politics in the Republic throughout the 1980s. Well before becoming Taoiseach, he had caused controversy. In 1970, when Minister for Finance, he had been accused – and acquitted – of conspiring illegally to import arms for use in Northern Ireland.

He was also charismatic, as this pen portrait by the historian J.J. Lee makes clear: "An accountant by profession, with a capacity to master a brief quickly, he had abundant flair and imagination, immense public self-control, an ability to cut through red tape with an incisiveness that infuriated those wedded to the corruption of bureaucratic mediocrity, and an energy capable of sustaining his insatiable appetite for power. He was plainly Taoiseach material. Yet, widely admired for his talents, he was also widely distrusted for his use of those talents.

"He radiated an aura associated in the public mind with a Renaissance potentate – with his immense wealth (discreetly acquired after his entry to politics), his retinue of loyal retainers, his Florentine penchant for faction fighting, his patronage of the arts, his distinctive personality, at once crafty and conspiratorial, resilient and resourceful, imaginative but insecure."

when it emerged that the attorney-general (the Government's chief legal advisor) had sought an injunction to prevent a 14-year-old rape victim having an abortion in England.

To many people, the proposal seemed both hypocritical and irrelevant since an estimated 4,000 Irish women travelled to Britain each year for abortions. But after a vitriolic public debate, the Constitution was amended to support the attorney-general's view and defend the right to life of the unborn.

The issue would not die down, and three proposals were put to the electorate. The first guaranteed freedom of travel (thereby ensur-

of travel and information, were passed. Abortion therefore remained legal, but in narrow and ill-defined circumstances, and the legislators were faced with tackling an issue that most of them had been all too happy to avoid.

Divorce at last

It was inevitable that the 1992 referendums would provide only a partial answer to a question with crucial implications for the role of the Church and, above all, for the status of women. A striking feature of the abortion debate was that it was carried on by powerful cliques – politicians, lawyers, clerics, doc-

ing that women could continue to go abroad for abortions). The second promised freedom of information "relating to services lawfully available in another state." The third, and most contentious, outlawed termination of pregnancy unless it was necessary "to save the life, as distinct from the health, of the mother." It also excluded the risk of suicide acknowledged by the Supreme Court.

After an acrimonious debate, this last proposal was defeated; the others, on freedom

LEFT: Charles Haughey, a charismatic prime minister discredited after he left office.
ABOVE: women protest against anti-abortion laws.

tors – consisting overwhelmingly of men.

But the ground was shifting significantly and a 1995 referendum on divorce gave the pro-divorce faction the slimmest of majorities: less than 1 percent. Such a result would have been inconceivable a decade earlier. Despite the closeness of the vote, enough politicians of all parties were sufficiently emboldened to ensure that divorce finally became legal in the Republic two years later.

Dublin's rebirth

The late 1990s saw Dublin transform itself into a fashionable "weekend break" destination for Europeans. The focus of publicity was on the Temple Bar district, an area near the Liffey where old warehouses had been converted into restaurants and nightspots reminiscent of London's Covent Garden.

Film makers, too, began to flourish. Neil Jordan, director of such hits as *The Crying Game* and *Michael Collins*, was the most prominent, but there was also a spate of local films which had begun with the launch of the Irish Film Board in 1981 and included such varied offerings as *Eat the Peach* (1986), the quirky tale of one man's bid to build a motor-cycle wall of death, and *The Field* (1990), a grim tale of life on the land in the 1920s.

With the Irish box office representing less than 0.5 percent of the global market there was limited scope for purely Irish films. So the government tempted in foreign producers with tasty tax breaks. This persuaded Mel Gibson, for instance, that, although his 1995 *Braveheart* portrayed a legendary Scottish hero, the stirring battle scenes would look no less patriotic if they were filmed in Ireland.

Ireland also began promoting itself as the Silicon Valley of Europe. Its combination of a youthful, well-educated workforce and generous grants and tax incentives lured more than 300 electronics companies to the Republic. Computer giants such as Dell and Gateway 2000 began assembling computers there, and Microsoft established its European operations centre in Dublin.

The brain drain reverses

The buoyant job market eroded one of the Republic's most distinctive characteristics: the fatalism with which young people emigrated – at a rate of some 30,000 a year in the 1980s – mainly to Britain and the United States. Suddenly many of those who had gone in the 1980s came home, flaunting the experience they'd gained abroad and grabbing many of the new jobs. This unaccustomed immigration had one negative effect: it meant that overall unemployment stayed high, at around 12 or 13 percent.

As the transformation of the economy became known abroad, Ireland became a magnet for refugees. Having exported people for centuries, Ireland was unprepared to import them, yet refugees from destinations

---

WHY EUROPEANS TOOK A FANCY TO DUBLIN

Politicians in Leinster House could hardly believe their luck as apparently endless grants flowed into economically disadvantaged Ireland from the European Union, But it got even better: ordinary Europeans seemed to love Ireland just as much as Ireland loved Europe and began arriving for weekend breaks, boosting hotels, bars and restaurants.

Europe's politicians felt enthusiastic about Ireland in the late 1980s partly because its support acted as a useful counterweight to the often antagonistic attitude of the British government led by Margaret Thatcher. Being small and remote lent enchantment, too: Ireland could never have got away with offering corporate tax incentives

that made a mockery of EU harmonisation if it had been a serious economic competitor to France or Germany.

But why did Dublin, despite its poor weather and high prices, become such a chic tourist destination in the 1990s? Part of its popularity could be traced to the success of bands such as U2 and Boyzone, and the impact made by Riverdance, the show that sexualised traditional Irish dancing. The Irish talent for making merry was also highlighted by the creation of more than 1,000 Irish theme pubs overseas, from Durty Nellie's in Amsterdam to O'Kim's in Seoul. Soon the message was transmitted by word of mouth: the real pubs in Dublin were even better.

as diverse as Romania and Zaire, learning of Ireland's comparatively liberal immigration laws, arrived in Dublin. Applications for asylum, which had been only 30 to 40 a year at the beginning of the decade, soared to several thousand a year.

Racism, previously not an issue in such a homogeneously white, Catholic city, began to become a problem as Dubliners saw immigrants as potential competition in the jobs market. Attacks on blacks and Asians in particular increased in frequency, but the initial political reaction was to keep quiet about the problem and hope it would go away.

But the Emerald Isle hadn't quite turned into the Garden of Eden. Dublin in particular was bedevilled by criminal racketeering, much of it centred on a lucrative drug trade. The scale of the problem became apparent in 1996 when the gangs gunned down Veronica Guerin, the country's leading investigative journalist.

As for the economic success, the pessimists – always a vocal breed in Dublin – predicted that the bubble would burst. The optimists, on the other hand, argued that, in adopting its new-found style and sophistication, the city had retained a deep pride in its historic iden-

Liberal attitudes

When, in 1997, a centre-right coalition of Fianna Fáil and the Progressive Democrats came to power, the coalition's leader, 45-year-old Bertie Ahern, was notable for being the first Irish Taoiseach to be separated from his wife and living with another woman. The fact that this situation was accepted by most people underlined how quickly Ireland had become a more liberal, pluralist society.

LEFT: Alan Parker's American-financed 1991 film of *The Commitments*, from the novel by Roddy Doyle.
ABOVE: the DART trains revolutionised travel between Dublin and outlying areas such as Dun Laoghaire.

tity – and the capacity to change, to re-invent itself for changing times, had always been a feature of that identity. This view was borne out by the enthusiastic adoption of the euro as Ireland's new currency in 2002, and by the continued renovation of the city centre though such projects as the new Millennium pedestrian bridge across the Liffey, the rejuvenation of O'Connell Street and the construction of the Spire of Dublin which sends a beam of light skyward as a proud new symbol of the city.

As the Dublin historian Peter Somerville-Large wrote: "The only constants are the sea, the play of light and the same green curve of hills the Vikings saw when they arrived." ❑

PEOPLE AND CULTURE

Mix charm, wit, congeniality and loquacity. Add a liking for sport, music, food and drink. You've got a Dubliner

Just over a million people live in Dublin city and county – almost one in three of the entire population of the Irish Republic. The city has been swollen greatly in recent decades by a marked population drift from country to capital. This means that many Dubliners have very recent rural roots, even though they are likely to profess a disdain for "culchies" (country people). Another demographic statistic is even more striking: more than 40 percent of the population is under 25. Dublin is a young city – and this fact has been an important element in the rapid social and economic changes of recent years.

Young people throng the city centre by day and night, giving it an infectious vitality. The streets are further enlivened by the many buskers and pavement artists. On a walk up Grafton Street, you're likely enough to encounter a string quartet, a blues guitarist, a jigs-and-reels band and a performing poet. The occasional horse still clip-clops through the city-centre traffic pulling a cartload of junk or scrap metal. Despite the outward face of prosperity in recent years, Dublin remains a city of sometimes disturbing social disparity.

Like its weather and many of its people, Dublin has a repertoire of shifting moods, and sometimes seems to be in two moods at the same time. Its streets can be full of bustle and yet there will be places where people linger easily to look around them or to talk – there is always plenty of that, for Dublin is a city of talkers. As the writer John Ardagh put it: "Human qualities come first – the gregarious intimacy, rare in a town of this size, the vivacious gossip, the cultural fizz, the wit and repartee at every social level."

The wit can be laced with venom, as the poet Sir John Betjeman discovered during a spell in Dublin. Returning to London, he said he felt he had escaped from a pool of cannibalistic crocodiles. Non-literary circles aren't much safer: whether you follow the letters page in the *Irish Times*, tune into Gay Byrne's long-running *Late, Late Show* on television, or merely listen to conversations in pubs, there's no denying that Dubliners enjoy being disputatious.

There's also a strong theatricality about their character. There's a recklessness, a tendency towards exaggeration. There's a love of "codology", the Irish equivalent of "leg-pulling". But there's an introversion, too, a proneness to melancholy and pessimism. You can sometimes sense this characteristic in a pub when, after the talk – once called "a game with no rules" – has achieved an erratic brilliance, the convivial mood abruptly changes to one of wistfulness and self-absorption, and you know it's time to leave. ❑

PRECEDING PAGES: rapt spectators at a Croke Park football game; Dublin remains a great place for book lovers. **LEFT:** there's a lot of history behind Dubliners, as here at the O'Connell Monument in the street named after the great 19th-century politician.

THE BIRTH OF THE CELTIC TIGER

An unexpected economic boom brought consumerism to Dublin in a big way.
But, beneath the surface, how much has really changed?

Open-air movies on balmy summer nights, cafe-bars serving the best cappuccino, any number of nightclubs and restaurants catering for almost every taste, 24-hour city centre convenience stores swarming with late-night "ravers" and an annual festival featuring Mardi Gras-style street theatre and spectacular fireworks displays. Put all of this together with a booming economy, the emergence of a confident contemporary architecture and the extraordinary asset of having the youngest population in Europe and what you get is Dublin, one of the most transformed cities in the world. All that's missing is a Mediterranean climate to match its mood.

Sitting out in the utterly modern Meeting House Square in the heart of Temple Bar watching Fritz Lang's silent film classic, *Metropolis*, with a sextet playing on a stage designed by Santiago Calatrava, it doesn't *feel* like the old Dublin at all, certainly not the introverted provincial backwater known to writers such as Brendan Behan and Sean O'Casey.

The European dimension

Dublin is now conscious of the fact that it's a *European* capital city which overtook Amsterdam and Prague in 1997 as the most popular place to spend a weekend. And this cultural change has come about not just because so much European Union money has been poured into the Irish economy in recent years; it is more to do with "attitude".

The Irish see themselves as "Young Europeans". Many of the younger generation have worked abroad, in cities like Berlin and Munich, Paris and Barcelona, as well as more traditional Irish haunts such as London, and they've now returned home in huge numbers to participate in Ireland's "Celtic Tiger" economy – bringing new ideas with them. As Dublin architect Sean O Laoire wrote, Eamon de

Valera would turn in his grave at "the new bourgeoisie debating the merits of extra virgin olive oil and sun-dried tomatoes" or, indeed, at "the late-night liggers, nightclub goers, strollers, revellers, down-and-outs, policemen, ambulances in one vast urban drawing room."

Dublin's bourgeoisie are notoriously fickle.

They flit around like butterflies, seeking out the trendiest restaurant of the moment, leaving a potential trail of liquidations in their wake. Loyalty is ephemeral in the "loads-a-money" consumerist binge sweeping the Irish capital; nothing is sacred anymore. If it's the Eden restaurant today, it's the Mermaid tomorrow.

Ireland has come an awfully long way. For years, the St Patrick's Day parade was a tacky procession dominated by blue-kneed American majorettes. Now it's a magical piece of European street theatre, with carnival groups gyrating along the civic thoroughfare from Christ Church to O'Connell Street.

Americans who come to Dublin expecting

LEFT: Powerscourt House shopping centre in South William Street has a wide variety of chic units.
RIGHT: sales pitch to tourists at O'Connell Bridge.

something more traditional seem quite taken aback by this heathen festival. To them, it's all just a bit too "foreign", with not a leprechaun in sight. Standing in College Green, as the spectacle swirled around them, one middle-aged US visitor said to his grey-haired friend: "Where are we? Jamaica?"

A new liberalism

Dubliners have shaken off the shackles of the Catholic Church. A succession of scandals, involving priests convicted of child sex abuse and even a bishop whose girlfriend had a baby, saw to that. The "liberal agenda" has tri-

buildings had been demolished to make way for a manic road scheme or an equally devastating "comprehensive redevelopment."

The inner city's population had slumped from 250,000 in the mid-1920s to just over 75,000 in 1986. Many streets in the historic core died after dark, as commuters rushed home to their semi-detached houses in the suburbs. Marginalised communities, particularly in the inner city public housing complexes, were gripped by the menace of hard drugs – particularly heroin – and this, in turn, led to an explosion of both petty and serious crime. Those who had been banished to new

umphed, with legalised contraception, divorce and homosexuality – and at a lower age of consent (16) than Britain.

Ireland today is a different country, far removed from the "priest-ridden" society of myth and reality; it is exorcising its demons and coming to terms with life in the age of the Internet. Those changes are more true of Dublin, with over a third of the Republic's population, than elsewhere and this has enabled it to become a confident capital city.

Looking at Dublin today, it's hard to believe that it was so down in the dumps in the early 1980s. The city was littered with weed-strewn derelict sites and surface car parks where

housing estates on the outskirts were also in despair, with jobless rates of up to 70 percent.

Then, something extraordinary happened. Partly to distract attention from how bad things really were, the authorities staged a "Millennium" celebration for the city in 1988. Nicknamed in typical Dublin style the "Aluminium", it had the effect of focusing attention on the historic core, making suburbanites realise at last that it really was worth saving.

The activities of ginger-groups such as the Dublin Crisis Conference helped change public policy. Indeed, it was at a resumed session of this conference in 1987 that the then Taoiseach (Prime Minister) Charles Haughey made a memorable pledge to spare the historic Temple Bar area from demolition.

For years, the national transport company – CIE – had been acquiring property in the area with a view to developing a new bus station and transportation centre. But CIE made the fortuitous error of letting the buildings it owned on attractively affordable rents and, before long, Temple Bar had become Dublin's Bohemian quarter, the city's very own "Left Bank."

There was some irony in the fact that all the

THE TEMPLE OF BARS

It has been estimated that, since 1991, around an acre of extra licensed space has been added to the redeveloped Temple Bar area.

Bar was designated as the city's new "cultural quarter". A state agency was set up to oversee its renewal and development, along the lines of an imaginative architectural framework plan prepared by some of Dublin's most talented architects. The aim was not only to erect contemporary buildings to house a range of new cultural facilities – such as The Ark, billed as Europe's first cultural centre for children – but also to create new public spaces of streets and squares and repopulate the area by providing high-quality apart-

art galleries, restaurants, alternative clothes shops and rock band rehearsal studios had sprung up in the shadow of the Central Bank, an aggressively modern free-standing office block on Dame Street. But after they established a firm foothold in the area, it became impossible to proceed with the plan.

Temple Bar's transformation

In 1991, when Dublin served a rather lacklustre year as European City of Culture, Temple

LEFT: eating and shopping in the Grafton Street area.
ABOVE: Temple Bar has rapidly developed into the Covent Garden of Dublin.

ments on the upper floors of new and refurbished buildings.

Some £22 million in European Union aid was secured to help fund the Temple Bar project. And since most of this money came from its tourism programme, there was an overwhelming impetus to justify the EU investment by putting "bums on seats" as quickly as possible. That's largely why the area became known as the "Temple of Bars." Small neighbourhood bars were turned into "mega-pubs" and every new hotel installed its own drinking emporiums at street level, with the inevitable result that Temple Bar became a "destination" for revellers, including English stag parties.

Though Bord Fáilte, the Irish tourism board, could barely bring itself to acknowledge their existence, these raucous stag party groups soon constituted a sizeable proportion of the visitors from Britain drawn here by low air fares. Many, even in the tourism trade, decided it was the type of business Dublin could do without and began to turn away the groups.

Simultaneously, the city has been attracting a different kind of clientele – the bankers, foreign exchange dealers, stockbrokers and insurance company executives who have flooded into the city's International Financial Services Centre, an onshore equivalent of one of those

offshore tax havens, built on the Liffey quays beside the Custom House.

It is far from the "exciting people place" originally envisaged in 1987. Surrounded by a ring-fence, both fiscal and physical, it stands apart from the north inner city, which remains one of Ireland's most socially deprived areas, yet its power-dressed form and shimmering glazed blocks constitute the most potent symbol of the "Celtic Tiger."

The Custom House Docks, where the International Financial Services Centre is located, might be more animated if the Irish Museum of Modern Art had been installed in a long, early 19th-century warehouse on the site.

Instead, the art gallery was despatched to the Royal Hospital, in Kilmainham.

All is not lost, however. In 1997, the Custom House Docks site was subsumed into a much larger 1,300-acre (530-hectare) redundant Docklands area controlled by a new development authority with a mandate to secure its social and economic, as well as physical, regeneration. The *laissez faire* lesson of London's docklands had clearly been learned.

The population boom

By far the most dramatic change in Dublin is the number of people now living in the city. Until 1990, there was not one private apartment available in the centre of Dublin. By 1998, more than 7,000 had been built – too many, sadly, of the "shoebox" variety in large schemes of 100-plus units which may become the tenements of the 21st century.

The influx of new residents – mostly single people in their twenties wanting to be close to where everything was happening – has had a profound impact. Old wards where the population had been falling relentlessly since the 1920s are brimming with new life and the shops and other facilities required to sustain it.

And while the vast majority of Dubliners still live in the suburbs, it is one of the objectives of the Docklands master plan to have at least 25,000 new residents in the area within a decade or so. Indeed, the aim is to create such a "beautiful environment" around the various water bodies of the Docklands that it may even appeal to families.

Keeping the human scale

Building height restrictions are being relaxed to allow for the erection of high-rise buildings in certain locations. Here again, however, the mistakes made from Pittsburgh to Sheffield have been taken on board; the elegance of new "sculptural forms" on the skyline is seen a primary consideration in a city which is still very much on a human scale.

There has already been an unprecedented boom in construction activity, reflected in the huge number of tower cranes helping to build yet more apartment blocks as well as hotels, leisure centres, office buildings, shopping malls and multi-storey car parks. Nobody knows when this boom may end, but in the meantime Irish builders are on the pig's back.

The strong performance of Ireland's economy – with growth rates in recent years higher than any other country in the European Union – has drawn the British chain-stores to Dublin in droves. Even the once-elegant Grafton Street, practically every indigenous outlet, with such notable exceptions as Bewley's Cafe and Weir's jewellers, has been taken over by the same chains. The oldest shop in Dublin, Read's Cutlers on Parliament Street, closed in 1997.

But a marvellous plan is under way for the

THE SAME SHOPS

With Argos, Boots, Debenhams, Dixons, Marks and Spencer, Tesco and Mothercare, the Jervis shopping centre could just as easily be located in Manchester.

people sleeping in the streets. The city also retains its ghettos, both at the core and on the urban periphery. After taking over as a very progressive city manager in 1996, John Fitzgerald pointed out that parts of the capital remain "stubbornly excluded from the present economic boom." And if Dublin can't do something about this now, with the State's coffers laden, "what hope in hell have we got when the inevitable downturn comes around?"

The people themselves have already fought

renaissance of O'Connell Street, turned into a Honky Tonk Freeway by burger and clip-joints. "Ireland's main street", rebuilt in the 1920s after the devastation caused by the 1916 Rising and subsequent Civil War, may return to its rightful place as the heart of the city.

Poverty remains

Dublin is not without its social problems. Despite the new-found wealth, there are still beggars on O'Connell Bridge and homeless

back. Communities which had been devastated by drugs have rediscovered their inner resources and banished the heroin dealers who had threatened to destroy them. In a way, this is also a symbol of the "can-do" attitude which began to pervade the whole place as it prepared for the uncertainties of the 21st century.

But the "Celtic Tiger" has its downsides, too. Traffic congestion in the city, fuelled by record sales of new cars, is fast making Dublin the most maddening capital in Europe. There are plans for a light rail system and a variety of other measures to improve public transport, all aided by European Union funds, but in the meantime private cars reign supreme. ❑

LEFT: exuberant performers dominate a Dublin pub.
ABOVE: all dressed up for Irish dancing, one of the many traditions not eradicated by increasing affluence.

THE POWER OF THE PEN

Dublin is indisputably a writer's city. So why have so many of its greatest writers packed their bags at the earliest opportunity?

No city has suffered more literary departures than Dublin, and no city has been more brutally criticised by its writers. Jonathan Swift felt himself "dropped in wretched Dublin". George Bernard Shaw complained of "a certain flippant, futile derision and belittlement peculiar to Dublin". "The blind and ignorant town," W. B. Yeats called it. James Joyce seems to have agreed: "How sick, sick, sick I am of Dublin!" he wrote to a friend. "It is the city of failure, of rancour and unhappiness. I long to be out of it."

Yet Dublin produced all of these and many more writers, not just by giving birth to them but by influencing them and, to various degrees, characterising how they looked upon the world and how they described it. Despite all the leave-takings, despite all the abuse, Dublin became a writers' city, and an astonishing number of truly great writers became Dublin's.

The impact of *Ulysses*

This phenomenon may have begun with Dean Swift's first satirical broadsides, launched from his house in the Liberties in the early 18th century, but its fullest expression was initiated on a summer's day two centuries later, when a proud, perhaps even arrogant young Dubliner first walked out with his future wife. The date was 16 June 1904, the Dubliner was James Joyce, and the expression of Dublin (and so much more) was to be *Ulysses*.

A cornerstone of 20th-century literature from its publication in 1922, the novel is also the great magnet for thousands of readerly pilgrimages to Dublin every year. Joyce's much quoted statement that, if destroyed, the city could be rebuilt out of his book has its own truth. The very spirit of the Dublin of that June day on which two men criss-crossed it in fussy, often ironic, always exquisite detail, is recreated in *Ulysses*. Joyce recovered from his

Dublin-sickness to the extent that the city became the stage and provided most of the cast for his imagination. The stories in *Dubliners,* the early novel *A Portrait of the Artist as a Young Man, Ulysses* and the orchestrated dream of *Finnegans Wake* describe it more intimately, more honestly and more gloriously

than any words – be they by Dickens, Balzac or Tolstoy – have ever painted a city.

"I tried," Joyce once said, "to give the colour and the tone of Dublin with my words; the drab yet glistening atmosphere of Dublin, its hallucinatory vapours, its tattered confusion, the atmosphere of its bars, its social immobility." His success brings more visitors along the route of Bloomsday – that day of *Ulysses* – every year (*see pages 86–87*). It has also influenced many other Irish writers, including Samuel Beckett, Sean O'Casey (in his autobiography) and Flann O'Brien.

Joyce puts the case for Dublin's quality of paradox as clearly as anybody has. This qual-

PRECEDING PAGES: actor, writer and wit Micheál MacLiammóir, joint founder of the Gate Theatre. **LEFT:** James Joyce. **RIGHT:** Oscar Wilde.

ity, this drab yet glistening atmosphere", this "tattered confusion" is at the root of the city's status as a literary capital. Dublin certainly has its geographical beauties and its structural grandeurs and its writers have praised them graphically. But the city's difficulties and contradictions made most of them writers in the first place.

British invasions made Dublin the most important town in Ireland and eventually the second city of the Empire. By the same token, they turned Dublin into a city never quite in tune with the rest of Ireland or the rest of the Empire. A writer could stay in Dublin and feel

what amounted to his political exile from court and London. Yet his political writings probably did more for Dublin and Ireland than any penned after him. *The Drapier Letters,* a series of letters supposedly by a Dublin tailor, forced England to cancel a deal which would have inflicted a cheap currency on Ireland.

This campaign alone made Swift a hero in Dublin, where he was known as the Hibernian Patriot, or, more colloquially and for years to come, as "the Dane" (a Dublin pronunciation of "Dean"). The "savage indignation" noted in his memorial in St Patrick's Cathedral made him apparently intolerant of the mass of Dubliners

out of place or leave Dublin, probably for London, where he would also be out of place. So nearly all the great works of Irish literature, from *Gulliver's Travels* through *The Importance of Being Earnest, John Bull's Other Island, Ulysses, The Plough and the Stars* to *Waiting for Godot,* have been composed with a very Dublin sense of detachment.

Swift's savage indignation

No one felt this detachment more than Jonathan Swift, born in Dublin in 1677 and Dean of St Patrick's Cathedral from 1713 until his death in 1745. A Dubliner, Swift was forever fulminating against Dublin and

he saw every day. They are recognisable in the Balnibarbi section of *Gulliver's Travels:* "the people in the street walked fast, looked wild, their eyes fixed, and were generally in rags..." In the pamphlet A *Modest Proposal,* Swift suggested, with savage irony, that the Irish should fatten their babies and sell them as tasty joints for the rich people's tables.

The great satirist was really directing the brunt of his fury at Britain's Establishment which presided with such cruel indifference over Ireland's suffering, though he was too positive not to criticise what he saw as local pusillanimity in the face of such thoughtless oppression. His desire for justice would have manifested itself anywhere; but his walks all over Dublin, his interest in its tradesmen, and the wild creative imaginings behind his ironies marked him out as a native son. He knew it himself. "I am only a favourite of my old friends the rabble," he told a friend, "and I return their love because I know no one else who deserve it." He left his money to build a lunatic asylum for Dublin.

Swift had studied at Trinity College. As the only university in Ireland then, Trinity concentrated the literary talents of the

SHERIDAN'S SATIRE

The Rivals and *School for Scandal* played Dublin within weeks of opening in London, satirising the lower ranks of English high society in a way that foreshadowed Wilde.

siast, the philosopher-bishop George Berkeley, who spent much of his life in Dublin, and the great statesman Edmund Burke (1729–97), who moved to England, like most significant Irish writers in the 18th century. Thomas Moore, born to an Aungier Street shopkeeper and his wife in 1779, followed the drift. The popularity of his sentimental song lyrics may seem incredible today, as may his friendships with Byron and the executed United Irishman Robert Emmet. But Moore sensed his city's dejection after the

educated, Anglo-Irish, Protestant classes in a city which also boasted a number of busy theatres. Most of the famous playwrights of late-Restoration and 18th-century drama – William Congreve, George Farquhar and Oliver Goldsmith – passed through Dublin. Richard Brinsley Sheridan's father, Thomas, managed a theatre in Smock Alley (now Exchange Street) until a particularly devastating riot in the stalls drove him and his family to England.

Trinity also produced Swift's fellow eccle-

failed 1798 rebellion and the Union with Britain which followed. On a visit, he described Dublin as "at length gay... but it is a kind of conscript gaiety".

The position of Moore's statue above what Samuel Beckett described as "the underground convenience in the maw of College Street" will endear him to most Dubliners more than the statue itself. Joyce's Stephen Dedalus was not the first to enjoy the coincidence of these toilets and the title of Moore's most famous lyric, *The Meeting of the Waters*.

Despite their proclivity for exile, Dublin's writers frequently connect with one another. It was Oscar Wilde's father, the eye and ear

LEFT: old volumes preserved in Marsh's Library.
ABOVE: Trinity-educated playwright Oliver Goldsmith.
ABOVE RIGHT: orator and politician Edmund Burke.

surgeon William Wilde, who first proved that a physical affliction rather than madness had killed Swift. Oscar's mother, Speranza, boasted as an ancestor the Reverend Charles Maturin, whose own grandfather had succeeded Swift as Dean of St Patrick's. Maturin's great Gothic novel *Melmoth the Wanderer* captured the imagination of the 19th century. This strange Dublin curate, a Calvinist who dressed like a dandy, nurtured his imagination by staying in his own city where, he felt, "the most wild and incredible situations of romantic story are hourly passing before modern eyes…"

But Dublin's 19th-century writers continued to leave the city. Bram Stoker, author of *Dracula,* followed his Trinity College colleague Oscar Wilde to England at about the same time as George Bernard Shaw emigrated. Shaw later wrote that "my business in life could not be transacted in Dublin out of an experience confined to Ireland." A character in his play *John Bull's Other Island* mentions Dublin's "horrible, senseless, mischievous laughter."

The legacy of Yeats

Born in Sandymount in 1865, William Butler Yeats associated himself with Sligo and a literature of myths and peasants, using Dublin

IRELAND'S BEST-SELLING BOOKS

Easons, the Dublin book retailer and wholesaler, compiled a list in 1998 of the top Irish classics of all time:

Gulliver's Travels by Jonathan Swift
The Vicar of Wakefield by Oliver Goldsmith
Castle Rackrent by Maria Edgeworth
The Complete Works of Oscar Wilde
The Complete Works of W. B. Yeats
Dracula by Bram Stoker
The Playboy of the Western World by J. M. Synge
The Complete Works of James Joyce
Three Plays by Sean O'Casey

Easons also compiled a list of Ireland's best-selling books of the 20th century. This was dominated by Maeve Binchy, the former *Irish Times* journalist who has ploughed the same furrow as Edna O'Brien did a generation earlier, though in a more sentimental way:

The Glass Lake by Maeve Binchy
Little Irish Cookbook by John Murphy
Evening Class by Maeve Binchy
The Copper Beech by Maeve Binchy
Waiting for Godot by Samuel Beckett
Borstal Boy by Brendan Behan
The Ginger Man by J. P. Donleavy
Peig by Peig Sayers
Irish Proverbs illustrated by Karen Bailey
Angela's Ashes by Frank McCourt

as the butt of many of his criticisms of modern, commercial life. Yet it was in Dublin that Yeats's Irish Literary Movement developed in the 1890s and flourished throughout the next, difficult half-century. George Moore, another exile, returned to the city he had once characterised as full of "bawling ignorance and plaintive decay", and the seeds of the Abbey Theatre were sown in the Antient Concert Rooms on what is now Pearse Street.

Those early days saw plays from Yeats,

WILLIAM BUTLER YEATS

W. B. Yeats (1865–1939) was more than a poet and playwright. He served from 1922 to 1928 as a senator of the Irish Free State and chaired a commission on coinage.

Dubliners enjoyed calling one of the great poets of the 20th century "Willy the Spooks", and W. B Yeats enjoyed haranguing the city for its stupid prejudices and selfishness: "You have disgraced yourselves again!" he cried to an organised demonstration against Sean O'Casey's *The Plough and the Stars* in 1926.

O'Casey headed across the Irish Sea himself a few years later, as annoyed by theatre politics as by the audiences. By then (like Joyce) he had portrayed Dublin as it had never been shown

Moore, Lady Gregory, Douglas Hyde and Edward Martyn. The Abbey itself was founded in 1904 and three years later a play about the west of Ireland by a Dubliner, another returnee, opened to riots in the audience. Some holy citizens were shocked by a reference to underwear; but John Millington Synge's *The Playboy of the Western World* confirmed the Irish Literary Renaissance and gave Dublin the status of a literary capital for all the world to see.

Not that Dublin took it entirely seriously.

LEFT: Bram Stoker first editions at Trinity College.
ABOVE: Dublin-born playwrights George Bernard Shaw (1856–1950) and Sean O'Casey (1880–1964).

before, setting his plays during the chaos of the 1916 Rising, the 1920 Black and Tans campaign and the 1922 Civil War. His characters survived in the poverty of the city's decayed Georgian tenement buildings, and spoke the wonderful robust, imaginative Dublin argot.

Although a youth and then an exile during the high years of the Irish Literary movement, Joyce was familiar with Yeats (who, like Shaw, couldn't finish *Ulysses).* The man who later joined WBY and GBS as a Nobel-prizewinning Dublin-born writer, Samuel Beckett, became friendly with Joyce in Paris in 1929. Though eventually writing in French, Beckett still sprinkled his work with references to

Dublin and to the suburb of Foxrock where his family lived. His combination of despair and humour has that Dublin aspect more immediately apparent in Joyce, O'Casey and, later, in Dublin's favourite performing writer, Brendan Behan; Dublin productions of Beckett's play *Waiting for Godot* prove the point.

In the late 1940s and 1950s writers such as Behan, the poet Patrick Kavanagh and the witty novelist Flann O'Brien circulated the pubs, a casual speakeasy called the Catacombs, and, occasionally, the law courts (honouring the city's celebrated tradition of literary litiga-

Doyle. For 14 years a teacher in the suburb of Kilbarrack, he captured in authentic dialogue the argot of North Dublin's working class in best-sellers such as *The Commitments* and *Paddy Clarke Ha Ha Ha*. A much bleaker view of Dublin was provided by Dermot Bolger in novels such as *Night Shift* and *The Journey Home* which cast a cold eye on the city's social ills without resorting to whimsy.

Dublin played host to most of Ireland's finest writers during the 20th century: Frank O'Connor; Austin Clarke, James Stephens, Liam O'Flaherty, Seamus Heaney and Louis

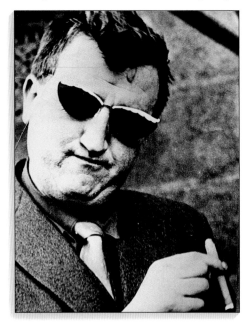

tion) in a virtually surreal parade of alcohol, poverty and dispute. J. P. Donleavy's novel *The Ginger Man* has described some of this ambience. It produced Behan's plays about Mountjoy Prison and the IRA, *The Quare Fellow* and *The Hostage*, Kavanagh's beautiful later lyrics, and O'Brien's comic masterpieces in the *Irish Times* and in books such as *At Swim-Two-Birds* and *The Third Policeman*.

The modern school

Although the "literary" novel has flourished in the hands of writers such as John Banville, the 1990s saw the rise of the "new urban realism", whose most successful practitioner was Roddy

MacNeice are just some of them. MacNeice's beautiful poem about the city explains the strange magic of its hold on the imagination:

> *...she holds my mind*
> *With her seedy elegance,*
> *With her gentle veils of rain*
> *And all her ghosts that walk*
> *And all that hide behind*
> *Her Georgian facades –*
> *The catcalls and the pain,*
> *The glamour of her squalor,*
> *The bravado of her talk.*   ❑

ABOVE LEFT: playwright and hell-raiser Brendan Behan.
ABOVE: award-winning novelist Roddy Doyle.

The Intoxication of Talk

Flann O'Brien, in his classic novel *At-Swim-Two-Birds*, captures the Dubliner's love of language: "We filled up the loneliness of our souls with the music of our two voices, dog-racing, betting and offences against chastity being the several objects of our discourse."

Of course, it doesn't by any means follow that a cartload of words is necessarily a good thing: it all depends on the horse that's pulling it. The Irish psyche – sardonic, tending towards defeatism – is the ideal one for a correctly jaundiced and entertaining view of the world; but, like everywhere else, benumbing bores abound.

In general, working-class people cut bolder images quicker, with blunter instruments, with more mime and other physical back-up. The middle class, with a larger vocabulary, are blander, less distinctly "Dublin", and less hectic. The upper class, from their fat fastnesses sited on the fringe of the bay, stretch their vowels like aching muscles, and there is the distilled but distinct roll redolent of the posh English: "My woife and I..."

The art of listening

To appreciate Dublin talk, sit back and let it wash over you, like music. It's the overall effect that counts, not an understanding of every peculiar phrase. Take, for example, this monologue faithfully transcribed from a native of Ballyfermot, a long-established working-class city suburb. It is just before Christmas – that time of dragons, traps and quicksand for those with a weakness for drink and, from his furtive, cobwebbed eyes it is obvious that the speaker has sunk deep into the quicksand the previous night. Up to his armpits, in fact – or, as they are colloquially called in Dublin, his oxters.

He says (translation provided where considered necessary): "Ah, how's the man? Listen, I can't stop. *(He stops.)* She's at war with me over yesterday. *(She: his wife – never, ever referred to as such.)* She sent me into town yesterday to buy the turkey with the mickey money. *(Mickey money: State children's allowance payment.)* I gets off the bus and who do I meet the first thing only the Hogger. You know the Hogger, Paddy Whatseesname's cousin, course you do, the fellah with the leg. *(A fel-*

low with a leg: a man who limps.)* Anyway, we said we'd go in for the one, you know yourself, with Christmas and all. *(Going in for the one: the ideal of entering a pub for a single, quick drink.)*

"So, I needn't tell yeh, you know yourself, the next thing I remember, the barman is calling time, the Hogger is up throwing shapes looking for a digging match off all comers and roaring out of him about the Black and Tans, and the night outside is as black as your boot. *(Throwing shapes: striking an aggressive stance. A digging match: fisticuffs.)* Well, I went home by rail – I held on to every shaggin' railings between the pub and home. I remember thinkin', if she's in the scratcher asleep, she

won't see the cut of me. *(The scratcher: the bed. The cut of me: my condition.)*

"Well, I wakes up this morning and the first thing I hear is her sayin' to me that I was at it again last night obviously, drinkin' what me children should be eatin'. How dare you, says I, I'd a quiet drink with an old mate. Oh yes? she says, real smarmy, and with that I opened me eyes and there I was, talkin' to her feet, after gettin' into the wrong end of the bed in the horrors of drink! Guilty as charged. Listen, where would I get a cheap turkey? Where? Sure that's miles away. Will we go in for the one anyway?"

It's magnificent, but is it English? Not exactly. But it's classic Dublin. ❑

RIGHT: in bars, talk is often more important than drink.

IN THE FOOTSTEPS OF LEOPOLD BLOOM, ESQ.

The action of James Joyce's Ulysses takes place on a single day in 1904. Each year on that day, 16 June, the novel's events are faithfully re-enacted

FÁILTE DUBHLINN

HERE, IN JOYCE'S IMAGINATION WAS BORN IN MAY 1866

LEOPOLD BLOOM
CITIZEN, HUSBAND, FATHER, WANDERER
REINCARNATION OF ULYSSES

Polls of literary critics have deemed *Ulysses* the greatest novel of the 20th century, although even in Dublin it is probably more honoured than read. Thematically based on Homer's *Odyssey*, it documents a 24-hour period in the lives of an Irish Jew, Leopold Bloom, and a budding writer, Stephen Dedalus, as they move around Dublin; the story reaches its climax when they meet.

The novel was published in 1922 in Paris by Sylvia Beach's Shakespeare & Co bookshop. It was banned in Britain and America – though never, curiously, in Ireland, though it was difficult to obtain there. The first Bloomsday celebrations took place in Dublin on 16 June 1954, the 50th anniversary of the events depicted in the novel. Initially they were designed to appeal mainly to academics, but after Joyce's centenary in 1982, they became increasingly popular so that now they are rivalled only by St Patrick's Day.

Participants, wearing what approximates to 1904 garb, trace the paths of the book's characters. After a Bloomsday breakfast in Sandycove, they can listen to readings delivered by costumed actors, lunch on Gorgonzola sandwiches and Burgundy in Davy Byrne's pub, walk through the northside, taking in Hardwicke Street, Eccles Street, Gardiner Street and Mountjoy Square, enjoy more readings at the Joyce Centre, and then discuss the book's finer points over a few pints.

There's plenty to discuss. As Joyce said, there are enough enigmas in *Ulysses* "to keep the professors busy for centuries arguing over what I meant, and that's the only way of securing your immortality." He'd be impressed that a website now hosts readings on 16 June from 18 cities all over the world.

▷ **PORTRAIT OF THE ARTIST**
Bloomsday Festival has now expanded to occupy an entire week when you can't escape James Joyce – even in the form of pavement art.

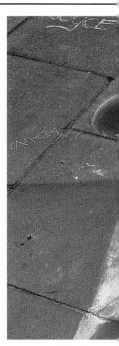

△ **GOING BY THE BOOK**
Robert Nicholson, long-time curator of Sandycove's Joyce Museum. Sylvia Beach, who first published *Ulysses* in 1922, opened it in 1962.

△ **IT'S THE 1904 SHOW**
Many pilgrims wear period costume, as do the actors positioned at strategic points.

▷ **PINTS OF VIEW**
Ulysses mentions so many bars that Bloomsday can easily turn into a pub crawl.

JAMES JOYCE 1882–1941

One of 10 children, James Augustine Aloysius Joyce was born at Rathgar, Dublin, and was educated at Belvedere College. He graduated from University College with a degree in modern languages in 1902.

In 1904 he lived briefly in the Martello Tower at Sandycove (above). The same year he met Nora Barnacle, a simple country girl, and moved abroad, living mainly in Trieste and Paris; they had a son and a daughter but did not marry until 1931. Eye troubles began in 1907, leaving him almost blind in later life.

Joyce remained an exile for the rest of his life. In Paris he mixed with writers such as Ezra Pound, Scott Fitzgerald, T.S. Eliot and Ernest Hemingway. As a young man, Samuel Beckett acted as his secretary. When war drove him out in 1940, he moved to Zurich, where he died a year later. Nora remained in Zurich, where she died in 1951.

△ **BLOOMSDAY BEST**
Edwardian dress is favoured, including boaters, watch chains, long skirts and parasols. But anything remotely close is accepted.

▽ **JOYCE'S WOMEN**
Joyce set *Ulysses* on 16 June, the day he first walked out with Nora Barnacle, later his wife and the likely basis for Molly Bloom in *Ulysses*.

△ **ON THE BEACH**
The book begins at Sandycove, where a *Ulysses* breakfast is served from 6am.

▷ **ON THE STREET**
Joyce's insouciant statue at Earl Street North is a familiar figure in central Dublin.

THE MUSIC SCENE

*You're spoiled for choice but you don't have to choose. Here it's permissible
to like the Dubliners and Clannad as well as U2 and Boyzone*

The sad tale of an impoverished street-trader who died of tuberculosis doesn't sound like the best material for a city's unofficial musical anthem but the 200-year-old haunting refrain of "Molly Malone" still resounds around the streets and pubs of Dublin today. It faces stiff competition, though: apart from being a capital of traditional Irish music; the host city of a record-breaking amount of Eurovision Song Contests and the place of world-famous recording studios, Dublin also spawned, in the group U2, the biggest rock band in the world.

The aura of U2 is enough to attract thousands of tourists to the city to re-trace the footsteps of Dublin's "fab four" and pay homage at all the different places around the city associated with the band. But, once here, people find there's more to Dublin than U2 and more to the city than rock music.

Musical tolerance

Whether it be the Celtic backdrop or the city's reputation as a place of "words and song", music is an essential part of the cultural fabric. From major rock extravaganzas staged in the city's rugby ground, Lansdowne Road, to an up-and-coming band of hopefuls playing in a corner of a bar or the ubiquitous traditional music "sessions" – as popular with locals as they are with tourists – Dublin moves and sways to a rhythm that other cities just don't possess. There's a tremendous pride in the city's – and indeed the country's – musical achievements, and music as a form of creative expression, whether it be pop or classical, is encouraged and facilitated by both government and citizens.

The peculiar social environment has produced an atmosphere where many different genres of music sit easily side by side. A large percentage of the city's population are from

the countryside and they have brought a rich heritage of traditional music with them – still evident in places like The Brazen Head pub on the city's quays which hosts "trad" sessions every night of the week.

The huge increase in population after World War II meant an unprecedented number of

teenagers coming of musical age in the 1960s when the showbands and local beat groups sought to satisfy demand in Dublin by playing cover versions of the hits of the day from the Beatles and the Rolling Stones.

It wasn't until the '70s, however, that the city could boast its first international music star. Phil Lynnot, a local Crumlin lad, and his band Thin Lizzy first scored a top 10 hit with their updated version of the folk song "Whiskey In The Jar" and then went on to become a world famous band with albums like "Live And Dangerous", still cited by many of today's young musicians as huge influences on their work. For the first time,

---

LEFT: U2 gained an international reputation for spectacular stage shows. **RIGHT:** the Cranberries had a more specifically Irish sound.

an Irish rock band was competing with more traditional groups like the Dubliners on the international stage and Thin Lizzy's success helped pave the way for The Boomtown Rats, led by Bob Geldof. The Rats (as they were locally known) scored big hits with songs like "I Don't Like Mondays" and "Rat Trap" before they exited stage left and left the way clear for the biggest and the best Dublin band of them all: U2.

From the Northside of the city, the four members of U2 were, and still are, a pivotal Irish music group. From number 1 albums in America, to sold-out world tours to the cover of *Time* magazine, U2 put Dublin firmly on the international music map. Virtually every venue they used to play concerts or record their albums in Dublin has become a tourist attraction in its own right.

The search for stars

As a result, most every record company in the world sent representatives to Dublin to find another bunch of teenagers who would hopefully live up to the "next U2" label. Dublin became known as "The City of 1,000 Bands" and you couldn't walk down a street in the city without hearing the clamorous sound of

THE U2 PHENOMENON

The U2 rock band is in some ways the Irish equivalent of the Rolling Stones: without relying on hit singles, it is hugely influential, its international concerts are built around gargantuan stage effects, and its members have a shrewd business sense (for example, their part-ownership of the stylish Clarence Hotel on Wellington Quay). The band was formed in 1976 by four students: singer Paul Hewson (known as Bono), guitarist David Evans (known as The Edge), bassist Adam Clayton, and drummer Larry Mullen. Top albums include *War* (1983), *The Joshua Tree* (1986) and *Achtung Baby* (1991). Their political involvement focuses on support for human rights.

some band rehearsing their songs. There never was a "next U2", of course, but with the band deciding to stay living in Dublin and taking every opportunity to support local talent, they have made a positive contribution to the city's musical infrastructure.

These days, Dublin has become a positively trendy city in which to live and record your album – musical acts as diverse as Nanci Griffith, Carole King, Def Leppard and Lisa Stansfield now call Dublin "home". One of the main attractions of the city is that, unlike most anywhere else in the world, Dubliners don't believe in hassling musical stars and for the most part let them walk the streets uninterrupted by hordes of autograph seekers.

Dublin's musical taste is nothing if not eclectic, and you can track down any type of music, from Country 'n' Western to '70s Disco to Heavy Metal to Euro-style pop. You wouldn't think, for example, that American soul music would find such a ready home in Dublin, but the success of Alan Parker's 1991 film *The Commitments* (based on a book by Roddy Doyle), which was about a group of young Dublin people who form a soul band, demonstrated how seriously music

LOCATING THE VENUES

Main sources of information are the country's leading music magazine *Hot Press* and the local listings guide *In Dublin*, both of which have eclectic coverage.

concerts and operas; Whelans, which is home to all types of folk/rock/pop acts; and the Olympia Theatre, which regularly showcases the best of local talent alongside major British and American acts.

One mistake worth avoiding is reminding people of how successful Ireland has been in the Eurovision Song Contest. Most people regard the saccharine pop tunes that the contest requires as an embarrassment and not truly representative of the country's/city's musical output. Ireland

is taken here, irrespective of whether it is traditional or imported. The most recent addition to Dublin's roster of successful international acts, Boyzone, have now become one of the biggest "boy bands" around, thanks to their pop-driven songs and massive female fan base.

With live music of all variety available seven nights a week, you can be spoilt for choice, but the main venues to look out for are The Point Depot, which hosts major international musical events; the National Concert Hall, which is mainly used for classical music

LEFT: Thin Lizzy, a pioneering 1970s band.
ABOVE: Boyzone, one of the top 1990s attractions.

has done so well in the contest because there are more songwriters/musicians in the country than there are in any other European country – it's the law of averages.

Audience participation

The main cultural differences you'll find in Dublin is that the playing of music is a very informal affair where audience participation is a welcome addition to the atmosphere of the evening. Music isn't a passive activity in this city and nobody will be bothered if you join in, suggest songs or simply banter with the musicians – especially in the more traditional types of music. The normal rules of etiquette apply for the more classical types of concert.

Outside of Dublin, Ireland has enjoyed a disproportionate amount of musical success for a country of just 4 million people. Acts such as Clannad and Enya from Donegal and the Cranberries from Limerick sell millions of records worldwide while "first generation" Irish acts like Shane MacGowan and the Kelly Family further increase the stock of successful Irish bands. Part of the reason why these acts make such an impression is that their music, no matter how contemporary in execution, still bears all the hallmarks of pure Irish traditional music. Clannad, for example,

sing a number of songs in the Irish language and their dreamy musical landscapes are rooted in their experience of growing up in the Donegal countryside.

While other countries experience a definite break between their folk and modern music bands, Irish bands tend to embrace their musical heritage and reflect it in their sound. While some American and British bands can sound homogeneous in that they could come from anywhere, there's always a sense of place with Irish bands and they play with an identifiable sound that owes as much to the past as to the present. Whether it be the folk-inflected rock music of the Hothouse Flowers or the bits of traditional music that seep into the hard rock sound of a Dublin band like the Hormones, it seems that Irish bands can bring something a bit extra to their sound.

The club scene

The biggest change in Irish music over the past few years, particularly among the younger people, is how "club" music has become the new and dominant means of musical expression. In European terms, Dublin is seen as a "clubbing capital" and venues like POD (Place of Dance) and The Kitchen (the night-club owned by U2) are two of the best places in the city in which to experience the modern musical sound of youthful Ireland. Local DJs are bringing out their own records on their own labels and dabbling in the contemporary genres of music known as Garage, Drum 'n' Bass and Trance.

There were fears that the rise of the clubs would be the death of live music – in that it's much easier for venues just to hire a DJ to spin records than a whole band with sound and lighting requirements – but commendably club music co-exists quite happily with live rock music and live traditional music. Because of the city's fascination with music and willingness to embrace the old as well as the new, it is no strange thing for people to start off a night's musical entertainment in a pub with live folk music before moving on to see a rock band play and finishing the night in a club to the sounds of dance music.

Where it's at

Visitors can feel free to drop their musical prejudices and sample what's on offer. No matter what time of day or what time of year, there is always something happening somewhere. Due to ever-changing fashions and the coming and going of musical venues, it pays to ask people for advice about what's hot and what's not. Or simply walk around the streets, stopping off outside anywhere you hear music coming from – it helps if you experiment and stay off the beaten track sometimes. Who knows, you might even end up at a secret U2 gig. ❏

LEFT: Enya transformed traditional Irish balladeering into the easy-listening sound of the 1980s and '90s.
RIGHT: the Dubliners, kings of the rousing chorus.

THE SPORTING LIFE

Football is the most popular spectator sport – not surprisingly,
since there are three different types to choose from

The story goes that, after a triumph by the Dublin county Gaelic football team in the All-Ireland final, an old man in the Liberties, the city's historic working-class quarter, was asked what he thought about the resurgence of "the Dubs". He retorted: "Dubs how-are-yeh! Sure they're a crowd of culchies from Fairview and Marino!"

By way of translation, one should know that *"how are yeh!"* is a Dublin expression of scorn and that *"culchies"* is a disparaging term for rural people. One should also know that Fairview and Marino are inner suburbs of north Dublin city. The old man was giving voice to local chauvinism by suggesting that only denizens of the Liberties deserved the name of "Dubs": but he was also expressing a common enough Dublin view that Gaelic football is a game for "culchies" and that the only proper game of football is soccer.

Various forms of football

In sport, as in everything else, Dublin is different from the rest of Ireland. In the provinces, by far the most popular sports are the "national games" administered by the Gaelic Athletic Association, especially Gaelic football, which looks to the uninitiated like a cross between soccer and rugby. But in much of Dublin city, "Gaelic" plays second fiddle to those other two forms of football – rugby, in the more affluent, mainly southside areas; soccer, in working-class areas.

And here comes a further twist: Dublin soccer fans are primarily interested not in Irish, but in English soccer, for the League of Ireland is in effect a poor relation of the English League. Like other small European countries, Ireland can offer only limited opportunities in domestic competition, so the best players are signed to overseas clubs, mainly in England. Dublin-born players who have won

international reputations include John Giles, Liam Brady and Frank Stapleton.

This explains why the team most popular with Dublin fans is Liverpool, which has several Irish players and is based in an English city often called the second capital of Ireland because so many of its inhabitants

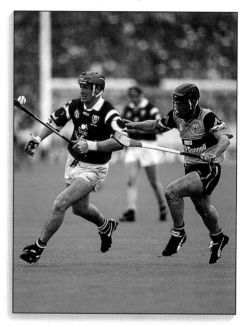

are of Irish extraction. Manchester United also has a big following for similar reasons.

The headquarters of Irish rugby is at Lansdowne Road stadium in Ballsbridge, which is the focus of intense interest each spring during the annual Five Nations Championship between Ireland, England, Wales, Scotland and France. (Rugby, incidentally, unlike soccer, is organised on a cross-border basis and the Ireland team includes players from both North and South.) Lansdowne Road is also regularly "borrowed" for international soccer matches.

The city's other great football cathedral, Croke Park, stands across the Liffey in the

---

PRECEDING PAGES: Gaelic football.
LEFT: passive crowd control at a football game.
RIGHT: Cork takes on Clare in a hurling match.

meaner streets of the northside. This is the Mecca of Gaelic games enthusiasts and the venue each September for the all-Ireland championship finals in the "national games": hurling and Gaelic football. National games reflect national character and both games are fast and furious, with possession of the ball changing constantly: whether you consider this a strength or a weakness, neither game can be played effectively in a defensive, counter-attacking style.

Hurling has an ancient lineage, being descended from a game played in prehistoric times by the legendary Cuchulainn. It has a

passing resemblance to hockey, but the ball can be hit in the air as well as along the ground, caught in the air or carried on the flattened end of the player's stick (the hurley). Skilled players can take the ball onto the hurley from the ground while running at full speed and carry it, balanced or bouncing, on the broad end before passing or scoring.

Dublin has no great tradition in hurling, the pre-eminent counties being Cork and Kilkenny. But Dublin county is a major force in Gaelic football, which attracts more spectators than any other sport in Ireland. Like hurling, the game has 15 players a side. Played with a ball similar to that used in soccer,

Gaelic football is to a great extent an invented game. The rules are therefore imperfect and subject to constant revision. Players can handle the ball, lift it off the ground with the foot, run with it while passing it between hand and foot, kick it, or fist it, or play it with the feet on the ground as in soccer. Its main flaw is that there is no clear method of dispossessing a player in possession. But it is a spectacular game, and attracts the biggest crowds of any sporting event in Ireland.

Other sports

Horse-racing has a strong following in Dublin, as throughout Ireland. There is a racecourse at Leopardstown, in the southern suburb of Foxrock, and several others within easy reach of the city. The highlight of the racing calendar is the Irish Derby, held in June at the Curragh, 32 miles (51 km) southwest of Dublin.

Golf, another national obsession, is played at many courses around the city; the major event is the Carroll's Irish Open, which is contested each June by the top international professionals.

Other popular sports include athletics, boxing and snooker. Greyhound racing attracts those who enjoy a "flutter" to evening meetings at Shelbourne Park and Harold's Cross. Even cricket has its devotees, despite its withering dismissal by the young Oscar Wilde on his arrival at Trinity College. "I refuse to play cricket," he said. "The postures are indecent."

International activities

Ireland's enthusiastic role as a member of the European Union has helped Dublin's image as a centre for international sporting activity. In 1998, for example, the world's greatest cycling race, the Tour de France, began in the city before proceeding down the east coast to Cork and then across the channel. A total of 198 riders and a 5,000-strong entourage took part. An estimated 900 million people in 130 countries watched the start of the race.

In the same year, Dublin also hosted the finish of the Tall Ships race from Vigo in Spain. Thousands of people lined the coast to witness the splendid spectacle of dozens of sailing ships majestically entering Dublin Bay. ❑

LEFT: greyhound racing, a good excuse for a "flutter".
RIGHT: moment of triumph at the Dublin Horse Show.

A FRESH APPROACH TO FOOD

In a city that likes its food, a few chefs aspire to be high priests.

Luckily, Dubliners are adept at cutting clerics down to size

The traditional image of Irish cuisine scarcely extends beyond potatoes, bacon and cabbage, washed down with a glass of Guinness. Those basic ingredients still exist, of course, but these days they're likely to be laced with cheese, wine, almonds, garlic and herbs, and the soggy stodge that once dispirited visitors has now been replaced with plates of food masquerading as a Monet painting. The standards of cooking in Dublin restaurants are often remarkably high. Trouble is, the prices are even higher.

A cheerfully pagan place at heart, with something of a Mediterranean temperament – though not, sadly, the climate – Ireland "discovered" food when package holidays introduced its citizens to the exotic ingredients used in Spain, Italy and Greece. They began experimenting with radical cooking methods and also realised that their indigenous cuisine had its merits too: stunningly fresh fish from unpolluted waters, prime beef and lamb, dawn-crisp vegetables and wondrously creamy dairy produce. Really, all Ireland has ever needed to import has been citrus fruit and wine.

Making it dramatic

Darina Allen, the doyenne of Irish cooking, has emphasised in her books and television programmes the virtues of simplicity and freshness and, with her indomitable mother-in-law Myrtle, has turned their cookery school at Shanagarry in Cork into Ireland's top gastronomic temple. But not every Irish chef has put her on a pedestal. Many, particularly in Dublin, subscribe to the Marco Pierre White philosophy, regarding a meal as a drama or a minimalist painting, to be produced with much flourish in return for an equally impressive sum of money.

One of the most talked-about chefs, Done-

gal-born Conrad Gallagher, trained in California before returning to Ireland to open his first restaurant, **Peacock Alley**, now located in the Fitzwilliam Hotel, St Stephen's Green. On a good night, Gallagher's soaring cuisine does for food what Michelangelo did for marble, but on a bad night the experience

can seem fussy and pretentious and there can be glitches on the wine list. Dare to complain, though, and you may swiftly discover that Gallagher does not subscribe to the philosophy that the customer is always right. He has also opened a brasserie, named after himself, on Merrion Street, close to the Dáil.

Rivalling Gallagher as Dublin's top restaurateur is Patrick Guilbaud, a Breton with attitude and the most spectacularly expensive wine list in Dublin (many of the wines cost hundreds of pounds and some cost thousands). The food at **Restaurant Patrick Guilbaud**, in Upper Merrion Street, is magnificent in the sternest, purest French tradition.

LEFT: a touch of style in Temple Bar.
RIGHT: Ireland's food guru Darina Allen.

These are not everyday eating places, of course, for the average Dubliner, who will complain at length about the outrageous cost of dining out while at the same time insisting on the weekly treat of a restaurant meal. A typical haunt might be **Dobbins Bistro** in Stephen's Lane which has established a reliable reputation since it was founded in the early 1980s and which is also a fun place, especially favoured at lunchtime by politicians and journalists, with sardonic sawdust on the floor in case anyone should take the business of eating out too seriously. Unlike the French, the

Gardens in the southeast suburb of Donnybrook, with its Irish art collection, fire in winter and fountain garden in summer – not to mention its wonderful prawns. The fashion-conscious are more likely to head for **The Tea Room** in the Clarence Hotel on Wellington Quay; the hotel is part-owned by members of U2 and the restaurant has understated mastery of both food and decor, catering for a variety of tastes.

The Irish are still a relatively carnivorous nation, and steak remains unrelentingly popular. Arguably the best steak in town can be found at **L'Ecrivain** on Baggot Street, a small,

Irish are not stiff or ceremonial about food and see no reason why they can't have lots of *craic* (rumbustious conviviality) and red wine with their fish if they want it.

For those seeking French food less rarefied than Patrick Guilbaud's, **Les Frères Jacques** on Dame Street offers a robust cuisine and a cheery yet correct atmosphere. Those with more conservative tastes may favour **Le Coq Hardi** on Pembroke Road, which has a legendary wine list much appreciated by certain politicians – there's even a discreet bedroom for those who have researched it a shade too thoroughly.

Art lovers will enjoy **Ernie's**, in Mulberry

very enjoyable restaurant with a tiny roof garden and a gifted chef-patron, Derry Clarke.

Mid-price places

For a combination of fun and good value, try **Roly's Bistro** in Ballsbridge, an instant hit with its affordable menu of Irish dishes served with classic French flair, or **Gotham Café** on Anne Street, one of several small, trendy spots with contemporary cuisine and gourmet pizzas. More exotically, there's the **Cedar Tree**'s Lebanese fare on Andrew Street.

Further uptown, on Leeson Street, **Sassi's Restaurant** has a lively Mediterranean spring in its step, with food to match the light, bright decor. **La Stampa**, on Dawson Street, a former guild hall, is beloved by narcissists for its huge mirrors, glittering chandeliers and trendy ambience. Wanna-bee model-girls are fond of **Fitzers Cafe**, a trendy chain with outlets in Ballsbridge, Dawson Street and Temple Bar.

Ethnic food

Dublin doesn't have a Chinatown like London or San Francisco, the balti craze that swept Britain made less of an impact here, and there's no Little Italy or Greek Street – indeed, the absence of a really good Greek

of regional cuisine, with little clear distinction between Pakistan, say, and Kurdistan.

Chinese restaurants flourish. The best by a long shot is **Wong's**, which has a branch in Ranelagh and another in Clontarf (both suburbs are easily reached by bus or taxi). Wong's takes its mission seriously, with a clear distinction between the styles of Canton, Szechuan and the other provinces. Unexpectedly, the branch in Clontarf serves superb sea bass – it can be inexplicably difficult to find really great fish in Dublin and why a Chinese restaurant should be your best bet is a mystery. Otherwise, if you're after

restaurant in the city is something of a puzzle. There are three Indian restaurants, however, which are much more than mere curry houses: the **Shalimar** on the corner of George's Street and Wicklow Street, the **Rajdoot** on Clarendon Street, and **Chandni**, which is a little distance out in Ballsbridge. The Rajdoot's reception area, with its brass bowls and dark wood, is particularly attractive, as are the turbanned, pantalooned staff. However, fans of Indian food may be surprised in Dublin to find a frequent mish-mash

fish, the **Lobster Pot** in the southeast suburb of Ballsbridge is reliable, although it's expensive and some find the cooking a little on the heavy side.

The Irish and Italians get on famously, so you'll find lots of excellent pizza and pasta at reasonable prices. The prize for the ultimate pizza goes to **Da Pino** on Parliament Street, while on Dame Street **Nico's**, a long-established restaurant, serves up its veal and spaghetti with a solemn, slightly wistful air. You won't find any opera-singing waiters or stunning saltimbocca in Dublin, no gilding or swagging or much Italian drama; the fun is created chiefly by the customers.

LEFT: Patrick Guilbaud, doyen of French cuisine.
ABOVE: Conrad Gallagher, an Irish chef with attitude.

Inexpensive places

If a social night out is as important to you as culinary quality, the **Mongolian Barbecue** in Temple Bar is great craic. You select the makings of your meal from a free-style array of ingredients and give them to one of the chefs at the open kitchen who grills them on a huge hotplate while you wait. And get talking to everyone in the melée. Because you compose your own meal, you can hardly complain it's not what you ordered.

Also very cheery and chatty is **Pizza Stop**, just off Balfe Street near the Westbury Hotel; owned by a Roman, it offers basic but beau-

tiful pizza and pasta in earthy, red-check and Chianti-flask surroundings.

Mao in Chatham Street, opposite the College of Music, caters for a hip student crowd and matches its sometimes very good Chinese fare with a range of Oriental beers. Along the same lines, **Yamamori** is a Japanese noodle house on George's Street, with big tasty bowls of teriyaki and other delights, washed down with sake. Because of the communal tables, this is a good place to meet people and get talking.

Another cheap and sociable place is at either of the two **university restaurants** at Trinity College and UCD Belfield – not many people realise that visitors are allowed in. The self-service food is not great gastronomy, but it's healthy and good value, in an interesting environment. Finally, the **Kilkenny Centre** on Nassau Street is great for lunch, as is the restaurant in the **National Art Gallery** on Merrion Square.

Taking it home

Seeking out gastronomic souvenirs is an old tradition with visitors to Dublin. "Where can I buy Milleen's cheese/buttermilk bread/smoked salmon/potato cakes to take home?"

The city's food speciality shops tend to be tucked away in odd places. Favourites are **The Big Cheese** in St Andrew's Lane just off Dame Street, **Magill's** on Clarendon Street, **Caviston's** in Sandycove (near the James Joyce museum), the **Epicurean Food Hall** opoosite the north end of the Ha'Penny Bridge, and the **Douglas Food Company** in the southern suburb of Donnybrook. All have interesting ranges of both native and foreign produce, as well as expert owners.

On Saturday mornings there's a food market in Meeting House Square in Temple Bar, which is frequented by entrepreneurs who drive up each week from far-flung parts of the country with their home-made cheeses, sausages, chutneys and so forth. It's not a very big market, but it's cheerful and there's always something new to be sampled.

Buying a range of good food requires a lot of leg-work – there's no massive food hall like Harrods in London or aromatic emporium such as Zabar's in New York. For bread, your best bet is either **Bewley's** on Grafton Street (for brown bread), or **Cooke's** at Castlemarket, off Clarendon Street, if you crave foccacia, tomato or olive concoctions.

But perhaps the best investment is one of Darina Allen's books, whether the *Simply Delicious* series or her large coffee-table tome *A Year at Ballymaloe Cookery School*. Daniel Day-Lewis's sister Tamsin, who spent her childhood summers in Ireland, has also written a delightful coffee-table memoir, *West of Ireland Summers*, packed with recipes for mystical, mouthwatering Celtic fare. ❑

LEFT: the range of Irish cheeses has vastly increased.
RIGHT: what Ireland is surrounded by.

PUBS

Irish theme pubs abroad lack one authentic ingredient found only in Ireland.
It's not the perfectly poured Guinness, it's the intoxicating talk

Pubs are to Dublin what canals are to Venice, and the popular association isn't hard to fathom. They have charm and character. They are warm and friendly. They can be pools of tranquillity or the setting for raucous merriment. And they serve fine food and drink. Odds are, long after your visit to Dublin is over, it's the pubs you'll remember.

Wander into the back room of the Palace Bar in Fleet Street in mid-morning and you enter a little sea of calm. On the walls are sketches and photographs of long-dead bohemians, for this room was a meeting place for writers and painters in the 1940s and '50s - the equivalent of New York's Algonquin Hotel. You can sip your favourite tipple and read your newspaper for hours while, outside the door, the city's traffic roars along Westmoreland Street.

Walk into Doheny and Nesbitt's old-fashioned pub on Baggot Street of an evening and the chances are you'll find an animated argument under way about politics or the economy. Nesbitt's is a haunt of civil servants, politicians and journalists. Cross the road to O'Donogue's and you're in the middle of a lively music session, with fiddle, banjo and tin whistle. Dublin pubs may be varied, but they have one thing in common. They're seldom boring.

A long tradition

Dublin has had a long association with pubs. Richard Barnaby, a 16th-century traveller, remarked on the "streates full of tavernes." In 1682, Sir William Perry observed that, of the 6,025 houses in the city, 1,200 were public houses selling intoxicating liquors. A century later, nothing much had changed. In 1798, Thomas Street, in the old Liberties area, numbered 190 houses, of which 52 were licensed to sell alcohol – more than one in four.

Part of the attraction of pub-life in Dublin is the people you'll find there. Dubliners love to talk and the pub serves as a meeting place for friends and acquaintances. It's a kind of club, but not one that looks coldly on strangers. Sit long enough at a bar-stool in Dublin and you'll be drawn into the conversation and your opinions sought as if you are one of the regulars. Indeed, Dubliners are so addicted to talking and drinking that at one stage the Government

decided that the only way to get people back to work in the afternoon was to close the pubs between 2pm and 3pm. This moratorium was dubbed "the Holy Hour" after a religious observance devoted to penance and prayer. Thankfully it has been abolished.

The Guinness mystique

Until recently Guinness stout, a heavy beer with a sharp, hoppy taste, was the standard drink in Dublin pubs. Serving a pint of Guinness demands skill. The glass must be held at the correct angle to the tap so that the beer runs down the inside of the glass. It is then left for several minutes to settle and finally topped up

---

LEFT: the Brazen Head, Dublin's oldest pub.
RIGHT: O'Donoghue's is a centre for traditional music.

again. It is rare to be served with a bad pint of Guinness in Dublin but you'll know a good one if the beer is cold and black and has a firm creamy head on top. Devotees say there is "eating and drinking" in it *(see pages 168–69)*.

In recent years, Guinness has seen its pre-eminent position challenged by a range of new, lighter beers and ciders. Because the vast majority of pubs are "family houses" – that is, individually owned and not tied to a particular brewery – they can provide a wide variety of brands and brews. It's not unusual to find Ger-man, Spanish, Japanese and Mexican beers on sale, along with a vast array of spirits. In a sense, Dublin pubs have become international.

Other quiet revolutions have been under way. Microbreweries have arrived, providing home-brewed beers for the discerning tippler who has grown tired of the mass-produced products of the big breweries. These are some-times slightly more expensive, but they offer distinctive flavour and taste. Micro beers to watch out for are: St Finians ale, D'Arcy's stout, Beckett's and Revolution ales, Cobble-stone lager, Black Biddy stout and Red Biddy ale. One of the most distinctive microbrew-eries is to be found on the edge of the trendy Temple Bar area at Parliament Street, where

HOW IRISH PUBS CONQUERED THE WORLD

If America can persuade the world to eat McDonald's hamburgers, can Ireland persuade it to drink Guinness? It seems to be doing just that, judging from the explosive international spread of "traditional" Irish pubs. There are more than 1,000 of them now, from Durty Nellie's in Amsterdam to Finnegan's in Abu Dhabi, from Shifty O'Shea's in Leicester, England, to O'Kim's in Seoul, Korea.

Most have rumbustious music, and some carry the theme to absurd lengths by incorporating in the decor such Irish Catholic icons as a pulpit and a confessional. But they all seem to have one thing in common: they sell lots of beer.

How did it all start? Some trace the trend to the 1994

World Cup when Irish football fans descended on bars around the world, creating the convivial atmosphere of a pub back home – and boosting the takings. The increasing popularity of Irish culture has helped things along.

Never slow to spot an opportunity, brewers such as Guinness set up companies to export the Irish pub con-cept. They'll help entrepreneurs anywhere in the world to design their hostelry – you can pick a standard model such as Country Cottage, the Victorian Dublin or the Brewery – and also to locate authentic fittings and recruit staff. But of course they're nothing like the genuine article back in Ireland.

the Porter House is located. Opened in 1996, the pub-brewery has won an award for its Plain Porter and now produces 160 kegs a week of porter, ale and lager. Its owners say that running a successful microbrewery is like running a restaurant, where the skill of the brewmaster, like the chef, is paramount.

Opening times

Most pubs open at 10am, with a handful, known as "early houses", opening at 7am. These are mainly located in the markets and docks areas of the city and are used by workers in the nearby industries, although the general

serving drinks at 11pm in the winter and 11.30pm in summer, with 30 minutes' drinking-up time before the doors are closed. However, there is a tendency for pubs to stay open longer in response to the demands of the tourist trade. A growing number of pubs in the city-centre now serve until 2am and there is a lobby to have them open even longer.

Food has become important. Whereas 20 years ago, pubs were mainly for drinking and socialising – and a customer would be lucky to get a stale ham sandwich – Dublin pubs now provide a range of keenly-priced, well-cooked meals, particularly at lunchtime. Indeed "pub

public will also be served. The "early houses" tend to be functional drinking places, lacking the style and comfort of city-centre pubs. The morning period in most pubs tends to be quiet, with trade picking up at lunchtime and falling off again in the afternoon, so if it's a quiet, reflective drink you seek, this is the time to go.

Dublin pubs come into their own in the evening, as people finish work or go for a night-out and they can become packed and noisy, particularly at weekends. They stop

LEFT: many trendy bars have opened in the city centre.
ABOVE: Hughes Bar is one of the places where Dublin people go to hear traditional music.

grub" can sometimes rival that of established restaurants and Dubliners now go as readily to the pub to eat as to drink.

When size matters

Pubs are also getting bigger. In the past they mainly consisted of one room, or bar, with perhaps a snug where women could go at a time when it wasn't polite for females to be seen drinking in public. They have been expanding so that many now have several bars on different floors and have become vast drinking emporiums where a customer could easily get lost. There is also a trend towards memorabilia, with old photographs, road signs, musical instruments, books and even farm utensils such as butter churns on display to add atmosphere. Older Dublin drinkers dislike this development and some argue that the cosy intimacy of the traditional pub is being lost. Thankfully, most pubs have been spared the scourge of pinball machines, juke-boxes and pool tables.

What to ask for

A word about pub etiquette. The standard measure for beer is the pint, so if you simply ask for a beer you'll be served a pint. However if you just ask for "a pint", you'll be served a pint of Guinness, so it's best to be specific about

what beer you want, when ordering drinks. If you want a half-pint, ask for "a glass."

Where to go? This depends very much on what you want. If it's a quiet drink in pleasant surroundings, try Neary's of Chatham Street with its distinctive iron arms holding street lamps outside. This is also a favourite pub for actors and showbusiness people from the nearby theatres. Doyle's at College Green, across the road from Trinity College, provides good food and service and some quiet corners. This is the local pub for journalists from the nearby *Irish Times*.

Bowes of Fleet Street is a small pub with a quiet, intimate atmosphere. The Bailey in Duke Street has a comfortable ambience and a reputation for style. Across the road, Davy Byrne's is famous for being mentioned in *Ulysses*, but it's no longer the modest establishment it was when James Joyce drank there. There's hardly a pub in Dublin where playwright Brendan Behan didn't drink, but one establishment is strongly associated with him. This is McDaid's on Harry Street, near the top of Grafton Street. It's a small, plain pub with a high ceiling but it was the meeting place for well-known writers in the 1950s.

Taverns with tunes

Many Dublin pubs provide traditional Irish music sessions. Standards vary, but it's rare to find a session that isn't entertaining. Some of the best music is to be heard in Hughes's pub in Chancery Street, at the rear of the Four Courts, Mother Redcap's Tavern in Christchurch Back Lane, near the cathedral and the Brazen Head in Lower Bridge Street, which has the oldest licence in Ireland (1666) and was once the haunt of rebels and revolutionaries. The nearby Merchant is also worth a visit for its set dance sessions. Times and nights vary, so it's advisable to telephone.

If you don't find yourself near any of these places, there's no need to worry. Just look around for the nearest hostelry where the locals look settled in, glasses raised; where the warm, inviting mutter of human voices locked in chat just grazes your ears as you enter. That's the place you're looking for. That's your local for the night. ❏

THE THEME PUB ARRIVES

One recent development is the arrival in Dublin of theme pubs. These are best described as drinking emporiums – Zanzibar, for example, on the north quays near the Ha'penny Bridge, can accommodate 1,200 people. This vast pub has an African/Arabian theme and is decorated with mirrors, lights, palm trees and giant urns. It is crowded each evening with Dublin's twenty-something trendsetters.

Other such pubs include Pravda in Lower Liffey Street, which has a Russian Revolution theme, and the Odeon Bar, situated in the old railway station in Harcourt Street with space for 1,000 drinkers.

Left: the other hand is holding a pint.
Right: who's buying the next round?

PLACES

*A detailed guide to the city and surroundings, with principal
sites clearly cross-referenced by number to the maps*

> *In Dublin's fair city*
> *Where the girls are so pretty,*
> *I first set my eyes on sweet Molly Malone.*
> *She wheeled her wheelbarrow*
> *Through streets broad and narrow,*
> *Crying, "Cockles and mussels, alive, alive, oh!"*

Today, two centuries after Molly was immortalised by an
anonymous versifier, her descendants keep alive the street-
market tradition. These days they wheel prams, battered
baby carriages outgrown by infants and now filled with a bewildering variety of fruit or firewood, bananas or bric-a-brac, toys
or trinkets. Their sharpwitted patter is equally bewildering, but
usually delivered with a charm that makes it all too painless for
you to part with your money.

Dublin is a city for walkers, a city of chance encounters, a
city where the people are as worth watching as the architecture. In the past it has had an untidy, abstracted kind of elegance,
as if its mind was on something more important than looking
attractive. Now, as the city restores and revitalises its shabbier
quarters, it has been given a facelift of spirit as well as of appearance, taking its place among the more vibrant capitals of Europe.

It is a divided city: divided by the River Liffey that flows
through its centre and by the social differences which the river
delineates. The split began in the early 18th century when the
rich moved north across the river from the old medieval city
with its teeming slums to the fine new terraces and squares such
as Henrietta Street and Mountjoy Square. Then the fashion set-
ters doubled back to establish enclaves on the southside in Merrion Square and Fitzwilliam Square. Next they drifted to the
suburbs of Ballsbridge and out along the coast to scenic spots
such as Dun Laoghaire and Dalkey.

But, whether they're northsiders or southsiders, people still
have time for the visitor. So get to know them, gaze at their
grand public buildings, their Georgian squares and their graceful lamp standards, walk through their galleries, their parks
and their gardens, wander into their bookshops and their pubs,
make excursions to the surrounding mountains and resorts, and
soon Dublin will feel like the most delightful place on earth.
What other capital city, after all, has a General Post Office as
a national shrine?   ❑

PRECEDING PAGES: the Grand Canal; O'Connell Bridge, looking north to O'Connell
Street; Ha'penny Bridge, free these days, the original footbridge over the Liffey.
LEFT: crying "Cockles and mussels" – the Molly Malone statue in Grafton Street.

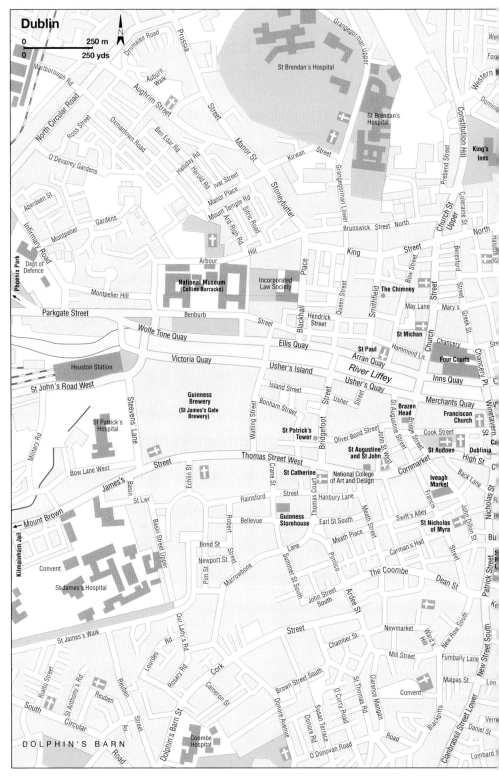

Dublin

St Brendan's Hospital

St Brendan's Hospital

King's Inns

National Museum (Collins Barracks)

Incorporated Law Society

The Chimney

St Michan

St Paul

Four Courts

Heuston Station

Guinness Brewery (St James's Gate Brewery)

Brazen Head

Franciscan Church

St Patrick's Hospital

St Patrick's Tower

St Augustine and St John

St Audoen

Dublinia

Thomas Street West

St Catherine

National College of Art and Design

Iveagh Market

Guinness Storehouse

St Nicholas of Myra

Convent

St James's Hospital

The Coombe

Convent

Coombe Hospital

DOLPHIN'S BARN

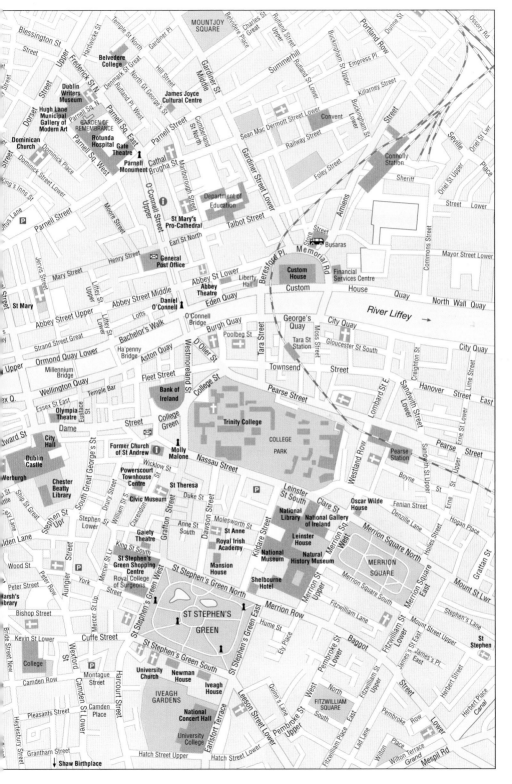

THE CITY CENTRE

Map on page 124

Within easy walking distance you can find the grandeur of the Bank of Ireland and Trinity College, the trendiness of Grafton Street and the tranquillity of St Stephen's Green

Dublin in the 18th century was concentrated between its two artificial waterways, the Grand Canal on the south side, with its series of delicate locks and bridges, and the Royal Canal on the north. It was bisected by the River Liffey with its elegant quays. As the century progressed, so did the speed and splendour of the building programme. By an Act of 1756, Dublin established the Wide Streets Commission, Europe's first town planning authority, which laid down practical and aesthetic guidelines for building development. Other bodies organised paving and lighting.

After the Act of Union transferred political authority to London in 1800, the Wide Streets Commission was disbanded, property values plummeted, and the great houses designed for fastidious aristocracy passed first into the hands of the professional middle classes, then became tenements housing Dublin's multitudinous poor. Conservation was not a major issue after Ireland achieved independence in 1921, and uncontrolled property development during the 1960s did irreparable damage to many of the city's elegant squares. Yet much remains.

The Bank of Ireland

College Green, where the city's north–south and east–west axes intersect, has a strong claim to be considered the centre of Dublin. It is flanked by two of the city's grandest 18th-century buildings, the Bank of Ireland and Trinity College.

You might think that the **Bank of Ireland ❶**, with its curving, columnar, windowless facade, exudes loftier ideals than those of commerce, and you would be right: it was begun in 1729 to house the Irish parliament and its builders could not have foreseen how brief would be its age of glory. Although at least four architects were engaged in designing and altering the building over about 80 years, it has a remarkable integrity of style. Edward Lovett Pearce planned the central section; James Gandon designed the east front in 1785; Francis Johnston altered both east and west sides during the conversion from parliament to bank after 1803.

The House of Parliament on College Green was at the centre of the great surge in prosperity and self-confidence among the wealthy Anglo-Irish of the 18th century, who grew increasingly restive about their subservience to England and began to dream of an independent nation. In 1783, under the inspiring leadership of Henry Grattan (1746–1820), its greatest orator, the parliament gained legislative independence under the English crown.

But the more radical ideals behind the American and French revolutions had also taken root in Ireland, culminating in the ill-fated 1798 rebellion. England reacted

LEFT AND BELOW: the Bank of Ireland.

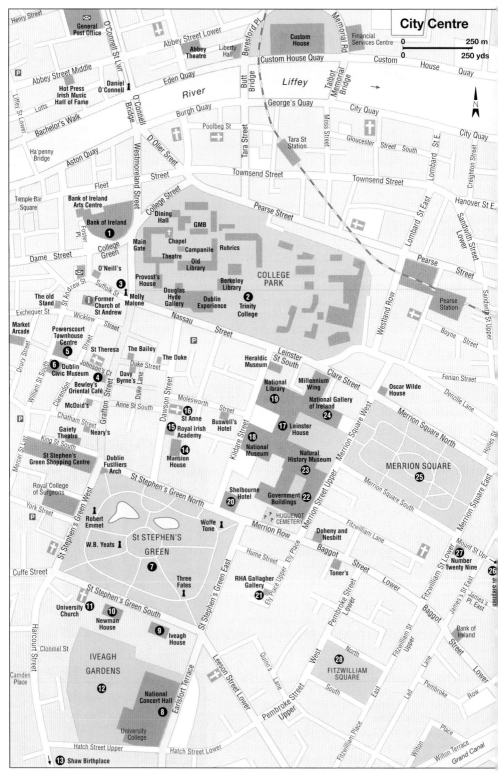

City Centre

by passing the 1800 Act of Union, dissolving the Irish parliament and bringing all power back to London, a move that had disastrous economic consequences for Ireland. The parliament's members, through a mixture of fear and bribery, acquiesced in its extinction and the building was sold to the Bank of Ireland for £40,000.

Above the Royal Arms on the main portico is a statue of Hibernia, with Fidelity and Commerce on either side. The east front, built as an entrance to the House of Lords, has a statue of Fortitude, flanked by Justice and Liberty.

Map on page 124

Past glories on display

The former House of Commons is now the bank's cash office, and bears little resemblance to its former self, but the House of Lords remains virtually untouched, with a splendid 1,233-piece chandelier and two grand Huguenot tapestries, illustrating the Siege of Derry in 1689 and the Battle of the Boyne in 1690, when the Protestant King William of Orange defeated the Catholic King James II of England on an Irish battlefield. It can be viewed during banking hours (Monday, Tuesday, Wednesday and Friday 10am–4pm, Thursday 10am–5pm, free) and there are excellent guided tours on Tuesdays only, at 10.30am, 11.30am and 1.45pm.

The Speaker's Mace from the House of Commons, which used to be called "Goose-pie" after its dome and dates from 1765, is also on view, as is Maundy money, the little coins which used to be given to the poor on the Thursday before Easter and could only be spent on that day.

The cannon and sentry boxes outside the building date from the early 19th century when a militia was formed to guard the bank. The present-day attendants – not military men, these – can be recognised by their distinctive attire: frock coats, scarlet waistcoats and tall hats.

Banking tradition.

BELOW: the Bank's grand chandelier.

Trinity students.

The **Bank of Ireland Arts Centre** in Foster Place, to the Dame Street side of the bank, houses The Story of Banking (Tuesday to Friday 10am–4pm, admission charge), an interactive exhibition on the building's history. This is also a venue for lunchtime and evening music recitals.

In the middle of College Green stands a statue of Henry Grattan. Although he was a member of the Protestant Ascendancy, Grattan espoused, in both the Dublin and London parliaments, the cause of Catholic Emancipation. His concept was that Ireland should be an independent country like England, with both of them sharing the same monarch within the British Empire.

Trinity College

Grattan is depicted frozen in mid-gesture, apparently addressing one of his ringing speeches to the facade of **Trinity College ❷**. Founded in 1591 by Elizabeth I on the site of a confiscated monastery, Trinity covers 16 hectares (40 acres) in the centre of the city on land reclaimed from the Liffey estuary. It doesn't quite have the grandeur of the Bank and was described by James Joyce in *A Portrait of the Artist as a Young Man* as being "set heavily in the city's ignorance like a dull stone set in a cumbrous ring."

Trinity remained an exclusively Protestant university for most of its history, having been set up by Queen Elizabeth to "civilise" the Irish and keep them from the influences of "Popery". The college has lost some, if not all, of its air of Ascendancy since the restriction on Catholic students was lifted in 1873. But until comparatively recently it was considered a dangerous place for church-going Catholics, and indeed it is only since 1970 that Catholics have attended in substantial numbers.

BELOW: Trinity College, with old library on right

STUDENT LIFE AT TRINITY

Trinity students have been associated over the centuries with an excess of hooliganism or privilege, usually both. The police still cannot enter Front Gate (Dublin's most popular rendezvous spot) unless invited in, but the students still pour out to make many of their social activities part of the city's as well.

The college has relinquished a fair degree of its mystique, especially since "The Ban" on Roman Catholics (by their own church) was lifted in 1970, but anyone in Dublin on a very special May night will remark on the queues of bow ties and ball gowns filing into the college around midnight for the Trinity Ball. The examination hall rumbles to rock, the podium in front of the new library beats to disco. At dawn, Dublin's cafés receive the wilting merrymakers.

The Ball comes as a climax to Trinity Week, an event much diluted by the modern move of annual examinations from September to June. Trinity Week still highlights the university's sporting profile, with the College Races on the traditional grass around College Park. This beautiful arena is more usually used for rugby and hockey in winter, and cricket in summer.

Students run tours of the college in summer— the only time you'll see them anywhere near the *Book of Kells*.

In academic circles, Oxford, Cambridge and Trinity were often mentioned in the same breath, and many English students who failed to make the first two ended up at "Trinners". Women students were admitted in 1903, earlier than in most British universities. Famous alumni include literary figures such as Oscar Wilde, Samuel Beckett, Thomas Moore, Sheridan Le Fanu, John Millington Synge, Oliver St John Gogarty and Bram Stoker. Politicians, rebels and statesmen such as Edward Carson, Douglas Hyde (Ireland's first president), Henry Grattan, Wolfe Tone and Robert Emmet also made their mark.

Most of Trinity's buildings date from the 18th century. The Palladian facade, surmounted by a surprisingly bright blue clock, was built between 1755 and 1759. The entrance is flanked by statues of two of Trinity's many famous alumni, the historian and statesman Edmund Burke (1729–97) and the writer Oliver Goldsmith (1728–74). Goldsmith is missing a pen that he once held, and it is rumoured that the college declined an offer from a well-known pen manufacturer to replace it. During term time, the poster-covered noticeboards at "Front Gate", inside the College Green entrance, give some idea of the varied activities that occupy the 7,000 students during and outside their lecture hours.

The main gate leads to a spacious, cobbled quadrangle, on the right of which is the **Theatre**, or Examination Hall (1779–91), which contains a gilt oak chandelier from the old parliament, a gilded black organ said to have been taken from a Spanish ship at Vigo in 1702, and many interesting portraits, including those of Elizabeth I (1533–1603), Jonathan Swift (1667–1747), George Berkeley, philosopher and bishop (1685–1753) and Edmund Burke.

Facing the Theatre across the quadrangle is its mirror image, the **Chapel** (1792), which today is used by all Christian denominations. Both Theatre and

Maps, pages 124, 128

TIP

Walking tours of Trinity – which include the fee to see the *Book of Kells* – start at the main gate on College Green (daily 10.15am–5pm, mid-April to October only).

BELOW:
Trinity College, founded in 1591.

The Virgin and Child, from the 9th-century Book of Kells.

Chapel were designed by Sir William Chambers, a Scottish neo-classicist architect who, oddly enough, never visited Ireland.

Beside the Chapel is the **Dining Hall** (1743), badly damaged by fire in 1984 but since restored. The 30-metre (100-ft) campanile which dominates the quadrangle was designed by Sir Charles Lanyon and erected in 1853 on a spot supposed to mark the centre of the medieval monastery church.

The red-brick building facing you beyond the campanile is **Rubrics** ("red brick"), the oldest surviving part of the college, built as living quarters around 1700. Oliver Goldsmith had rooms here, and John Ruskin so approved of the building that he commissioned the architect, Benjamin Woodward, and his stonecarvers for the Oxford Museum of Natural History. The walls of **Graduates' Memorial Building** (GMB), which separates Botany Bay (where some of the students' rooms are located) from the front square, have echoed to raised voices in many a heated college debate, whilst countless games of cricket, rugby and hockey have been played on College Park.

The Book of Kells

To the right of Rubrics is the **Old Library** (1712–32), where Trinity's greatest treasure, the **Book of Kells**, is kept in the Treasury (Mon–Sat 9.30–5pm, Sun June–Sept 9.30am–4.30pm, Oct–May noon–4.30pm, admission charge). The *Book of Kells* ("Kelly's Book", as it has been called by some less informed visitors) is a magnificently decorated copy of the gospels in Latin, created by unknown scribes at Kells, County Meath, around 800 – or possibly written at a monastery on the island of Iona, off western Scotland, and brought to Kells for safety from Viking raids. It is the greatest artefact of the flowering of Irish culture between the 7th and 9th centuries, the era when Ireland was famed as "the island of saints and scholars" and Irish monks re-Christianised Europe after the Dark Ages. In 1007 a writer described the book as "the most precious object of the Western world". Being both priceless and fragile, the book is kept in a plate-glass case and only two pages are displayed at a time.

Other illustrated manuscripts in the Treasury include the 7th-century *Book of Durrow*, the 8th-century *Book of Dimma* and the 9th-century *Book of Armagh*. An accompanying exhibition explains the creation of these remarkable works and places them in historical and cultural context.

Upstairs from the Treasury is the breathtaking **Long Room**, almost 64 metres (209 ft) in length and containing some 200,000 of the college's oldest books on two floors of shelves lining each side and rising to a lofty, barrel-vaulted ceiling. Precious books and manuscripts from the library's collections are displayed in cases down the centre of the room, flanked by marble busts of great thinkers and writers such as Plato, Cicero, Newton, Boyle and Goldsmith. The bust of Jonathan Swift is particularly fine. Priceless manuscripts include Greek and Latin tracts, works on Egyptian papyri, Irish texts from the 16th and 17th centuries and one of William Shakespeare's earliest folios.

Under the Library Act of 1801, Trinity became one of four libraries in Britain and Ireland to receive by en-

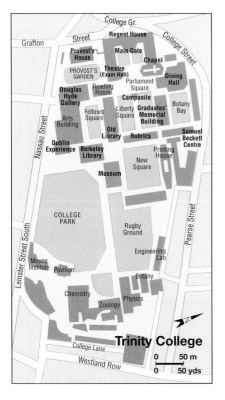

Trinity College

titlement a copy of every book published in the two countries. Although a boon for students and researchers, this entitlement caused some storage problems for the college librarian. Seven libraries, spread over the campus and beyond, house something like 3 million volumes and at one point the amount of shelving was increasing by half a mile a year.

Map on page 128

The Long Room also contains Ireland's oldest harp, probably 15th-century, for long erroneously known as "**Brian Ború's Harp**" (Brian, high king of Ireland, died in 1014). This is the harp which appears on Irish coins as an emblem of bardic society.

The modern concrete building beside the Old Library is the **Berkeley Library** (1967), designed by Paul Koralek and described by the author Brendan Lehane as "an annexe of shuttered concrete that has a claim to be the best modern building in Ireland." It is named after Bishop George Berkeley, the great 18th-century philosopher who came to study at Trinity in 1700 at the age of 15 and later served for a time as the college librarian. Regarded by some as the precursor of Einstein and the father of higher education in America, Berkeley, who was born in Kilkenny, was also a distinguished scientist, economist, psychologist and writer.

Brian Ború's Harp.

He tried unsuccessfully to found a college in Bermuda "for the education of the sons of English planters and of native Indians." Being 1,600 miles (2,500 km) from mainland colonial America, it proved to be an impractical institution, and he subsequently donated part of his library to Yale and Harvard. He also advised his friend, the American philosopher Samuel Johnson, on the founding of what is now Columbia University of New York, donated his residence to Newhaven College, Connecticut, and helped to found the Uni-

BELOW: Trinity College's Long Room Library.

versity of Pennsylvania. A reformer who held strong views on Irish economic nationalism and self-sufficiency, he is honoured less in Ireland than in the United States, where both the University of Berkeley, California and Berkeley Divinity School, Newhaven, are named after him.

Douglas Hyde, the son of a Protestant clergyman and a Trinity graduate, was a principal founder of the Gaelic League, set up in 1893 to champion the Irish language. In 1933 he became Eire's first president.

The same architect designed the adjacent Arts Block, which faces onto Nassau Street and houses the **Douglas Hyde Gallery**, a venue for contemporary art exhibitions. In the same building during the summer is the **Dublin Experience**, a 45-minute audiovisual introduction to the city (late May to early October daily every hour 10am–5pm). The playing fields on College Park, behind the Berkeley Library, are a relaxing place to stroll.

A left turn on leaving Trinity by the main gate brings you past the **Provost House** (1759), "the most perfect house in Dublin," according to Maurice Craig, author of *Dublin 1660–1860*. Unlike most of Dublin's other great Georgian houses, it still serves its original purpose and is the home of the college head. The main interior features are the entrance hall, the octagonal staircase and the saloon, and its paintings include a portrait of Queen Elizabeth I and a Gainsborough portrait of the Duke of Bedford. Its design is an adaptation by John Smyth of the Burlington House built in London for General Wade.

Grafton Street

BELOW: Grafton Street, Dublin's chic shopping venue.

Past the Provost House is the entrance to **Grafton Street**, named after an 18th-century viceroy and now the southside's main shopping and social artery. A bronze statue ❸ at the junction with Suffolk Street depicts **Molly Malone**, the fictional 18th-century fishmonger supposedly buried in St Werburgh's Church and eternally commemorated in the city's most famous song, "In Dublin's fair

city" (*for picture of statue, see page 118, for lyrics of song, see page 119*). Her generously sculpted bosom has prompted some to wonder how its designer, Jean Rynhart, managed to transplant silicon into bronze and, with typically dry Dublin wit, the statue is universally known as "the tart with the cart".

But a leisurely walk up Grafton Street, which was pedestrianised in 1982 and more recently paved with red bricks, should soon persuade the visitor that the girls are still so pretty: the street is constantly thronged with people, many of them young, many of them seemingly here (especially on Saturday mornings) just to see and be seen. In the summer, artists often produce chalk pictures on the pavement near the statue – a precarious business, given the climate.

More than anywhere else, Grafton Street exudes a sense of Dublin's knack for seeming to bustle and dawdle at the same time. Admittedly, it has lost a little of its character in recent years as rising rents have forced out some long-established traders and UK-based multiples have moved in. The former premises of Dublin's most prestigious store, Brown Thomas, is now occupied by Marks and Spencer, while Brown Thomas has moved across the street, displacing another old Dublin firm, Switzers. But the atmosphere of Grafton Street is a world away from, say, the joyless commercialism of London's Oxford Street and a stroll along it, especially if it's sunny, never fails to lift the spirits, with its flower-sellers, talented buskers and crowds of cheerful strollers.

Halfway up the street on the right is **Bewley's Oriental Café ❹**, one of a chain of old-fashioned shop-restaurants that have long been a Dublin institution (*see feature on the following page*). Most of the food is unremarkable, but the bitter, milky coffee is still one of Dublin's distinctive tastes, and you can eat a meringue or a cherry bun or the inimitable Mary cake at a marble-topped table and soak

Map on page 124

A favourite place to go when clubs close.

BELOW: Powerscourt Townhouse Centre.

The Bewley's Experience

As much a piece of Dublin as Guinness stout, the Ha'penny Bridge or the River Liffey itself, Bewley's Oriental Cafés – in Westmoreland Street, Mary Street, Grafton Street and South Great George's Street – have been haunts where generations of Dubliners meet, eat, drink tea or coffee and, above all, talk.

The Bewley family, Quakers by belief, arrived in Ireland in 1700, fleeing religious persecution in England. They settled in the midland counties and migrated to Dublin at the end of the 18th century. In about 1840 Joshua Bewley opened a teashop in Sycamore Alley, off Dame Street, near where the Olympia Theatre now stands. Later, he moved to nearby South Great George's Street.

His two sons, Charles and Ernest, joined the business. Ernest was ambitious and believed that the firm was not big enough to support the three of them. Impatient for expansion, he left to start a poultry farm and rejoined the family firm after his brother emigrated to New Zealand.

At the turn of the century, Ernest bought premises at 19–20 Fleet Street, intending to open a bicycle shop. But it became a café instead. Coffee, the sales of which were then small, was supplied by Ernest's cousin. When they fell out, Ernest bought one hundredweight (about 50kg) of coffee from a wholesaler and "shook in his shoes" in case he never sold it.

Milk from a herd of Jersey cows he had introduced to his farm in Rathgar was soon being served in the café, a bakery was started, and in 1916 the adjoining shop in Westmoreland Street was opened. Decorated in Oriental style, this café had a doorman who helped elegant ladies from carriages and motor cars. And it was one of the first cafés in the country with a "No Smoking" sign.

In 1927 Ernest Bewley fulfilled a life-long ambition when he opened his shop and café at 78–79 Grafton Street, on the site of Samuel Whyte's famous school where Robert Emmet, Thomas Moore, Richard Brinsley Sheridan and the Duke of Wellington had been pupils.

In 1971 Bewley's employees were given the option of buying shares in what became known as "the Bewley Community Ltd" – the first example of such industrial democracy in Ireland. It was typical of the family's philanthropic spirit, manifested by Victor Bewley, who ran the firm after his father died in 1932. Victor championed the cause of itinerants, providing four halting-sites in the grounds of his house in Brittas, Co. Dublin.

In the mid-1980s, however, with the firm hit hard by changing tastes and increasing competition, the employees sold their shares to Campbell Catering, and the cafés began going over to self-service.

The Grafton Street branch retains Harry Clarke's *Birds of Paradise* stained-glass window, and the Westmoreland Street branch has the original wooden pews popular with writers such as James Joyce, Brendan Behan and Flann O'Brien. ❑

LEFT: the way it was... Museum Café at Bewley's in Grafton Street.

up the atmosphere. Insomniacs and night-clubbers are well catered for: the premises stay open until 5am on Fridays and Saturdays and 1am other nights.

Next to Bewley's, at Number 79, is the site of Whyte's Academy, the celebrated school whose pupils include Richard Brinsley Sheridan, Thomas Moore, Robert Emmet, and Arthur Wellesley (better known as the Duke of Wellington).

Map on page 124

Stylish shopping

Johnson's Court, a narrow alley running along the side of Bewley's, leads to the **Powerscourt Townhouse Centre ❺** (open 9am–6pm weekdays with late opening on Thursday until 7pm). This is an architecturally splendid three-storey collection of 80 stylish shops, cafés and restaurants stacked around an enclosed courtyard under the roof of the former townhouse built in 1771–74 by Viscount Powerscourt, who was once MP for Co. Wicklow. It mixes rococo and neoclassical styles and contains some of the finest plasterwork in Ireland. The enclosed courtyard at its heart hosts Wednesday-lunchtime concerts of light music and jazz, and has a balcony made from 18th-century pitched pine beams from an old Guinness malting house.

If you walk through the centre, exiting on William Street South, on your left, at number 58, is the small **Dublin Civic Museum ❻** (Tuesday to Saturday, 10am–6pm, Sunday 11am–2pm, free entry), which has a range of artefacts relating to the city's history, including the damaged head of Admiral Lord Nelson from the O'Connell Street pillar toppled by the IRA in 1966 as their contribution to marking the 50th anniversary of the Easter Rising. There are also interesting prints of the great 18th-century streets, and a copy of the 1877 by-laws of St Stephen's Green which forbid entry not only to those "in an intoxi-

The son of Viscount Powerscourt sold Powerscourt House to the government in 1811. It was used as stamp duty offices until 1832, when it was bought by a wholesale warehouse company. It became a modern shopping centre in 1981.

BELOW:
Davy Byrne's bar on Bloomsday.

St Stephen's Green.

cated, unclean or verminous condition" but also to "any dog which may be reasonably suspected to be in a rabid state."

Two other upmarket shopping malls run off Grafton Street: **Royal Hibernian Way**, which links Grafton Street to Dawson Street, via Duke Lane; and the **Westbury Centre**, beside the Westbury Hotel in Harry Street, which can also be entered from Johnson's Court. There is also an interesting covered market linking Drury Street to South Great George's Street.

Notable pubs

Grafton Street's tributaries contain several notable pubs. **Davy Byrne's** in Duke Street was immortalised by James Joyce in *Ulysses* when Leopold Bloom stopped there for a Gorgonzola cheese sandwich with mustard washed down with a glass of Burgundy, but these days the pub is frequented by a young set who are probably not intimately acquainted with Joyce's work.

The Bailey, facing it across the street, used to be favoured by a literary and bohemian set but has also been taken over by the young and voguish. **McDaid's** in Harry Street was a haunt in the 1950s of well-known writers such as Brendan Behan and Patrick Kavanagh. **Neary's** of Chatham Street, with its Victorian-style marble-topped bar, mahogany surrounds and brass lighting, still attracts a theatrical crowd.

St Stephen's Green

BELOW:
feeding time in St
Stephen's Green.

At the top of Grafton Street you face the Fusiliers' Arch, the main entrance to **St Stephen's Green ❼**, a delightfully informal park bordered by elegant houses. The arch commemorates the 212 soldiers of the Royal Dublin Fusiliers who died

in the Boer War (1899–1902). Delightful though St Stephen's Green itself is, its setting was partially spoiled by the thoughtless 20th-century development which ruined the integrity of the Georgian buildings on two sides of the park. But much interesting architecture remains, and it is worth walking the four sides of the green to view such splendid buildings as the **Shelbourne Hotel** (*see page 146*) on the north side.

Also on the north side are the United Services Club (1754) at number 8, the St Stephen's Green Club (1756) at number 9, the University Club (1776–78) at number 17, and the Friendly Brothers' House at number 22. Just beyond the Shelbourne, a small 17th-century cemetery contains the remains of some of the Huguenots who fled from persecution in France in the reign of Louis XIV.

The park's west side – straight ahead as you leave Grafton Street – was particularly ruined by the property developers, apart from the neo-classical **College of Surgeons** (built in 1806 and extended in 1825–27), whose library contains more than 30,000 volumes. The bullet scars on its Doric columns date from the 1916 Easter Rising, when the building was occupied by the flamboyant Constance Markievicz, an Irish nationalist married to a Polish count and the first woman elected to the British House of Commons (though she wouldn't take her seat). Immediately to your right is the **St Stephen's Green Shopping Centre**, a curvilinear steel and glass erection of the late 1980s.

The 9-hectare (22-acre) green, formerly an open common where public executions were held, was enclosed in 1663, but it was not surrounded by buildings until the late 18th century, when it became one of the most fashionable spots in Dublin – the north side was known as the Beaux' Walk. In the early 19th century, railings and gates were added and an annual entrance fee was

Map on page 124

Shelbourne Hotel.

BELOW:
St Stephen's Green shopping centre.

imposed. Thanks to pressure and money from the Guinness family, the gardens were laid out as a public park in 1880 and are a great place for relaxing and people-watching.

The green contains several interesting statues, including one of the park's main benefactors, Sir Arthur Guinness, and (just outside the railings) one of the patriot Robert Emmet (1778–1803). The sculpture of the poet William Butler Yeats was created in 1967 by Henry Moore. There's a duck pond, a children's playground, and a Victorian bandstand where lunchtime concerts are held in summer. Just inside the park at the north-eastern corner is a memorial to the victims of the devastating 1845–48 potato famine.

Near the green's central fountain is a garden for the visually impaired; the plants are labelled in braille. At the south-west corner is the Park Keeper's cottage, which dates from the time when the green was used as grazing land for the Lord Mayor's sheep and cattle.

Famous residents

Leading off the east side of the green are **Hume Street** and **Ely Place**. Number 4 Ely Place was once the home of George Moore. The writer and surgeon Oliver St John Gogarty (1878–1957), the model for "stately, plump Buck Mulligan" in James Joyce's *Ulysses*, lived in number 25, which is now part of the art gallery of the Royal Hibernian Academy (*see page 147*). Number 8, Ely House, facing Hume Street, is the headquarters of the Catholic organisation, the Knights of Columbanus, which some feel has echoes of freemasonry. In former times, the house was frequented by W. B. Yeats, the poet George Russell (more commonly known as AE) and the patriot Maud Gonne.

BELOW: buskers in Grafton Street.

Map on page 124

At the south-east corner of St Stephen's Green, by the Leeson Street exit, is the **Three Fates statue**, presented by West Germany in 1966 as thanks for Irish aid after World War II. The monument, cast in bronze, was designed by the Bavarian sculpture Josef Wackerle.

From here, you can detour briefly along **Earlsfort Terrace** – opposite the gates of the green – to see the **National Concert Hall** ❽. This is the city's principal venue for classical music, housed in the former headquarters of University College Dublin (UCD), which is now based in a modern campus at Belfield, in the southern suburbs. The building, begun for the Great Exhibition of 1865 and later enlarged, has been nicely remodelled and has first-rate acoustics. There is a pleasant café/restaurant off the foyer.

Georgian townhouses

Back on the south side of St Stephen's Green, at number 80, is **Iveagh House** ❾, which dates from 1730 and was the earliest Dublin building designed by the fashionable German architect Richard Cassels (also known as Castle) and once the home of the Guinness family. Together with number 81, it now houses the Department of Foreign Affairs.

Numbers 85 and 86 comprise **Newman House** ❿ (June to August, Tuesday to Friday noon– 5pm, Saturday 2–5pm, admission charge; closed September to May, except by appointment). These two Georgian townhouses were acquired in the mid-19th century for the Catholic University of Ireland, forerunner of University College Dublin. John Henry Newman (1801–90), the English theologian and writer who had famously converted from Anglicanism, was its first rector and the poet Gerard Manley Hopkins was Professor of

"It is almost a definition of a gentleman to say that he is one who never inflicts pain," wrote John Henry Newman. The cardinal was also the author of some famous hymns, such as "Lead, Kindly Light, amid the encircling gloom."

BELOW: Newman House saloon.

Classics here from 1884 to 1889. The college's alumni include Patrick Pearse, Eamon de Valera and James Joyce – the place is the setting for several scenes in Joyce's *Portrait of the Artist as a Young Man*.

But the main attraction for the visitor is to see the houses' interior plasterwork, probably the best of its kind in Ireland and an indication of the strong influence that continental styles had on Irish craftsmanship. **Number 85** was built in 1738 as a small but splendid town villa for Hugh Montgomery, a wealthy Ulster landowner and member of parliament. The walls and ceiling of the ground-floor Apollo Room and first-floor Saloon feature marvellous baroque decorations by the Swiss Lafranchini brothers. When the Saloon was converted for use as a chapel, the Jesuit fathers censored the more voluptuous female forms on the ceiling by painting on costumes.

Number 86, which is much larger, was begun in 1765 for Richard "Burnchapel" Whaley, a raging anti-Catholic (hence the nickname) whose son, Buck, was a notorious rake and flamboyant member of the Hell Fire Club. He once jumped from a first-floor window of the house into a coach – for a wager, of course. Given the Whaleys' sectarian views, it is quite an irony that their house should have become a centre of resurgent Catholicism – one of its rooms, dominated by a heavy Victorian table lined with chairs, is known as the Bishops Room because the Church prelates held meetings there.

The plasterwork of number 86, by Robert West, is rococo, featuring flowers, musical instruments, birds and winged monsters rather than human figures. The upstairs room where Hopkins lodged – unhappily – for five years until his death in 1889 is preserved as it was in his day – cassock flung on chair, spectacles on mantlepiece, letters and manuscript (facsimile) on his desk. Also apparently frozen

The Hell Fire Club was founded in 1735 by Richard Parsons, first Earl of Rosse, in the Eagle Tavern, Cork Hill. The devil is said to have turned up for one function – a nice piece of image-making by the colourful members.

BELOW: the first-floor saloon of Newman House. **BELOW RIGHT:** University Church.

in time is the **Physics Theatre**, where James Joyce once attended lectures.

Next to Newman House is the small **University Church ❶** (1856). Because Dr Newman (whose bust you can find on the right-hand side) felt that Gothic was an insufficiently Christian style, it was designed under his direction by John Hungerford Pollen in a remarkably colourful neo-Byzantine style, with some pure Muslim references. Today, fashionable couples get married here.

Continue along the south side of St Stephen's Green and turn left into **Harcourt Street**, where Edward Carson, the great Ulster Unionist leader and prosecutor of Oscar Wilde, was born in number 4. A left turn into **Clonmel Street** leads into the leafy **Iveagh Gardens ⓬**, smaller and quieter than St Stephen's Green, with pleasant fountains and gravel paths.

Map on page 124

Where Shaw was born

This is a restful spot in which to end a tour of this part of the city, but admirers of the playwright George Bernard Shaw (1856–1950) will summon energy to walk for another 10 minutes or so – to the top of Harcourt Street, then right along Harcourt Road – to visit the **Shaw Birthplace ⓭**, the writer's modest childhood home at 33 Synge Street (May–Sept, Mon–Sat 10am–5pm, Sunday 2–6pm. Closed 1–2pm. Admission charge. Out of season group tours: tel: 872 2077).

Shaw, the product of an unhappy marriage, grew up in genteel poverty, his father having failed to prosper as a grain merchant, and left Dublin in 1876, when he was 20, to spend the rest of his life in England. Since he didn't begin to make a real impact as a writer until the 1890s, there's little in his birthplace from his writing years. But the house – carefully restored – is worth a visit if only because it gives a good impression of Victorian middle-class home life. ❑

Shaw, having become a literary lion in England, referred to Ireland as a "wretched little clod, broken off a bigger clod, broken off the west end of Europe."

BELOW: the Shaw Birthplace.

GEORGIAN DUBLIN

Map on page 124

This area takes in two of the city's major cultural institutions, the National Museum and the National Gallery, as well as some of the best-preserved Georgian terraces

O n the northern side of St Stephen's Green, **Dawson Street**, first laid out about 1709, has some late Georgian houses. On your right, walking away from the Green, is the **Mansion House** ⓮, the official residence of Dublin Lord Mayors since 1715. The house was built in 1705 in the Queen Anne style, and the ornate wrought iron and stucco on the exterior are Victorian additions.The resulting architectural style was despised by W. B. Yeats. The Round Room, built at speed in 1821 for King George IV's visit, is one of the city's largest public meeting halls, and it was here that the first Dáil (independent Irish parliament) assembled in 1918 to defy British rule by ratifying the rebellious declaration of independence of 1916.

Just down the street is the headquarters of the **Royal Irish Academy** ⓯, originally built in 1770 and converted in 1852 to its present use as the headquarters of the country's leading academic society, dedicated to promoting the study of the sciences, literature and antiquities. Among the precious manuscripts in its library (Monday to Friday 9.30am–5.30pm) are the 12th-century *Leabhar na hUidre* (*Book of the Dun Cow*), the 14th-century *Book of Ballymote*, and the early 17th-century *Annals of the Four Masters*.

Beyond it **St Ann's Church** ⓰ (Sunday to Friday 10am–4pm), a venue for concerts as well as services. The church was founded in 1707 but the Norman-style facade dates from 1868. Beside the altar are shelves designed for holding loaves of bread for distribution to the poor. Notable past parishioners include the revolutionary Wolfe Tone and Bram Stoker, author of *Dracula*.

Leinster House

Turn right and walk along **Molesworth Street**, which contains **Buswell's Hotel**, a favourite watering hole for politicians. Facing you at the end of the street is **Leinster House** ⓱, the home of the Irish houses of parliament, the Dáil and Seanad. It was designed by Richard Cassels and built in 1746 as the Duke of Leinster's town house. In 1815 it was sold to the Royal Dublin Society as its headquarters, but in 1922 the first independent government of the Free State chose it as its parliament and banished the RDS to the suburb of Ballsbridge.

The Seanad (Senate) meets in the north-wing saloon, with its stuccoed walls and ceiling. According to the author Brendan Lehane, the similarity between the design of this house and the White House in Washington DC may stem from the fact that the latter's architect, James Hoban, was born in Carlow in 1762 and trained in Dublin. You may be shown around Leinster House when the Dáil isn't sitting; apply at the Kildare Street entrance.

PRECEDING PAGES: Georgian doorways, Fitzwilliam Square. **LEFT:** the foyer of the Shelbourne Hotel. **BELOW:** classic townhouses.

The National Museum on Kildare Street.

BELOW: Mansion House, seat of the city's government.

The National Museum

Leinster House is flanked by two buildings with columnar entrance rotundas; these are the National Museum (to the right) and National Library, both of which were built in 1890 and are typical of the formal, imperial architectural statements being made all over Europe at the time. For that reason, perhaps, their fine design was undervalued in the early years of the Republic, and the museum was at one point in danger of being rebuilt as government offices.

The **National Museum** ⑱ (Tuesday to Saturday 10am–5pm, Sunday 2–5pm. free) has a splendid columnar hallway with a mosaic floor depicting the Zodiac, and contains a collection of Irish antiquities imaginatively displayed within a necessarily confined space. Its highlights include some stunning pre-Christian gold jewellery and early Christian artefacts, notably the 8th-century Ardagh Chalice (an elaborately decorated silver bowl used to pour wine during religious services and found in a field in Co. Limerick in 1868), the delicately crafted 8th-century Tara Brooch (*pictured on page 27*) and the 12th-century Cross of Cong (made of wood, bronze and silver and designed to hold a fragment of wood said to have come from the cross on which Christ died). St Patrick's Bell, between 1,200 and 1,500 years old, is said to have belonged to the patron saint himself.

During Ireland's turbulent history, it was often prudent to bury valuables in bogs, and farmers have over the years dug up some magnificent gold artefacts. Among those on display are gold collars and jewellery dating to the 8th century BC, a bronze war trumpet and other weapons from the 1st century BC, and a hollowed oak longboat over 15 metres (50 ft) long. The museum also has an Egyptian room containing a mummy, and an interesting section on Viking Dublin. The 1916 Room documents the 20th-century struggle for independence

and includes James Connolly's blood-stained vest. Collections of decorative arts, ceramics and musical instruments have been moved to the museum's extension at Collins Barracks (*see page 193*).

Map on page 124

The National Library

The **National Library of Ireland** ⑲ (Monday–Wednesday 10am–9pm, Thursday & Friday 10am–5pm, Saturday 10am–1pm; free), built between 1884 and 1890, has a precious collection of Irish manuscripts and first editions of authors such as Swift, Goldsmith, Shaw, Yeats and Joyce, as well as maps, prints and old newspapers. The spacious, domed reading room – featured, inevitably, in *Ulysses* – is worth a visit for its atmosphere alone, and you can obtain a one-day reader's ticket. To research your Irish ancestors, you can also visit the Genealogical Department on the first floor, which offers a free service for personal callers. The helpful staff will show you how to search their records, books and computer database, and can provide a list of professional researchers available for hire.

Further down Kildare Street, on the corner of Nassau Street, is the **Heraldic Museum** (Mon-Wed 10am-8.30pm, Thurs-Fri 10am-4.30pm, Sat 10am-12.30pm; free), built in 1859–61 and until 1971 home to the Kildare Street Club. The weather-beaten stone carvings on the windows include birds, monkeys playing billiards (barely distinguishable, some jested, from the right-wing club members), and a hare being chased by a dog. Inside, one of Dublin's finest interiors was destroyed in 1971 when a fine staircase hall with intricate carvings of snakes, snails and butterflies was removed to make way for toilets and a lift. The museum, of particular interest to those concerned with the development of knightly orders and insignia, has collections of banners, shields and coats of arms.

The National Library was so named in 1877 when the state took it over. It had been the Royal Dublin Society Library, set up in 1836 as a public library free to respectable persons.

BELOW:
signs of life at the National Museum.

Shelbourne Nubian.

BELOW: you can view the National Gallery's portraits while ascending the spiral staircase.

The Shelbourne Hotel

A left turn at the top of Kildare Street brings you past the **Shelbourne Hotel ⑳**, dating from 1824, but completed in its present splendid form, with the entrance guarded by statues of two Nubian princesses, in 1865. The Constitution of the Irish Free State, precursor of the Republic, was drafted here in 1922. The Lord Mayor's Lounge is a favourite rendezvous for afternoon tea, underlining the fact that Dublin's hotels are much more than places to stay – they have an important role in the social life of the city's middle class, being used as places to meet, eat and drink, gossip and see whom you might see – and nowhere is this more true than at the Shelbourne.

The hotel was built by John McCurdy, the most fashionable hotel designer of the time, for the Jury family, whose name lives on in a modern hotel chain. It occupies the site of Kerry House which, in 1798, was one of Dublin's "torturing barracks" where rebels and suspects were detained. In 1922, the constitution of the Irish Free State was drafted in the Constitution Room.

Among the hotel's many famous guests were Amanda McKittrick Ross (1860–1939), whose artlessly colourful prose gained her recognition as "the world's worst novelist". A rather better novelist, William Makepeace Thackeray (1811–63), wrote about the hotel in his *Irish Sketch Book*, and the Anglo-Irish novelist George Moore (1852–1933) featured the hotel in *A Drama in Muslin*.

Across the road from the hotel, at the north-eastern entrance to St Stephen's Green, is a striking statue by Edward Delaney of the 1798 nationalist leader **Wolfe Tone**, known irreverently as "Tonehenge". Continuing along Merrion Row you pass on the left a small **Huguenot Cemetery**, dating from 1693, founded by refugees from religious persecution in France under Louis XIV,

DISHING THE DIRT IN "DUBLIN 4"

Although it regards itself as a relatively classless city, Dublin has – like London or New York – its clique of intellectuals, mostly from the media, politics and the professions, who eat together and drink together. These "chattering classes" are collectively known as "Dublin 4".

The name derives from the prosperous suburbs of Ballsbridge and Donnybrook which come within the postal district of Dublin 4 and contain both the headquarters of RTE, the national broadcasting company, and the campus of University College Dublin. But the centre of activities of the "Dublin 4" set is actually in the heart of the Old City, between St Stephen's Green and the Liffey. A favourite watering hole is the Shelbourne Hotel, where politicians from the Dáil, actors from the nearby theatres, academics and media celebrities mingle in the Horseshoe Bar. Doheny & Nesbitt's and Mulligan's are two favoured pubs.

In this milieu, everyone seems to know everyone else and, in addition to the gossip, a good deal of business can be informally conducted over a pint of Guinness or a glass of Jameson's. Some find the atmosphere more than a little claustrophobic, though, and some envy the media types who have successfully shifted their careers to London. But then the Guinness isn't nearly as good there…

Map on page 124

who brought many valuable crafts to Dublin. Further along on the right is the black-and-white front of **O'Donoghue's pub**, where the celebrated folk group The Dubliners first belted out their ballads in the 1960s.

Next turn on the right is **Ely Place**, which has strong literary associations. The poet George Moore lived at number 4 and W. B. Yeats pursued his occult investigations at number 8, Ely House, which in his day was the headquarters of the Irish Theosophical Association. It is now the home of the Knights of Columbanus, a Catholic version of the freemasons. Oliver St John Gogarty, poet, surgeon and chronicler of literary life (model for the character Buck Mulligan in Joyce's *Ulysses*) lived at number 25, now demolished to make way for the incongruous modern brick and plate-glass building housing the **Royal Hibernian Academy's Gallagher Gallery** ㉑ (Tuesday to Saturday 11am–5pm, Thursday to 8pm, Sunday 2–5pm). This is the venue for the springtime show of work by members of the RHA as well as for various temporary exhibitions.

Back at the foot of Ely Place, there are two notable pubs to the right along Baggot Street: **Doheny and Nesbitt's** and **Toner's**. Both are time-worn places, always packed at night, frequented by politicians, journalists and lawyers.

Otherwise, carry straight on into Merrion Street Upper, passing the guarded gates of the heavily domed **Government Buildings** ㉒, which contain the office of the Taoiseach (prime minister, pronounced *tee-shuck*) and the Cabinet room. Both can be seen by guided tour (Saturday only 10.30am–12.30pm, 1.30–4.30pm; free; tickets available 10am– 4pm from the National Gallery). The Duke of Wellington, victor over Napoleon at Waterloo, was born in this street at number 24, though he was hardly proud of his Irish origins. "Just because you were born in a stable doesn't make you a horse," he remarked.

Classic Georgian.

BELOW: the Taoiseach's office in Upper Merrion Street.

Further along on the left is the **Natural History Museum** ❷❸ (Tuesday to Saturday 10am–5pm, Sunday 2–5pm; free) a musty but interesting place (nicknamed the "Dead Zoo") displaying mammals, birds and fish from Ireland and abroad as well as a skeleton of the long-extinct Great Irish Deer. The famous explorer David Livingstone delivered the opening lecture in 1857.

The National Gallery of Ireland

The National Gallery of Ireland.

A left turn on leaving the museum, past the lawns of Leinster House, brings you to the **National Gallery of Ireland** ❷❹ (Monday to Saturday 9.30am–5.30pm, Thursday to 8.30pm, Sunday noon–5pm; free). The statue in front is of the Irish railway tycoon William Dargan (1799–1867), who organised the 1853 Dublin Exhibition on this site and used the profits to found the gallery's collection. Inside, another statue honours the Dublin-born playwright George Bernard Shaw, who said he owed his education to the gallery and left it a third of his estate. This effigy, by the Polish sculptor Paul Troubetzkoy, was Shaw's own favourite.

Apart from a representative range of Irish painting, the gallery contains a small collection of Dutch masters, fine examples of the 17th-century French, Spanish and Italian schools, and a good English collection which includes major works by Gainsborough. Many of the old masters were donated by Sir Hugh Lane (1875–1915), a noted collector and curator of the gallery who was drowned when the *Lusitania* was hit by a German torpedo off the coast of Ireland. Currently the most celebrated painting is *The Taking of Christ* by Caravaggio, rediscovered in the Jesuit House of Study in 1990.

BELOW: the National Gallery.

Visitors should not miss the chance to encounter Irish artists of the 19th and early 20th centuries, such as James Arthur O'Connor, Nathaniel Hone, Sir

illiam Orpen, Walter Osborne, William Leech and Roderic O'Conor. A Yeats allery is devoted primarily to the works of Jack B. Yeats (1839–1922), brother ' the poet. The new Millennium Wing provides an additional 4,000 sq. metres ·r special exhibitions, a virtual reality gallery and other services. The National allery's restaurant is justly popular.

1errion Square

Map on page 124

merging from the gallery, you stand on the west side of **Merrion Square** ㉕, 1e of Dublin's finest. Laid out in 1762 , it has had many distinguished inhab- ants. Number 1, on the north-west corner, was the boyhood home of Oscar 'ilde; Daniel O'Connell lived at number 58; W. B. Yeats, who was born in e seaside suburb of Sandymount but grew up mainly in London, lived at num- ·r 52 and later at 82, after he became a senator of the Irish Free State; Sheri- 1n Le Fanu, author of the seminal vampire story *Carmilla*, lived at number 70. The **Oscar Wilde House**, together with the adjoining house, is now owned ⁄ the American College Dublin (a branch of Lynn University of Florida), hich is restoring it. Oscar's parents were celebrated in their own right: Sir 'illiam Wilde was a surgeon, amateur archaeologist and historian; Jane rancesca Wilde was an ardent nationalist well-known for her poetry and flammatory articles under the pen-name 'Speranza'. The ground and first oors of the house, which contain Sir William's surgery, study and Speranza's ·awing room, are open for guided tours (Monday, Wednesday and Thurs- 1y at 10.15am and 11.15am; admission free). From the middle of Merrion Square's attractive central gardens – open to the ıblic – the surrounding streets betray no sign of modern-day intrusions. As

Oscar Wilde's statue in Merrion Square's park.

BELOW: the drawing room at number 29 Fitzwilliam Street.

Map on page 124

Work on the Grand Canal began in 1755 and the first 12 miles (20 km) were opened in 1763. Railways eroded the canal's business in the 19th century and the last boats were withdrawn in 1959–60.

BELOW: the poet Patrick Kavanagh contemplates the Grand Canal.

you walk along the east side of the square – the side opposite the gallery – the intersection with Mount Street Upper offers a fine architectural view towards the cupola of **St Stephen's Church** ㉖ (1825), known because of its shape as the "Pepper Canister".

Ahead lies **Fitzwilliam Street**, the longest Georgian Street in Dublin, and the scene in 1965 of an infamous act of state vandalism, when 26 houses on its eastern side were demolished – thus destroying the street's unique integrity – to make way for a new Electricity Supply Board headquarters. Perhaps out of shame, the ESB in recent years helped to restore **Number Twenty Nine** ㉗ (Tuesday to Saturday 10am–5pm, Sunday 2–5pm; free) to house a kitsch exhibition of "Home Life in Dublin, 1790–1820" – upper middle-class home life, it should be said.

It is worth walking on up Fitzwilliam Street, at least as far as **Fitzwilliam Square** ㉘, the smallest, latest (1825) and best-preserved Georgian square in the city. Among its former residents were William Dargan, founder of the National Gallery (number 2), and Jack B. Yeats (number 18).

Returning down Fitzwilliam Street, turn right along **Baggot Street,** passing two notable modern edifices: on the left, the big, boxy, steel-and-glass administrative offices of the **Bank of Ireland** (including an exhibition hall used for contemporary art shows); and further along on the right, the headquarters of **Bord na Mona**, which oversees the extraction of peat from state-owned bogs. The bridge ahead offers a pleasant view along the **Grand Canal**, once an important commercial waterway connecting the capital with the River Shannon. A granite-sided seat on the Mespil Road side of the canal commemorates the poet Patrick Kavanagh (1905–67); one of his poems, inscribed in the stone, describes the pleasures of the spot (less peaceful now than in his day). ☐

The Role of Religion

The first-time visitor to Dublin cannot help being struck by the number of churches. A good many belong to the Church of Ireland (Protestant Episcopalian), traditionally the religion of the old Ascendancy. Several are attached to other Protestant denominations such as Presbyterian and Methodist. But the overwhelming majority are Roman Catholic, reflecting that religion's domination of the city's Christian belief.

The Archdiocese of Dublin, an ecclesiastical territory which includes the city and county of Dublin, most of County Wicklow, and parts of Counties Wexford, Carlow, Kildare and Laois, has a population of 1.2 million, of whom more than 1 million are Catholics. Not all are practising – in fact, the Catholic Church is concerned at the fall in church attendance, particularly among young city dwellers. But, by international standards, the number who turn up to Mass is still very high indeed.

The Catholics of the Archdiocese are served by more than 220 churches. In addition, there are chapels and oratories attached to the many religious communities of nuns, priests and brothers. When these are added in, the places of catholic worship total nearly 700.

To the visitor, the most visible sign of religious faith (although rarely seen among the young) is the popular habit of "blessing yourself" – making the Sign of the Cross with the hands when passing a church. This is a sign of respect for and devotion to the Holy Sacrament within, which Catholics believe to be not merely a representation but the true Body of Christ. "It sort of reminds me of what we're all here for," is how one elderly man explains the custom. "I always did it and I'm not going to stop now."

Although Dublin has two cathedrals – St Patrick's and Christ Church – both have belonged to the Church of Ireland since the Reformation in the 16th century. The Catholic Archbishop's seat is in the Pro-Cathedral in Marlborough Street, right in the heart of the city. It is a measure of the priority given to religion by many Dubliners in their daily lives that six Masses are celebrated on weekdays, beginning at 7.45am before work begins.

Outside, in the city's hospitals, schools and social service offices, nuns are reporting for work. There are 276 convents in Dublin and its environs and, although vocations are significantly declining, nuns still play an important role in education and social work. So, too, do the Christian Brothers, the Brothers of Don Bosco and the Salesians – and the priests of more than 100 religious societies. It's not difficult to understand why clerical garb is frequently seen on the streets, and in shops, restaurants and theatres.

People now question the role of the Catholic Church much more than they used to, and referenda on issues such as abortion and divorce have shown that Dubliners in particular do not toe the church line. But most people still accept, actively or passively, the importance of religion itself. ❑

RIGHT: religious observance is stronger in the older generation than among young Dubliners.

THE OLD CITY

Maps on pages 156 &158

Dublin Castle and the two great cathedrals – Christ Church and St Patrick's – convey a potent sense of the city's history. For many, the Guinness brewery is also a place of worship

I t was here that it all started, not in the year 988 as the 1988 Millennium celebrations tried to suggest, but more than a century earlier. Norwegian Vikings settled on the banks of the Liffey in 841; their battles with their Danish counterparts came to an end 11 years later with the arrival of Olaf, who united the two sides and founded the Norse kingdom of Dublin.

Many street names date back to medieval Dublin. The majority are named after the saints to whom the people of the Middle Ages were devoted: Michael's Hill, Nicholas Street, Patrick Street, Francis Street, John's Lane, James's Street, Werburgh Street, Bride Street, Thomas Street. All of these still run along, or connect with, the spine of old Dublin, which goes from east to west from Christ Church and Dublin Castle in the direction of Kilmainham, where once there stood the vast priory lands of the Knights of St John of Jerusalem.

It was in the street here, on the ridge above the Liffey, that the Vikings and the Gaels of Ireland intermixed to become the Hiberno-Norse. It was here, too, that Dublin, because of clerical rivalry, in the 12th century became the only town in Christendom to have two great cathedral churches. And it was here, too, that the Black Death raged in 1347. The old town has seen kingdoms and republics proclaimed. King James had his capital here before the Battle of the Boyne in 1690, and King William afterwards. Around these streets walked Jonathan Swift, the Dean of St Patrick's, and George Frederick Handel, the great arias of his *Messiah* echoing in his brain.

PRECEDING PAGES: Dublin Castle's state apartments. **LEFT:** a catholic collection of antiques for sale. **BELOW:** a stone head on Dublin Castle's chapel.

Dame Street

As time passed, Old Dublin gradually lost its importance and the city centre moved eastwards. When the Irish Free State was founded in the 1920s, the centre of government moved out of Dublin Castle, from which the British had ruled the entire island, and into Leinster House. Today, the centre point of the city is College Green, and **Dame Street** runs as an umbilical cord from the new city to its dishevelled old mother.

The street nowadays is a place of commerce, of banks and insurance companies. It is dominated by the modern hulk of the **Central Bank**, a layered cake of concrete and tinted glass which forms an incongruous umbrella for Temple Bar, the thriving arty quarter that lies behind it (*see pages 171–173*). Dubliners seem either to love or to hate the building, which was designed by Sam Stephenson in 1978.

Dublin Castle

With your back to Trinity College, continue past the bank. A left turn opposite the Olympia Theatre leads into the lower yard of **Dublin Castle ❶**. It was here, on the old main gate, that the English rulers would

impale the heads of rebellious Irish chieftains. Today, the first impression is of a strange architectural mixture. To your left is a modern office block. Uphill diagonally to your right, a massive medieval stone tower (the **Record Tower**) is flanked by a neo-gothic church and a red-brick Georgian wing with an archway below. Walk through the archway into the elegant cobbled quadrangle of the upper yard, and the picture becomes clearer:

Dublin Castle is essentially an elegant 18th-century palace with earlier remnants: the original Norman castle, dating from 1202, was largely ruined by fire in 1684. Above the main entrance to the upper yard stands a statue of Justice, holding the symbolic scales – "her face to the Castle, her back to the nation", as disgruntled Dubliners were wont to remark. This site was the centre of English rule in Ireland for seven centuries and, fittingly, it was here that the British administration handed over power to the new Free State government of Michael Collins in 1922.

The Record Tower.

The State Apartments

The castle's sumptuous **State Apartments**, prominent among the jewels of Dublin, are open to the public (except on major state occasions such as Anglo-Irish or European summit meetings) and the guided tour should not be missed (Monday to Friday, 10am–5pm, Saturday and Sunday 2–5pm, admission fee).

From the entrance hall a staircase leads to Battleaxe Landing, where guards armed with axes once barred the way. You then pass through a series of elegant drawing-rooms with finely decorated plasterwork ceilings (rescued from now demolished 18th-century houses). These were formerly bedrooms used by royal visitors, but one of them has a starkly contrasting association: the 1916

BELOW: the Chapel Royal, Dublin Castle.

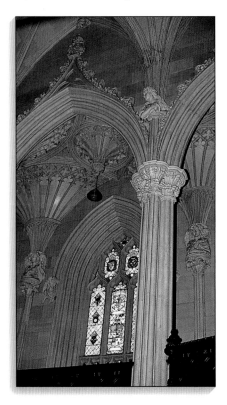

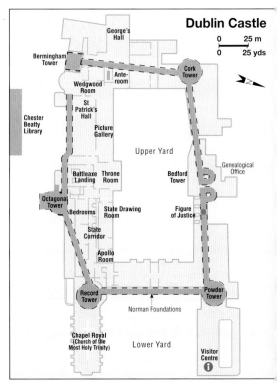

Dublin Castle

socialist rebel James Connolly lay wounded here after his capture. He was later taken to the stonebreakers' yard of Kilmainham Gaol, strapped to a chair, and executed by firing squad. In another of these rooms is an impressive Van Dyck portrait of the Countess of Southampton.

Other highlights of the State Apartments include the Grand Staircase, made of Connemara marble; the **Throne Room**, where English monarchs received their loyal subjects during visits to Ireland – George V was the last monarch to use the elaborate throne, which is more than 200 years old; the **Drawing Room**, decorated in French 18th-century style; and **St Patrick's Hall** (where presidents of Ireland are inaugurated), which has splendidly vivid ceiling paintings by Vincent Waldre showing St Patrick preaching to the Irish, Henry II receiving the Irish chieftains, and George III accompanied by Liberty and Justice. The **Bermingham Tower**, which dates from 1411 and was rebuilt in 1775, was formerly the state prison.

The tour finishes in the Undercroft of the lower yard where, in the most interesting section of all, you descend below ground to view recently excavated remnants of a Viking embankment and sections of the 13th-century **Powder Tower** and moat. Across the yard, the neo-gothic exterior of the **Chapel Royal** (1807–14, now the Catholic Church of the Most Holy Trinity) is decorated with more than 90 carved heads. These include the sovereigns of England, bishops and assorted worthies. St Peter and Dean Swift guard the north door and Brian Ború and St Patrick the east door. Inside, carved panels and stained-glass windows display the arms of English viceroys from 1173.

If you have time to spare before or after the tour, it's worth taking a look at **City Hall ❷** (Monday to Friday, 8.45am–5pm), which stands on Dame Street,

Maps on pages 156 &158

A formal 19th-century ball in Dublin Castle.

BELOW: the drawing room of the State Apartments.

just by the exit from the castle's upper yard, facing down Parliament Street. It's an imposing, Corinthian structure designed in 1769 for a £100 prize by the London architect Thomas Cooley. Originally the Royal Exchange, it served as a military depot, a prison and torture centre for rebels in 1798, and as a corn exchange, before Dublin Corporation took over in 1852.

The entrance rotunda features a splendid illuminated dome. On the mosaic floor is the city's coat of arms, with its Latin motto, "Happy the city where citizens obey" (clearly referring to somewhere less anarchic than Dublin). There are a number of statues, including those of Henry Grattan and Daniel O'Connell. The vaulted rooms beneath City Hall provide an atmospheric setting for an interesting exhibition on Dublin's history. *The Story of the Capital* is told through interactive computer screens, models, and displays of regalia such as the Great Sword, the Great Mace, the Lord Mayor's chain and other civic treasures. There is a separate side entrance (Monday to Saturday 10am–5.15pm, Sunday 2–5pm; admission fee).

Follow signs across the gardens to the **Chester Beatty Library** ❸ (Monday to Friday 10am–5pm, Saturday 11am–5pm, Sunday 1–5pm, closed Monday October–April; free). Budget some extra time here to fully enjoy this fascinating collection of illustrated medieval manuscripts, rare books, Arabic texts, Japanese and Chinese scrolls and art treasures from the Far East, Middle East, Persia and India. Among the highlights are ancient Biblical papyri dating from the 2nd to 4th centuries AD, some of earliest surviving gospel texts; jade books and snuff bottles from China, and Tibetan tankas on coarse linen cloth, while video screens show how the ancient arts, such as the calligraphy of the Koran, were achieved.

Image of India from the Chester Beatty Library.

BELOW: Christ Church Cathedral.

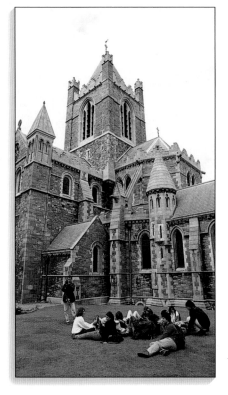

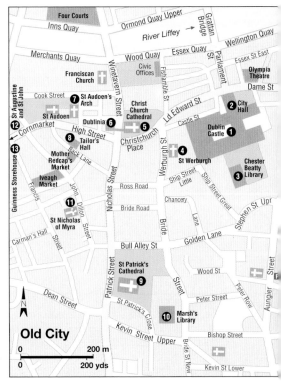

Map on page 158

The collection was donated to Ireland by Sir Alfred Chester Beatty (1875–1968), a New York-born tycoon who travelled extensively in the Middle and Far East and collected oriental artefacts, especially manuscripts. He retired to Ireland and became its first honorary citizen in 1957.

Now walk back through the lower yard of Dublin Castle, following the signpost to the Garden, laid out on the location of the dark pool on the river Poddle which gave the city its name. The red-brick tracery decorating the circular lawn is supposed to symbolise the eels which once abounded in the pool.

Leave the castle grounds by the nearby Ship Street gate and turn right along Werburgh Street, passing the **Church of St Werburgh ❹**. The first church was an Anglo-Norman structure named after the daughter of the King of Mercia but two fires devastated it and it was last rebuilt in 1784. Its frontage mixes Ionic and Corinthian architecture and it has a fine carved pulpit. The composer and pianist John Field (1782–1837), creator of the nocturne, was baptised here. Field spent most of his adult life in Russia and is entombed in Moscow. Lord Edward Fitzgerald, a leading figure of the 1798 rebellion, was interred in the crypt; the body of Major Henry Sirr, who captured him, lies in the adjoining graveyard.

At the top of the street, ancient and modern Dublin stand uneasily cheek by jowl: the brutal, bunker-like 1980s Civic Offices of Dublin Corporation, and the sombre, greystone buttresses of Christ Church Cathedral – one of two Protestant cathedrals in a mainly Catholic city which still lacks a Catholic cathedral.

The **Civic Offices** are a sorry monument to a major conservation controversy of the late 1970s: excavations for their foundations uncovered important relics of Viking settlements on Wood Quay, centre of the original Viking town, and a popular campaign was mounted to have the site preserved. Unfortunately, the city planners won the battle and the hated offices were built, after the Viking remains had been removed.

Sam Stephenson, the architect responsible for the new Civic Offices, has said: "Public buildings need to be large and assertive, to make a big statement. And a lot of nonsense is talked in defence of old buildings, which seem to acquire a veneration for beauty just by being old."

BELOW: lectern in Christ Church Cathedral.

Christ Church Cathedral

Standing on the hill of Dublin, **Christ Church Cathedral ❺** (daily 10am–5pm, except during services; admission fee) was founded by Vikings in 1038 and is fronted by a green churchyard in which there are remains of the old chapter house built in 1230. The neo-gothic exterior of the cathedral was created in a lavish and flamboyant manner in 1875 at the expense of a wealthy Dublin whiskey distiller, Henry Roe, who donated £230,000 (about £23 million/US$37 million at current values) to save the cathedral. It was a generous gesture – though probably partly motivated by a desire to outdo Sir Benjamin Lee Guinness, head of the celebrated brewery, who had funded the restoration of the nearby St Patrick's Cathedral – but it meant that Christ Church now bears little resemblance to the original building, the only cathedral of Norse foundation in Britain or Ireland.

There had been many restorations over the centuries, however. The cathedral was extensively rebuilt from 1172 under Archbishop (later Saint) Laurence O'Toole and Richard de Clare ("Strongbow"), leader of the Anglo-Norman invasion of Ireland. The central tower was built around 1600 after storm and fire

A candle burns in Christ Church Cathedral.

damage to the steeples. Many historic scenes were enacted in the cathedral. In 1394 England's Richard II received the homage of the kings of Ulster, Munster, Leinster and Connaught. Lambert Simnel, the 10-year-old pretender to the English throne, was crowned here by his supporters in 1487. King William III gave thanks here after winning the Battle of the Boyne in 1690. His gift of gold, along with other artefacts, are on display in the Treasures of Christ Church exhibition, which also explains how the Vikings built the original church.

The impressive interior dates mostly from Mr Roe's restoration, except for the north wall of the nave (which dates from the 13th century and has a visible tilt), the transepts and the west bay of the choir. But there are many interesting ancient artefacts, all clearly signposted and annotated. These include the tomb of a knight said traditionally to be Strongbow, who died in 1176. The tomb itself bears an effigy in chain armour which experts think may be that of an Earl of Drogheda. A smaller effigy alongside is said to represent Strongbow's son, put to the sword by his father when, though still a boy, he showed cowardice during an ambush.

There is a 15th-century brass lectern from which the Bible was read in English for the first time in Ireland; the holes in the lectern once held the chains which secured the holy book against theft. In the Peace Chapel of St Laud are beautiful medieval floor tiles, which the Victorians copied throughout the cathedral from portions of old tiling unearthed during rebuilding. On one wall of this chapel is a heart-shaped iron casket containing the heart of St Laurence O'Toole.

In the vast underground crypt, the oldest intact structure in Dublin, you can see remnants of the original Viking wooden construction as well as many fascinating oddities, such as the stocks in which local offenders were locked for ritual public humiliation, and a mummified cat and rat, found trapped in an organ pipe, one presumably chasing the other. When the cathedral fell on hard times in the 16th and 17th centuries, the vaults were used as wine cellars and drinking taverns and the nave became a market.

The cathedral choir, incidentally, is first-rate, and is worth catching at Evensong (see noticeboard for times).

BELOW: trying out the stocks for size.

Dublinia

The cathedral is connected by a covered bridge across St Michael's Hill to the former Synod Hall, which now houses **Dublinia ❻** (April to September, daily 10am– 5pm; October to March, Monday to Saturday 11am– 4pm, Sunday 10am–4.30pm, admission fee), an exhibition run by the non-profit Medieval Trust which explores the period between the coming of the Anglo-Normans and the suppression of the monasteries in the 16th century. (Admission to Dublinia includes entry to the cathedral via the bridge, but you can also enter Christ Church directly.)

The atmosphere of medieval Dublin is re-created through a series of tableaux (Anglo-Norman invasion, Black Death, etc). Exhibits include a scale model of the old city, various life-size reconstructions, including the interior of a cobbler's shop and a merchant's kitchen, artefacts from the Wood Quay excavations, and a multi-screen presentation every 30 minutes.

The Malton Room displays a set of James Malton's fine 18th-century prints of Dublin. Malton was English-born but lived in Dublin for at least a decade, probably in the 1780s. His watercolours effectively capture the city and its people at a time of great change.

From the top of the 60-metre (200-ft) St Michael's Tower, you can enjoy a panoramic view over the city.

Map on page 158

The St Audoen churches

A little further along **High Street**, two churches stand side by side, both named after St Audoen, a 7th-century bishop of Rouen in France. The first, a grandiose 19th-century affair, is Catholic; the second, topped by a Norman tower and fronted by a small, pleasant park, belongs to the Church of Ireland.

The **Catholic Church of St Audoen** is famous in recent Dublin lore for Father Flash Kavanagh, a priest who read the Mass more quickly than anyone else and drew large congregations of the less devout who wished to get their Sunday obligation over with as quickly as possible and be home for lunch before venturing out to afternoon soccer matches. The church was built in 1846 and the Corinthian columns were added in 1899. The giant turtle shells on either side of the door were brought home from the South Pacific by a sea captain and given to his brother, the parish priest.

The **Church of Ireland St Audoen's** was founded by the Normans in the 12th century, probably on the site of an earlier church dedicated to the Irish saint Columba, and is Dublin's only surviving medieval parish church. The font is 12th-century, and the tower contains three bells dating from 1423. There's an exhibition in the guild chapel (June–September, 9.30am–5.30pm; fee).

The Great Bell in the Catholic Church of St Audoen is named the Liberator after Daniel O'Connell. It signalled his release from jail and also tolled his funeral knell in 1847.

LEFT: the Dublinia experience. **BELOW:** the medieval Church of Ireland St Audoen's

Jonathan Swift

The self-penned epitaph on his tomb in St Patrick's Cathedral reads: "He is laid where bitter indignation can no longer lacerate his heart. Go traveller and imitate if you can one who was, to the best of his powers, a defender of Liberty."

Jonathan Swift was dean of the Cathedral from 1713 until his death in 1745 but is better known throughout the world as the author of *Gulliver's Travels*, a political satire often presented in sanitised form as a children's tale. In Ireland, however, Swift is also celebrated as a champion of the poor, a tireless critic of the iniquities of English misrule, and a model of the patriotic Anglo-Irishman. In one pamphlet, *A Modest Proposal,* he suggested, with savage irony, that the children of the Irish poor might be fattened and slaughtered as tasty joints for rich people's tables. In another, he urged the Irish to burn everything English except their coal.

Swift's parents, both English, had settled in

Dublin, but his father died suddenly in 1667 without seeing his unborn son. The boy's uncles ensured that he was well educated and he graduated from Trinity College in 1682 "by special grace" – a term implying that he had transgressed the university's rules.

In 1669 he moved to England to join the household of a diplomat, Sir William Temple, a distant relative of his mother's. He acted as secretary to Temple, who was writing his memoirs, and took full advantage of Temple's fine library. Here he also began his mysterious, intimate friendship with Esther Johnson, the daughter of Temple's widowed housekeeper. Variously described as his platonic companion, his lover, secretly his wife, or even a member of his family, Esther became the "Stella" to whom he later wrote a famous series of letters chronicling his reactions to early 18th-century public affairs. She is buried beside him in St Patrick's Cathedral.

Swift returned to Ireland intermittently between 1669 and 1699, when Temple died. During one visit, he was ordained as an Anglican priest and was soon afterwards appointed vicar of Kilroot, near Belfast. His witty writings won him recognition in London – notably *A Tale of a Tub*, a satire on "corruptions in religion and learning" – and he became acquainted with such prominent literary figures as Joseph Addison, Sir Richard Steele and William Congreve.

He became the chief pamphleteer for England's ruling Tory party and was rewarded in 1713 with the position of dean of St Patrick's Cathedral. When George I came to the English throne in 1714, the Tories' influence declined and Swift, out of favour, transferred his energies to Ireland. In 1726, he published *Gulliver's Travels*, which has since divided critics, some regarding it as a comic masterpiece satirising human folly and others as the work of a misanthrope. Essentially, it represents Swift's belief in 17th-century rationality, rejecting emotion in favour of common sense.

Ill health in his later years led some to consider him insane. But he is remembered in Dublin as a patriot and an indefatigable champion of the common people's rights – even though he felt more at ease with Tory grandees than with the common people. ❑

LEFT: Swift's bust in St Patrick's Cathedral.

The steps on the far side of the church lead down to the restored **St Audoen's Arch ❼**, the only surviving gate of the walled medieval city.

Just across High Street from St Audoen's, Back Lane leads to **Tailors' Hall ❽**, the city's only remaining guild hall, which now houses the headquarters of An Taisce, Ireland's National Trust, dedicated to preserving natural and architectural heritage. In 1792 the Catholic Convention, or "Back Lane Parliament" met here, with Wolfe Tone as secretary, to press demands for relief from the Penal Laws. The hall was also used for meetings of the revolutionary United Irishmen. Also in Back Lane is **Mother Redcap's Market** (Friday–Sunday 11am–5.30pm), a haunt for antiques hunters and foodies.

St Patrick's Cathedral

At the end of the lane, a right turn brings you into Patrick Street towards the granite spire of **St Patrick's Cathedral ❾** (March–October 9am–6pm daily, slightly shorter hours in winter; fee). Founded in 1191 but restored many times since, it stands on the oldest Christian site in Ireland. Originally, two branches of the River Poddle (now under ground) created a small island on which the church was built, and St Patrick is said to have baptised converts in a well which rose north of the tower in today's gardens. An ancient Celtic cross marking the well was unearthed in 1901 and is now preserved in the southwest corner of the nave. Like Christ Church Cathedral, St Patrick's has belonged to the Church of Ireland since Reformation times.

The 45-metre (147-ft) tower, out of square with the cathedral walls, was built in 1381 and the spire was added in the 18th century. The English conqueror Oliver Cromwell, passing through in 1649, used St Patrick's as a stable for his

Map on page 158

The first mention of a Tailors' Hall dates to 1539. A wooden hut replaced it in 1583, and the present building, completed in 1707, became the city's most fashionable venue for balls.

BELOW: St Patrick's Cathedral.

army's horses. By the mid-19th century, the cathedral had become dilapidated and was restored in 1864 through the generosity of the brewer Sir Benjamin Lee Guinness, whose donation is remembered by a bronze statue near the southwest door. The alterations were extensive and included the addition of flying buttresses. Not everyone appreciated the improvements and for a time the cathedral was dubbed "the Brewer's Church". Sir Benjamin's son, Lord Iveagh, funded further restoration and presented a peal of 10 bells, and there is a monument to Sir Benjamin's daughter displaying the rubric, appropriate for a brewing family, "I was thirsty and ye gave me drink."

St Patrick's and the surrounding area are inextricably linked with Jonathan Swift, who was dean for 32 years (*see page 162*). The cathedral contains Swift's grave, and next to it that of his beloved Stella. His pulpit is preserved and a bust close by is thought to be life-like. Other artefacts include medieval brasses, the helmets, swords and banners of the Knights of St Patrick, and the tattered flags of Irish regiments of the British Army (most of which were disbanded when the Irish Free State was founded). It is said that some of the first shots in the American War of Independence were fired at one of the flags. The banners of the Royal Dublin Fusiliers may be of particular interest to Australian visitors. The "Dubs", as they were known, were drawn to a great extent from the crowded, deprived area near the cathedral known as "the Liberties" (because it lay outside the jurisdiction of medieval Dublin). The regiment fought with distinction alongside Australian and New Zealand forces in the Dardanelles at Gallipoli in World War I and locals say that in the Coombe, the area's winding main thoroughfare, there was no house in April 1915 whose door was not draped in black crêpe.

There is also an elaborate 1632 monument to the Boyle family, the Earls

St Patrick's contains memorials to many famous Irishmen, including Turlough O'Carolan, the 17th-century harpist; John Philpot Curran, a popular orator and politician (1750–1817); the composer and violinist Michael William Balfe (1808–70); and Douglas Hyde (1860–1949), who became Ireland's first president in 1938.

BELOW: a pharmacy in the Liberties.

of Cork. This monument was originally erected beside the altar by the "great" earl (1566–1643), but Viceroy Wentworth ordered it to be moved because the congregation, he said, could not worship without "crouching to an Earl of Cork and his lady… or to those sea nymphs his daughters, with coronets upon their heads, their hair dishevelled, down upon their shoulders." One of the children in the monument is Robert Boyle, the physicist who propounded Boyle's Law (which states that, at a fixed temperature, the pressure of a confined ideal gas varies inversely with its volume). There are many monuments to politicians and clergymen, and one to Turlough O'Carolan, last of the great Gaelic harpists and bards.

Near the west end of the nave is the medieval **Chapter House Door**, which has a rough hole cut in it. In 1492, when two great Anglo-Irish families were feuding, the Earl of Ormonde took refuge in the Chapter House from the Earl of Kildare and his followers. Kildare cut a hole in the door and thrust his arm through it; Ormonde took his hand, and the peace was made. Thus did the phrase "chancing your arm" enter the English language.

Map on page 158

Marsh's Library.

Marsh's Library

Leaving the cathedral, turn left along St Patrick's Close, where a gateway in the wall leads to **Marsh's Library** ⑩ (Monday, Wednesday, Thursday and Friday 10am– 12.45pm, 2–5pm, Saturday 10.30am–12.45pm, closed Sunday and Tuesday; admission fee). This is Ireland's oldest public library, founded in 1702 by Archbishop Narcissus Marsh, and unchanged ever since.

Its 25,000 volumes and 200 manuscripts include some early printed books dating back to the 15th century. The two galleries of dark oak bookcases are laid

BELOW: the star of the St Patrick's Day parade in Dublin.

out in an L-shape, with the small reading room at the apex. At one end are three wired alcoves or "cages" into which readers of precious volumes were locked. Among many fascinating items is Swift's copy of Clarendon's *History of the Great Rebellion*, with the dean's pencilled notes in the margins.

Continue along St Patrick's Close into Kevin Street Upper and turn right. Cross the road junction into Dean Street, then turn right into **Francis Street**. You are now in the heart of **the Liberties**, so called because the Cathedral and its precincts stood outside the medieval city walls and were therefore beyond the Lord Mayor's jurisdiction. The area has a distinct and colourful working-class character, but it is gradually being "gentrified" by young professionals. In recent years many antique shops have opened along Francis Street.

The **Church of St Nicholas in Myra** (1832) ⑪, half-way up the street on the right, was built to celebrate Catholic emancipation in Ireland and was once the city's principal Catholic church; it also had jurisdiction over the Catholics of the Isle of Man, continuing a link which had been established in Viking times. Further up the street, the red-brick **Iveagh Markets** (1902) deals in food, crafts, clothes and bric-a-brac.

At the top of Francis Street, turn left into **Thomas Street West**, passing on your right the **Church of St Augustine and St John** (1872) ⑫, known locally as John's Lane Church and designed by Edward Welby Pugin. It was built with granite from Dalkey, just south of Dublin, with decorative red sandstone from Wales. The 60-metre (200-ft) spire is Dublin's tallest. Next door, the **National College of Art and Design** is housed in a former distiller's premises.

Further down Thomas Street West is the renovated facade of **St Catherine's Church**, in front of which the brave but foolhardy rebel Robert Emmet was

BELOW: the Church of St Augustine and St John.
RIGHT: tracing the history of Guinness.

hanged, then beheaded, in 1803. Emmet, a Protestant doctor's son, led a botched and hopeless attempt to take over Dublin Castle, but his defiant speech at his trial ensured his place in the republican pantheon: "Let no man write my epitaph… when my country takes her place among the nations of the earth, then, and not until then, let my epitaph be written."

Map on page 158

The Guinness brewery

Hereafter Thomas Street West, leading into James's Street, is dominated by the massive bulk of the **Guinness brewery**. It is the biggest in Europe, churning out 2½ million pints of its celebrated black stout every day. The brewery stopped admitting visitors some years ago, but instead you can get an informative and entertaining inside look at Ireland's favourite brew at the enjoyable **Guinness Storehouse ⑬** (daily 9.30am–5pm; admission fee). This is no ordinary brewery tour, but an imaginative exhibition on all aspects of making and selling Guinness. Set in a renovated 1904 warehouse – the first steel-framed building in the British isles – the Storehouse spreads over six floors surrounding a central glass atrium shaped like a giant pint. Encased in the floor of the atrium is the original 9,000-year lease signed by Arthur Guinness when he founded the brewery in 1759. Creative displays from a gushing waterfall and enormous vats of barley, to a walk-through 600-barrel copper vat explain the brewing process. There are humorous exhibits on Guinness advertising campaigns and its place in Irish culture, all enhanced by soundtracks and multimedia effects. Best of all, at the top is the Gravity Bar with the finest 360-degree view in the city. Your ticket entitles you to a complimentary pint – probably the best-tasting Guinness to be had anywhere, since it hasn't had to travel. The perfect end… ❑

Beer has long been associated with St James's Gate, one of the old outer gates to the medieval city. In 1670 the site was leased to Alderman Giles Mee, who owned a brewhouse in the vicinity.

BELOW: the Circular Bar on top of the Guinness Storehouse.

THE BLACK ART OF SELLING STOUT

Guinness may no longer be Irish-owned, but slick marketing has maintained its image and Dublin's pubs still claim to pull the best pint in the world

"When I die," said Sebastian Dangerfield, the wayward hero of J. P. Donleavy's novel *The Ginger Man*, "I want to decompose in a barrel of porter and have it served in all the pubs in Dublin. I wonder would they know it was me?"

Maybe not, but they'd probably send it back, because Dublin drinkers are notoriously fastidious about how the temperamental dark brew is poured and it must taste exactly right. Guinness is easily the predominant porter, whose name derives from its popularity with market porters in London, where the drink was invented. It became known as stout when Guinness introduced in the 1820s an "extra stout" (i.e. much stronger) version.

The company itself is now part of the massive London-based conglomerate Diageo, which brews Guinness in 50 countries and sells it in another 100. Often the drink is so modified to suit local tastes that Dublin aficionados would barely recognise it, and innovative marketing has even stretched to promoting it in the Caribbean – improbably but successfully – as an aphrodisiac.

Guinness has maintained its popularity by slick advertising designed to appeal especially to the young and by rigorous quality control in pubs. It further promoted its name in 1955 by publishing *The Guinness Book of Records* – the ideal means of settling bar-room disputes over trivia.

△ **CATCHING THEM YOUNG**
To prevent Guinness being seen as an old person's drink, marketing targets drinkers in their twenties.

▷ **HORSE SENSE**
The celebrated slogan "Guinness gives you strength" gave birth to a series of memorable adverts.

▷ **THE REAL THING**
Guinness, it's said, always tastes best in Dublin. One key is the pure, soft water taken to the St James's Gate Brewery not from the River Liffey but from reservoirs in the Wicklow Mountains.

THE CHANGE FROM CASK TO CAN

△ **THE GOOD OLD DRAYS**
Before the dominance of the diesel engine, dray horses delivering barrels of Guinness to pubs were a familiar sight in Dublin.

▽ **GOOD HEALTH!**
The company's most famous slogan, first used in 1929, didn't convince advertising regulators or the Dublin commentator below.

It is the addition of a small amount of roasted barley which gives Guinness its distinctive colour and taste. All the ingredients used in the St James's Gate brewery – Irish-grown barley, water, hops and yeast – are traditional. No artificial ingredients are added; although they might make the stout easier to ship, store and pour, they would affect the taste.

The mystique of "pulling a good pint" (which involves constant temperature in a pub's cellars, the distance from cask to tap and the frequency of the flow) was diminished slightly in 1989 by the launch of Canned Draught Guinness. Purists were outraged by this concession to the take-home trade.

Guinness, however, said the drink's creamy head and smooth taste remained unaltered, the result of its new "In-Can System". This meant placing a plastic widget in the can. When the can is opened, beer bubbles out of the widget as pressure is released. Result: a creamy head.

◁ **HOW IT ALL BEGAN**
In 1759, at the age of 34, Arthur Guinness leased a small disused brewery at St James's Gate for 9,000 years at £45 a year. Beer was then rarely drunk in rural Ireland, where whiskey and gin reigned. He died in 1803, leaving his son to develop the family firm internationally.

TEMPLE BAR

*It's vibrant, crowded, slightly phoney and very overpriced.
But Dublin's trendiest area, which almost became a bus
station, has instead turned into a tourist honey-pot*

Temple Bar is a network of small streets full of artists' studios, galleries, apartments, clothing and music stores, restaurants, cafés, pubs, craft shops and cultural centres. It lies along the south bank of the river just west of O'Connell Bridge, bounded to the south by Dame Street, to the east by Westmoreland Street, and to the west by Fishamble Street, and takes its name from William Temple, a 17th-century provost of Trinity College whose family mansion once stood here. Its renewal is comparable, on a smaller scale, to that of London's Covent Garden or Paris's Les Halles, and marks a welcome and overdue shift away from the benighted planning policies of earlier decades.

The fate of Temple Bar could easily have been very different. In the 1970s the state transport authority, CIE, began to plan a huge bus depot in the area, then a run-down former tradesmen's quarter. They bought up buildings for demolition, but in the meantime rented out many small shops and buildings on short leases to artists, designers, booksellers and restaurateurs. The area soon developed a lively Bohemian atmosphere and in the 1980s, local traders and residents, as well as conservation groups, began to lobby for its preservation.

The then prime minister, Charles Haughey – a keen patron of the arts – espoused the cause of Temple Bar; the bus depot scheme was dropped, and instead the authorities drew up a plan to restore and develop the area as a cultural quarter, offering a range of tax breaks and incentives to attract new residents and businesses.

The rate of development in the area in the past few years has been such that the bohemianism that gives it its charm risks being swamped by commercialism, self-conscious arty-smartness, and phoney olde-worldness (re-cobbled streets, pseudo-antique streetlights, etc). Some residents have complained about the loud and lively nightlife and there is concern that the enlargement of existing pubs and the development of new ones mean that the name Temple Bar may acquire a new level of meaning. But there's no denying that the area has a great "buzz".

LEFT: Temple Bar Square. **BELOW:** Ha'penny Bridge.

Finding your way

There is no "best route" through Temple Bar; it's essentially a place for browsing. But the map indicates a trail taking in the main points of interest. The area's renewal has been planned around two new public squares: **Temple Bar Square**, seen as a meeting point for shoppers, and **Meeting House Square**, a cultural centre and performance space.

Just off Temple Bar Square, **Merchant's Arch ❶** – a favourite spot for buskers – leads to the river quay and the **Ha'penny Bridge** (1816) – so-called because of the toll once charged for crossing it. This cast-iron pedestrian walkway across the Liffey has become one

*The fashionable
Eden Restaurant.*

of the best-known symbols of the city. It has also become a valuable link between Temple Bar and the bustling shopping streets of the Henry Street area across the river. On the north side of the bridge is one of those park-bench sculptures much liked in Dublin; this one features two women with shopping bags and has inevitably been dubbed "the hags with the bags".

The route from Temple Bar Square to Meeting House Square goes through the newly built Curved Street, which houses the **Arthouse ❷**, a multimedia centre for the arts) and the **Temple Bar Music Centre ❸**, which is both a training centre/workshop and a venue for concerts. You emerge in Eustace Street, where you can pick up details of current events at **Temple Bar Properties** (No. 18). Opposite is the **Ark ❹**, a cultural centre for children. Just up the street from the Ark, No. 6 marks the entrance to the **Irish Film Centre ❺**, an arthouse cinema with a bookshop, café/restaurant bar and film archive.

Alongside the Ark, a narrow passageway leads into Meeting House Square, an outdoor performance venue used in summer for concerts, theatre and film showings. On the south side is the **Gallery of Photography ❻** (Tuesday–Saturday 11am–6pm, Sunday 1–6pm; free), which shows both Irish and international works and has a range of postcards and books. On the north side is the **National Photographic Archive ❼** (Monday–Friday 10am–5pm, Saturday 10am–2pm; free), which presents themed exhibitions from the National Library of Ireland's collection of 300,000 photographs. Just beyond, on Essex Street East, is **DESIGNyard ❽**, an applied arts centre displaying and selling Irish and international jewellery, glass, ceramics and furniture.

Continuing westward along Essex Street East, you pass the rear of the Clarence Hotel, which fronts onto the river quay on the site of the original Custom House

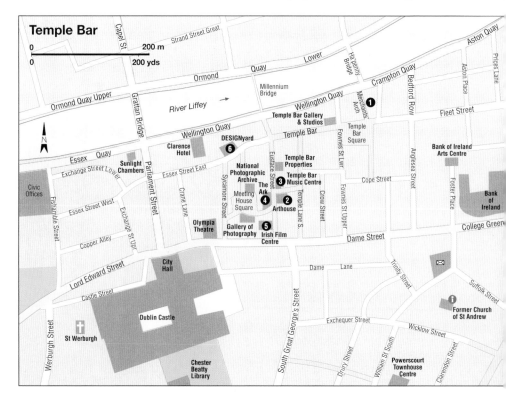

Map on page 172

(which was replaced by Gandon's 18th-century masterpiece further downstream). The hotel's current owners include members of the U2 rock band, and its stylish **Octagon Bar** is a fashionable meeting place.

A few metres further on, you cross Parliament Street. At the riverside end of the street is Sunlight Chambers, a building with a beautiful Victorian frieze displaying the way of the world according to Lever Bros soap manufacturers: men's toil makes clothes dirty, but women's toil (and, of course, Sunlight Soap) makes them clean again.

Welcoming the Messiah

Beyond Parliament Street, Essex Street leads down through what was the old Viking quarter. It ends at its junction with **Fishamble Street**, the medieval "fish shambles", or market, which winds upwards from the quay alongside the Civic Offices. This otherwise unprepossessing street is celebrated as the venue of the first performance of Handel's *Messiah*, conducted by the composer in 1742 in the Charitable Music Society's Hall, long since demolished. Because the hall was cramped and the attendance large, ladies were asked not to wear hooped petticoats and gentlemen not to wear their swords. *Messiah* was an instant success in Dublin, though London audiences remained cool towards it for several years.

A new hotel, named after the composer, stands beside the actual site, which is marked only by a battered plaque on a disused building. But since the 250th anniversary year of 1992, the birth of *Messiah* has been honoured annually on 13 April. Members of one of the city's leading choirs, Our Lady's Choral Society, stand on the spot at noon, the time of the first performance, and sing a selection of choruses from Handel's masterpiece. ❏

One of the area's most popular attractions, Dublin's Viking Adventure, an "interactive experience" of life in Viking Dublin, had just gone out of business at the time of writing, but there were hopes that it might be revived under new ownership.

LEFT: set dancing in a Temple Bar pub.
BELOW: murals in Temple Bar.

THE NORTHSIDE

*Commercialism has robbed O'Connell Street of its grandeur,
but buildings such as the Custom House, the Four Courts
and the General Post Office retain their dignity*

Map
on page
178

This route begins at **O'Connell Bridge**, designed as Carlisle Bridge in the 1790s by James Gandon, the greatest architect of 18th-century Dublin. In 1880 it was widened (so that today its breadth exceeds its span) and two years later it was renamed in honour of Daniel O'Connell, the great 19th-century leader of constitutional nationalism, whose statue dominates the entrance to O'Connell Street.

The bridge affords fine views into O'Connell Street and upstream along the river to the gracefully curving Ha'penny Bridge. But the view downstream to the Custom House, probably Dublin's finest 18th-century building, is badly blocked by a Victorian railway viaduct. For a decent sight of the Custom House facade, walk east along Burgh Quay, on the south bank of the river, and under the railway. Then, for a closer look, cross the river by Butt Bridge.

The Custom House

The **Custom House ❶** was commissioned by John Beresford, the greatly hated First Commissioner of the Revenue (i.e. colonial taxman-in-chief) and designed by Gandon. Completed in 1791, it was immediately recognised as a masterpiece; one contemporary writer remarked: "It is in every respect a noble edifice, in which there is no fault to be found except that old Beresford is sumptuously lodged in it." The building was a major centre of British power in Ireland for 130 years, until it was gutted by fire in 1921, during the War of Independence. When it was restored under the new Irish government, the interior was radically altered and the central dome was rebuilt in grey Ardbraccan stone from County Meath, rather than the original white Portland stone from Dorset, in England.

Gandon, born in London of a French father and a Welsh mother, looked to France for architectural models and it is easier to imagine the Custom House transposed to the banks of the Seine than those of the Thames. The dome is topped by a statue of Commerce. The keystones over the arched doorways flanking the Doric portico represent the Atlantic Ocean and 13 principal rivers of Ireland. Gandon went on to design O'Connell Bridge, the Four Courts, the eastern portico of Parliament House (Bank of Ireland) and the King's Inns.

Today the Custom House contains offices of the Department of the Environment and Customs and Excise. The **Visitor Centre** (Monday to Friday 10am–12.30pm, Saturday and Sunday 2-5pm, closed Monday, Tuesday and Saturday November to mid-March; admission fee) is sited just inside the main riverside entrance, one of the few areas of the interior to survive the fire. Apart from the intrinsic beauty of its neoclassical rooms, staircases and vestibules, the centre

PRECEDING PAGES:
the James Larkin
statue in O'Connell
Street. **LEFT:** the
O'Connell Monument. **BELOW:** the
Custom House.

Liberty Hall.

offers interesting exhibitions on Gandon and on the work of the various government departments, British and Irish, which have occupied the building – revenue collection, Victorian workhouse administration, public health, transport and, more recently, environmental protection.

The tall, 1960s edifice just upstream of the Custom House is **Liberty Hall**, headquarters of the country's largest trade union, the SIPTU (the Services, Industrial, Professional & Technical Union). Its more modest predecessor was a nerve-centre of the labour struggle in the early 20th century. Continuing towards O'Connell Bridge, a right turn into Marlborough Street brings you past the **Abbey Theatre ❷**, Ireland's national playhouse. The present building was erected in 1966; the original was destroyed by fire. The Abbey, founded in 1904 by W. B. Yeats, Lady Gregory and their collaborators, was central to the cultural renaissance of the time and earned a worldwide reputation through the great works of Synge and O'Casey and for its players' naturalistic acting style.

A left turn along Abbey Street brings you to O'Connell Street. Cross over and continue along Abbey Street Middle to the **Hot Press Irish Music Hall of Fame** (daily 10am–6pm; admission fee). Associated with the long-running Dublin music magazine, the music and video exhibits takes you through the highlights of contemporary Irish music, from Van Morrison to U2 to Boyzone.

O'Connell Street

Return to **O'Connell Street**. Laid out in the mid-18th century as Sackville Street, this was once one of Europe's most elegant promenades and the latter-day rash of discount shops, fast-food restaurants, amusement arcades, bland modern buildings, billboards and signs cannot quite obscure its inherent grandeur. Much of the original street was wrecked by British artillery during the 1916 Rising and it suffered further ruin in Civil War engagements of 1922. Decently rebuilt thereafter, it then suffered from poorly policed modern development. Now, an ambitious regeneration scheme is restoring O'Connell Street to its former glory.

The street was once dominated by a tall column topped by a statue of Admiral Nelson, erected in 1815 to mark the famous sea victory over the French at Trafalgar (and pre-dating the similar edifice in Trafalgar Square, London, by 32 years); but unidentified republicans demolished it (neatly) by an explosion in 1966 to mark the 50th anniversary of the Rising. In 2002, the **Spire of Dublin ❸** was erected on the site of the former column. Constructed of rolled stainless steel and rising 120 metres (390 ft) in height, the top 12 metres (39 ft) of Dublin's newest monument is a luminous tip which can be seen for miles around. Like its predecessor, it will serve as an emblem for the city.

Construction of the spire necessitated the removal of one of Dublin's

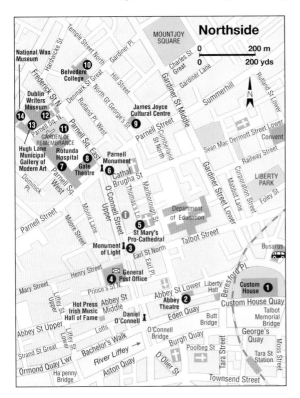

most famous fountains, the aquatic sculpture of Anna Livia, the goddess of the River Liffey who features in Joyce's *Finnegans Wake*. Erected in 1988 as part of the city's millennium celebrations, it was immediately dubbed "The Floozie in the Jacuzzi". After restoration, it will be relocated in Croppy's Memorial Park, at the junction of Parkgate Street and Wolfe Tone Quay.

Map on page 178

The other **statues** lining the centre of the street depict (from the bridge end): Daniel O'Connell (1775–1847); William Smith O'Brien (1803–64), leader of the Young Ireland Party; Sir John Gay (1816–75), proprietor of the *Freeman's Journal* and organiser of the city's water supply; James Larkin (1876–1947), a great trade union leader; Father Theobald Mathew (1790–1856), the "Apostle of Temperance"; and Charles Stewart Parnell (1846–91), inspiration of the late 19th-century Home Rule movement.

By the end of 2003, a new pedestrian plaza with trees and sculptured lighting will grace the front of the street's centrepiece – the imposing Ionic portico (1815) of the **General Post Office** ➍ (Monday to Saturday 8am–8pm, Sundays and holidays 10am–6.30pm). The building was seized by the rebels of Easter 1916 as their headquarters and it was here that they proclaimed the republic in ringing terms, to the initial bemusement of Dubliners – a reaction, in Yeats's words, "changed utterly" by the subsequent execution, one by one, of 15 captured insurgent leaders. The GPO's pillars are still pock-marked by bullets fired during the fighting. Inside, the rebels are commemorated by a fine bronze statue of the ancient hero Cuchulainn, with the text of the Proclamation of the Republic emblazoned on its base.

Henry Street, which turns off O'Connell Street just past the GPO, is the northside's main shopping street. Its tributary, **Moore Street**, is filled with fruit and

Statue of Sir John Gay, who organised the water supply.

LEFT: the General Post Office.
BELOW: the Spire of Dublin.

*The Parnell
Monument.*

BELOW: flower seller
in Moore Street.

vegetable stalls staffed by colourful and cacophonous women, and with a remarkable battery of butchers' shops. Outdoor markets have been a feature of
the city since medieval times and many of the traders here represent generations of their line. It's well worth visiting for a dose of down-to-earth Dublin.

Crossing O'Connell Street near the Spire of Dublin, you can walk down narrow Cathedral Street to visit **St Mary's Pro-Cathedral** (1816–25) ❺, the city's
main Catholic Church (daily 8am–6.30pm). The original plan was for it to stand
on O'Connell Street, but opposition from the Protestant ascendancy relegated
it to its cramped, backstreet site. Both facade and interior are severely neo-classical. John McCormack, the great tenor (1884–1940), was a member of the
church's Palestrina Choir, which can be heard at 11am Mass each Sunday.

The surrounding area was once a notorious red-light district known as "Monto"
(a contraction of Montgomery Street): it was here that Stephen Daedalus wan-
dered in search of sin in Joyce's *A Portrait of the Artist as a Young Man*, "his heart
clamouring against his bosom in a tumult." A statue of the author leaning la-
conically on his walking stick can be seen at the mouth of nearby Earl Street North.

The north end of O'Connell Street is dominated by the **statue of Parnell**
❻. "No man has the right to fix the boundary to the march of a nation...", the
stirring gilt inscription begins. It is an oft-noted irony that the figure of Parnell appears to be pointing towards the **Rotunda Maternity Hospital** ❼, erected
in 1752 as the first purpose-built maternity hospital in Europe. It was funded
by concerts held in the adjoining Assembly Rooms to the right of the hospital,
which today house the **Ambassador Cinema** and the **Gate Theatre** ❽. The
Gate was founded in 1928 and rivals the Abbey for first-class productions of the
classics (*see panel below*). It was here that the teenage Orson Welles bluffed

THE ABBEY AND THE GATE

Although housed in a nondescript 1966 brick building, the Abbey Theatre is, in effect, Ireland's national
theatre, with all the expectations and theatrical in-fighting
that such a status carries with it. It was set up in 1904 by
W. B. Yeats and Lady Gregory as a major component of
the Gaelic Revival and its principal purpose was to stage
new Irish plays such as Synge's *Playboy of the Western
World*, which caused a riot in 1907.

The Gate was created in 1928 by the actor-producer
Micheál MacLiammóir and his partner Hilton Edwards
with the purpose of producing important foreign drama in
Dublin. Playing on the well-known gay relationship
between the couple, local wags referred to the Gate and
the Abbey as Sodom and Begorrah.

The "Begorrah" approach of the state-subsidised
Abbey can still be very successful – as it was, for example, with Brian Friel's *Dancing at Lughnasa*, which went
on to become an international hit. But critics are divided
over whether the Abbey should be a bit less conservative
and the theatre has had a fair turnover of artistic directors.
The Gate, however, continues to present classics with a
sure touch, and it is left to burgeoning fringe theatres to
stage more experimental work.

his way into making his first professional appearance. Also at this end of O'Connell Street is the **Gresham Hotel**, built in 1817, destroyed during the Civil War and rebuilt in 1927 to accommodate the future famous, from Dwight D. Eisenhower to Ronald Reagan, from Richard Burton to Bob Hope.

Map on page 178

James Joyce Centre

Turn right along Parnell Street, then left into **North Great George's Street**, an address which is regaining its cachet as many of its grand Georgian houses are rescued from decades of decrepitude. At number 35 is the **James Joyce Centre ❾** (Monday to Saturday 9.30am–5pm, Sunday 12.30– 5pm; fee), located in a beautifully restored late 18th-century town house which features in *Ulysses* as the venue for dancing classes run by a character named Denis J. Maginni.

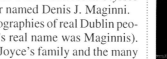

The centre's most interesting exhibit is a set of biographies of real Dublin people fictionalised in Joyce's masterpiece (Maginni's real name was Maginnis). There are also photographs and storyboards about Joyce's family and the many different homes they inhabited. And, in a suitably Joycean collision of fact and fiction, you can view the front door of number 7 Eccles Street, home of Leopold Bloom and his wife Molly, the central characters of *Ulysses* (the house itself was demolished). Obviously, the centre is primarily for Joyce enthusiasts, but others will enjoy viewing the fine interior with its splendid ceilings by Michael Stapleton, one of the great Dublin stuccodores.

An illustrious venue.

Facing you at the top of the street is **Belvedere College ❿**, the Jesuit school attended by the teenage Joyce (1893–98) and featured in *A Portrait of the Artist as a Young Man*. The streets around here are full of Georgian and Victorian buildings, some shabby, others restored to their former beauty; Great Denmark

LEFT: James Joyce statue in Earl Street North. **BELOW:** Mountjoy Square

The Children of Lir.

Street itself leads uphill through Gardiner Place to Mountjoy Square, another example of faded grandeur, partially restored. But our route takes us in the other direction, down Great Denmark Street to emerge, opposite the landmark spire of **Abbey Presbyterian Church**, on the corner of Parnell Square.

Turn left and walk a few yards downhill to enter the **Garden of Remembrance ⑪** (daily, dawn to dusk), laid out in 1966 around a sunken cruciform lake to commemorate those who died for Irish freedom. The imposing sculpture by Oisin Kelly is based on the myth of the Children of Lir, who were changed to swans. A poetic inscription calls on the "generations of freedom" to "remember us, the generations of the vision".

Dublin Writers Museum

Back on the north-east corner of the square, beside Abbey Presbyterian Church, is the **Dublin Writers Museum ⑫** (Monday to Saturday 10am–5pm, Sunday 11am–5pm; fee). In this fine 18th-century house, again with plasterwork by Stapleton, the museum displays photographs, paintings, busts, letters, manuscripts, first editions and other memorabilia relating to celebrated writers such as Swift, Shaw, Yeats, O'Casey, Joyce, Beckett and Behan, though it's rather short of material on more recent authors. The first-floor **Gallery of Writers** is splendidly decorated; there is also a pleasant café and an interesting bookshop.

BELOW: the
Gallery of Writers
in the Dublin
Writers Museum.

Back on Parnell Square North, just a few yards from the Writers Museum stands the **Hugh Lane Municipal Gallery ⑬** (Tuesday to Thursday 9.30am–6pm, Friday and Saturday 9.30am–5pm, Sunday 11am–5pm; free). The gallery's nucleus is the mainly Impressionist collection of Sir Hugh Lane (nephew of

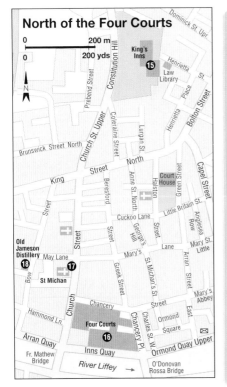

North of the Four Courts

Yeats's Abbey Theatre collaborator Lady Gregory), who died when the liner *Lusitania* was torpedoed in 1915. Because of Dublin's tardiness in providing a suitable home for the paintings, he handed them over to the National Gallery in London and a codicil in his will bequeathing them to Dublin was held to be invalid. The dispute was resolved in 1959 by a compromise under which the collection was shared and paintings are rotated between Dublin and London.

Map on page 178

Apart from well-known French names including Courbet, Monet, Degas, Rouault and Bonnard, there are works by important Irish artists such as Nathaniel Hone, Sarah Purser, John B. Yeats and Jack B. Yeats (father and brother of the poet), Louis Le Brocquy and Robert Ballagh. The striking Irish Impressionist Roderic O'Conor is well represented. There are also temporary exhibitions of contemporary work. In 1998 the gallery painstakingly dismantled the London studio of the Dublin-born artist Francis Bacon and faithfully reconstructed it here (fee).

Leaving the gallery, a right turn into Granby Row leads past the **National Wax Museum** (Monday to Saturday 10am–5.30pm, Sunday noon–5.30pm), which has a predictably eclectic mix of wax models (patriots, prelates, pop stars).

A left turn brings you along Dorset Street and Bolton Street, a depressing inner-city streetscape of drab Corporation flats, run-down houses and bleak workshops. On the right, shortly after crossing the junction with Dominick Street, you find **Henrietta Street**, a short cul-de-sac that is the oldest and once perhaps the finest of the city's Georgian streets, the home of archbishops, peers, and Members of Parliament. It is now, sadly, decrepit. A plaque on the wall of **Number 7** offers a pithy lesson in social history: the house was built in 1730 by Nathaniel Clements, noted architect and Member of the Irish parliament, and he

Painting of W. B. Yeats in the Dublin Writers Museum.

BELOW: an exhibit at the Hugh Lane Municipal Gallery.

Dublin's oldest pub.

TIP

The Four Courts are
open to the public
Monday to Friday
11am– 1pm and
2–4pm.

BELOW:
the Four Courts.

lived here in "Parisian splendour". But in 1908 all the fine doorcases and chimneypieces were removed by one Alderman Meade, who turned the house into a tenement housing 70 people. He did the same for several other houses in the street.

The impressive building at the top of Henrietta Street is the **King's Inns** , the Dublin inns of court, where, in the English tradition, newly qualified barristers must eat a prescribed number of meals. The inns (not open to the public) were designed by Gandon and built at the turn of the 19th century. You can walk through the gardens when the gates are open.

The Four Courts

Continue along Bolton Street, bearing left down Capel Street, once one of Dublin's most fashionable addresses but now occupied mostly by furniture shops. This was the city's main north–south axis until the O'Connell Bridge was built. At the bottom, turn right along the river quay to reach another Gandon masterpiece, the **Four Courts** ⑯. The 137-metre (450-ft) wide building, erected between 1786 and 1802, houses Ireland's High Court, finished in polished Austrian oak, and Supreme Court, finished in walnut panelling with walnut seats.

Great damage was done in 1922 in the first fighting of the Civil War when troops of Michael Collins's new government shelled the building, which had been barricaded by anti-Treaty republicans, from across the river. Before surrendering, the rebels blew up the Public Records Office, symbolically wiping out the colonial past by destroying many priceless documents including the full records of the Irish Parliament. Restoration was completed in 1932.

The dominant lantern-dome is fronted by a six-columned Corinthian portico surmounted by the statues of Moses, Justice and Mercy, and flanked by two wings enclosing courtyards. One architectural authority has written that the Four Courts are "masculine in feeling", while the Custom House expresses the feminine aspect of Gandon's mind.

To get a proper view of the building's proportions, cross the river to Merchant's Quay. Here, just opposite the Four Courts, is a large church known as "**Adam and Eve's**", which is reputed to be the only one on earth named after a pub. A tavern known as Adam and Eve's once stood on the site and in penal times Masses were held secretly in a room behind it. The official title is the Church of the Immaculate Conception. At the junction with Bridge Street, you may wish to inspect the **Brazen Head**, the city's oldest pub, which claims to have been founded in 1198, though the earliest proven reference to it dates from 1613. The present building probably dates from 1754 and in the 1790s it was the headquarters of the United Irishmen. The desk of Robert Emmet, who tried unsuccessfully to capture Dublin Castle in 1803, is preserved in the house. Many writers, such as Brendan Behan, drank here.

St Michan's Church

Recross the river via **Father Mathew Bridge** and continue up Church Street to visit **St Michan's** ⑰, built in 1095, probably on the site of an earlier Viking church, and for several centuries the only church on the north bank of the Liffey (Mar–Oct, Mon–Fri

Map on page 182

10am–12.30pm, 2–4.30pm; Nov–Feb, Mon–Fri 12.30–3.30pm, Saturdays all year !0am–12.45pm; closed Sunday; free). The present structure dates from the late 17th century, but it was much restored in 1821 and again after the Civil War. The impressive organ, built in 1724, is still in use – Handel is believed to have played it at rehearsals for the première of *Messiah* – and the original keyboard, removed during an overhaul in the 1950s, is on display. At the front of the organ gallery is a marvellous oak carving of 17 musical instruments.

But St Michan's best-known attraction is its **underground vaults** (admission fee). Here, coffins were stacked in a number of arched chambers; in one, several coffins have fallen and broken open, revealing mummified corpses, brown and leathery, preserved for hundreds of years through chance environmental conditions – the air in the vaults is very dry because of the absorbent limestone walls and there is also speculation about a high level of methane because the church stands on a former marsh. Also in the vaults are the death mask of the patriot Wolfe Tone and the tomb of two brothers named Sheare, put to death for their part in the 1798 rebellion. A copy of the death warrant, describing in detail the gruesome recipe for their slow execution, is mounted beside their coffins.

Time for a stiff drink? Leaving the church, continue up Church Street, then left into May Lane. Just ahead, on Bow Street, is the **Old Jameson Distillery ⓲**, a museum sited in an old warehouse of the 1791 distillery (daily 9.30am– 5.30pm; fee). The tour in this re-created distillery follows the process of whiskey making, which dates to the 6th century in Ireland. The surrounding area, Smithfield Village, is one of the city's oldest neighbourhoods. Behind Jameson's, alongside the cobbled Smithfield Market, is an old brick tower called **The Chimney ⓳**. Buy tickets at the Chief O'Neill Hotel to ascend to the top for a splendid view over the city. ❏

BELOW: St Michan's Church vaults.

KILMAINHAM JAIL AND PHOENIX PARK

Map on page 190

The jail preserves grim reminders of the Republic's birth, but its claustrophobic effect evaporates in one of the world's largest city parks, a museum of modern art, and a conservation-conscious zoo

The gloomy grey bulk of **Kilmainham Jail** ❶ (sometimes written as Kilmainham Gaol) was intimately connected with Ireland's struggle for independence from its construction in the 1790s until it ceased to function as a prison in the 1920s. Now a visitor centre, it offers uniquely vivid insights into the history of Irish nationalism and into the grim social conditions of 19th-century Ireland (April to September, daily 9.30am–4.45pm; October to March, Monday to Saturday 9.30am– 4pm; Sunday 10am–4.45pm; fee).

A long line of rebels and patriots, including Robert Emmet, Charles Stewart Parnell, Patrick Pearse and the other rebels of 1916, spent time within these walls; some of them died here. Some scenes for the 1993 film *In the Name of the Father* were filmed in the jail, whose historical significance may have helped Daniel Day-Lewis when he played one of the "Guildford Four" wrongly imprisoned for 14 years for a 1974 pub bombing in England. Less aptly, the location has been used in pop videos by U2 and Sinead O'Connor.

PRECEDING PAGES: caretakers at Kilmainham Jail.
LEFT: Phoenix Park.
BELOW: interior of Kilmainham Jail.

Visitors are first invited to browse in the museum, which explores 19th-century notions of crime, punishment and reform through a series of imaginative and well-captioned displays. The upstairs section is devoted to the nationalist figures, some famous, some obscure, who were imprisoned here, many awaiting their execution. A guide then leads visitors into the vaulted east wing of the jail, with its tiers of cells and overhead catwalks, and upstairs to the prison chapel, where an excellent audiovisual summary of the nationalist struggle is shown. Within this chapel, one of the 1916 leaders, Joseph Plunkett, was married only hours before his execution; he was allowed to spend just 10 minutes with his bride.

Visitors are then brought to the "**1916 corridor**", containing the cells that housed the captured leaders of the Rising, and finally led to the stone-breakers' yard where 14 of them were shot between 3 and 12 May of that year. The shots fired in this yard signalled the beginning of the end of British rule in most of Ireland, for the executions transformed the rebel leaders in the public mind from misguided and troublesome idealists into heroes and martyrs, and lit the spark of the War of Independence. Tragically, there were later executions in the jail, during the 1922 Civil War which immediately followed Independence. The last prisoner to be held in Kilmainham was Eamon de Valera, leader of the losing faction in the Civil War, but who survived to become prime minister and president of independent Ireland. A visit to Kilmainham Jail is in some respects a grim experience, but an impressive and moving one.

Stained glass at the old Royal Hospital.

The Irish struggle for independence occurred against the backdrop of a much wider and bloodier struggle and it is easy to forget that, while a few hundred lost their lives in the 1916 rising, nearly 50,000 Irishmen died on the battlefields of World War I. They are commemorated at the **Irish National War Memorial Park ❷**, laid out with ornamental gardens by Edwin Lutyens on a pleasant slope overlooking the River Liffey at Islandbridge. If you have time to spare, it is worth the detour: turn right on leaving the jail, then left on South Circular Road, cross the railway and turn left. It's a fine spot for a picnic.

Irish Museum of Modern Art

Back at the road junction near Kilmainham Jail, you see the ornamental gateway which leads, via a long avenue, to the **Royal Hospital Kilmainham ❸**, built in 1680–84 – not as a hospital in the modern sense of the word, but as a splendid retirement home for soldiers. It predated the similar institution at Chelsea in London (home of the famous "Chelsea Pensioners"). Severely classical in style, reminiscent of Les Invalides in Paris, it forms a quadrangle around a generous central courtyard.

The building served its original purpose for nearly 250 years; then, after Irish independence, it was used as a temporary police headquarters and as a storehouse for museum exhibits while discussions dragged on about how best to use it. Eventually it was splendidly restored in the 1980s and in 1991 it was designated, amid some controversy, as the home of the new **Irish Museum of Modern Art**, which now occupies the hospital's east wing (Tuesday to Saturday 10am–5.30pm; Sunday noon– 5.30pm; free). The permanent collection is, so far, rather patchy, but the temporary exhibitions are often interesting. Al-

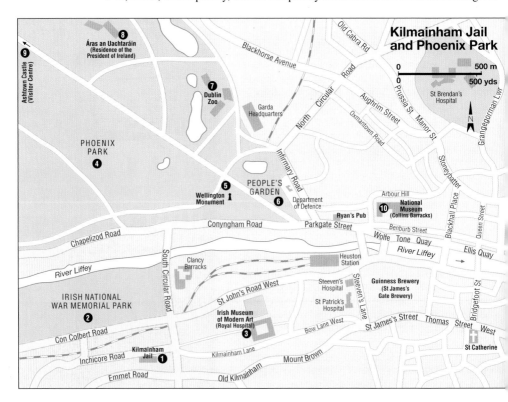

though the conversion of the building is tasteful, the plate-glass insertions undoubtedly spoil the quadrangle and there is something incongruous about avant-garde installations in such an atmospheric old setting; you may find it either jarring or stimulating. There is a café on site and there are guided tours to other sections of the Hospital, including the impressive, pine-panelled Great Hall and the magnificent, baroque Chapel (Jun–Sept 10am–4.45pm; fee). The geometric gardens to the north side of the hospital are currently being restored.

Leaving the Royal Hospital by the eastern gate, turn left to walk along Steeven's Lane, which runs between the Guinness Brewery and the 18th-century Steevens's Hospital. Passing **Heuston Railway Station** (1846) to your left, with its projecting Corinthian columns and twin flanking domed campanile, you cross the Liffey and turn left towards Phoenix Park, passing one of Dublin's finest Victorian pubs, **Ryan's** of Parkgate Street, which has a magnificent mahogany central bar and a series of snugs for private drinking.

Phoenix Park

Phoenix Park ❹ (daily 6.30am–11pm) now stretches before you. Less than 3 km (2 miles) from the centre of Dublin, it is one of the world's largest city parks (712 hectares/1,760 acres), more than five times as big as London's Hyde Park and more than twice the size of New York's Central Park. (A word of warning: camping in the park is forbidden and is highly risky; likewise, do not linger after dark.) The name of the park does not derive from the legendary reincarnatory bird, but is a corruption of the Gaelic *fionn uisce* ("clear water").

Its history as parkland dates from the English Crown's seizure of the lands of the medieval priory of Kilmainham. On the priory lands north of the Liffey,

Map on page 190

The Irish Museum of Modern Art.

BELOW: the Royal Hospital's grounds and gardens.

*Phoenix Park
in bloom.*

a vice-regal country residence called The Phoenix was erected in the early 17th century. In 1662, further lands were acquired for the purpose of creating a royal deerpark of more than 800 hectares (2,000 acres) around the residence. The supervision of the park was entrusted to a ranger and two keepers, chosen from "persons of the proper station and politics". The present-day layout of the park is largely the creation of Lord Chesterfield, an 18th-century viceroy of Ireland, who considered the park to be "a crude uncultivated field", had it landscaped according to formal, Augustan principles at his own expense, and opened it to the public in 1747. One result was that robberies and duelling were soon rife.

The park's main gate is at its southeastern corner, off Parkgate Street, opposite Heuston station. Inside, all of the park's principal features are signposted. To the left of the entrance is the **Wellington Monument ❺**, a 60-metre (200-ft) obelisk erected after the Battle of Waterloo in honour of the Dublin-born British general who preferred to play down his Irish connection.

To the right of the entrance is the **People's Garden ❻**, with colourful flowerbeds banked steeply around an ornamental lake. The adjoining buildings, designed by James Gandon, are now used by the Department of Defence. The nearby **Garda Headquarters** contains a small police museum.

Dublin Zoo

BELOW:
the Wellington
Monument.

Next on the right comes **Dublin Zoo ❼**, the third oldest public zoo in the world (1831), noted for the successful breeding of lions – it claims to have bred the lion famous for introducing MGM movies. The zoo (March to October, Monday–Saturday 9.30am–6pm, Sunday 10.30am–6pm; November to February, Monday–Saturday 9.30am–5pm, Sunday 10.30am– 5pm) has a fine collection of tropical animals, an African reptile house, a large natural lake containing waterfowl, and a "City Farm" with goats, lambs, rabbits, hens and guinea pigs for viewing at close quarters. In recent years, the emphasis has shifted towards conservation and nurturing endangered species for eventual return to the wild.

Beyond the zoo is **Áras an Uachtaráin ❽**, the residence of the President of Ireland, built in 1751 as a viceregal lodge, and greatly enlarged in 1815 to serve as the viceroy's home. On 6 May 1882, Lord Frederick Cavendish, newly-arrived Chief Secretary for Ireland, and T. H. Burke, the Under-Secretary, were stabbed to death within sight of the House. Four members of "The Invincibles" – an extremist rebel secret society – were hanged in Kilmainham Jail for the "Phoenix Park Murders", which had dire consequences for Anglo-Irish relations. The murderers had been informed on by a colleague, James Carey, who was pardoned by the authorities and boarded a boat to Cape Town. But, in a twist that has odd echoes of a later political assassination, Carey was shot dead on the boat; his murderer was later executed in London.

Towards the north end of the park, also to the right of the main road, is the 17th-century **Ashtown Castle ❾**, a 17th-century tower house renovated as the site of the **Phoenix Park Visitor Centre** (mid to end-March 9.30am–5pm, April to May, 9.30am–5.30pm; June to September, 9am–6pm; October 9.30am–5pm, No-

Map on page 190

vember to mid-March, Saturday and Sunday 9.30am–4.30pm). An exhibition includes a reconstruction of the Knockmaree Cist, a tomb housing two 5,500-year-old skeletons; these were discovered in 1838 in the southern part of the park. There is also a video covering the area's general history, and a café/restaurant.

To the left of the main road is the **US Ambassador's residence**, formerly the Chief Secretary's Lodge. Behind that house lies the "Fifteen Acres", an open space actually of 80 hectares (200 acres) containing playing fields for football, hurling, cricket and polo; these were the duelling grounds for 18th-century gentlemen. Overlooking this expanse is the raised altar built for the 31st Eucharistic Conference in 1932 and a stark, 27-metre (90-ft) cross to mark the spot where Pope John Paul II celebrated an open-air Mass attended by 1 million people in 1979.

National Museum extension

Leaving Phoenix Park by the main gate and returning to the city centre along the north side of the quays, you pass on your left the forbidding grey blocks of **Collins Barracks ⓾**, built in 1704 as the Royal Barracks and, until 1997, the oldest continuously occupied purpose-built barracks in the world. The buildings have been converted for use as an extension of the National Museum (Tuesday to Saturday 10am– 5pm, Sunday 2–5pm, admission free). This annexe displays the museum's collections of Irish silver, glassware, china, textiles and furniture, and has sections on musical instruments and Japanese art.

The Curator's Choice galleries display some of the finest works in the collection, on a rotating basis. Also fascinating are the Out of Storage galleries, which contain an amazing assortment of artworks and objects, juxtaposed in strange harmony and available for further study via touch-screen computers. ❑

TIP

You can get to the zoo by bus number 10 from O'Connell Street or buses number 25 and 26 from Abbey Street Middle.

BELOW:
out for a stroll in
Phoenix Park.

THE SOUTHERN SUBURBS

*Past the village of Blackrock and the port of Dun Laoghaire
can be found a series of gorgeous bays and charming
seaside towns such as Dalkey and Killiney*

Map
on page
198

Travelling out through Merrion Square North, along Northumberland Road past the squat, circular block of the **US Embassy** (1964), looking rather like a cake, you reach the prestigious suburb of **Ballsbridge ❶**. The large grey-stone buildings to the right on Merrion Road, just past the bridge which gives the area its name, are the headquarters of the **Royal Dublin Society** (nearest DART station: Sandymount), which has long played an important role in the city's social and cultural life.

The RDS was founded in 1731 by 14 Dublin gentlemen to promote "husbandry, manufactures and other useful arts and sciences" and its members created the cores of the National Library, the National History Museum, the National College of Art and the Botanical Gardens at Glasnevin. The society had a series of headquarters before buying Leinster House in 1815, from which it was evicted in 1923 to make way for the new Irish parliament.

The RDS then moved to its present grand premises in Ballsbridge, where it had been holding its annual agricultural Spring Show and Dublin Horse Show since 1881. The Horse Show – one of the world's great equestrian competitions, staged in August – remains an important date in the city's social calendar, though the Horse Show Ball is no longer a prime marriage mart for the well-heeled. The RDS is also an important venue for trade exhibitions, conferences and concerts, both classical and pop. Just past the RDS is the bleak new **British Embassy**.

PRECEDING PAGES:
sheep at the Royal
Dublin Society's
spring show. **LEFT:**
looking down on
Bray. **BELOW:** wait-
ing for the action at
Dublin Horse Show.

Around the coast

The main road south soon skirts the coast at **Booterstown ❷**, giving fine views across Dublin Bay. An important marshland bird sanctuary occupies an unlikely site between the busy dual-carriageway and the railway. Just past Booterstown DART station on the right is **Blackrock College**, where Eamon de Valera, Ireland's first president, studied and later taught; among more recent alumni was Bob Geldof, rock singer and inspirer of the Band Aid famine relief concert.

To the left of the road is a nicely landscaped public park. **Blackrock village ❸** (DART: Blackrock), which has some interesting shops, pubs and restaurants, is basically a dormitory suburb. In the 18th century it became known as a popular venue for the new-fangled sport of sea-bathing. **St John's Catholic Church** has windows by stained-glass artists Harry Clarke and Evie Hone. A large boulder on the forecourt of a supermarket commemorates the site of Frescati House, home of the patriot Lord Edward Fitzgerald, who died in the 1798 uprising. The house and almost 3 hectares (7 acres) of wooded grounds were bought by property developers in 1969. The actor Micheál MacLiammóir,

founder of the Gate Theatre, told a protest meeting in 1971: "Man does not live by bread alone, nor does a nation live by supermarkets alone." But his plea was in vain and eventually, despite a continuing public outcry, the property was redeveloped in 1983.

Dun Laoghaire

Blackrock is bypassed by the main road, which leads on to the large town of Dun Laoghaire (pronounced *Dunleary*), Ireland's principal ferry-port.

TIP

The main places of interest in Dublin's southern suburbs can be reached by buses departing from Eden Quay, beside O'Connell Bridge, and by the DART suburban trains.

Dun Laoghaire ❹ (DART: Dun Laoghaire) was rechristened Kingstown in honour of a visit by King George IV, who departed from here in a rather inebriated state in 1821 at the end of a visit to Ireland. It reverted a century later to its original name, which dates back to an ancient fort, said to have been the residence of Laoghaire, a High King of Ireland and one of St Patrick's converts to Christianity. The town, with its colourful and elegant terraces, retains overtones of imperial elegance. The harbour, with its long, granite piers each more than a mile long reaching out to embrace the sea, was built between 1817 and 1859 to plans by a Scotsman, John Rennie. It is the headquarters of several prominent yacht clubs. The east pier (near the town centre) glows with a fine golden colour in the evening sun and is popular for promenading.

The **Maritime Museum of Ireland** (May to September, Tuesday–Sunday 1–5pm, tel: 280 0969 for other times; fee) is in Haigh Terrace (turn left off the main street after the shopping centre), housed in the former Mariners' Church, with its finely crafted oak ceiling. Probably the most important historical exhibit is the "yole" (French longboat) used for ferrying senior officers. It is the only surviving relic of the unsuccessful invasion fleet, accompanied

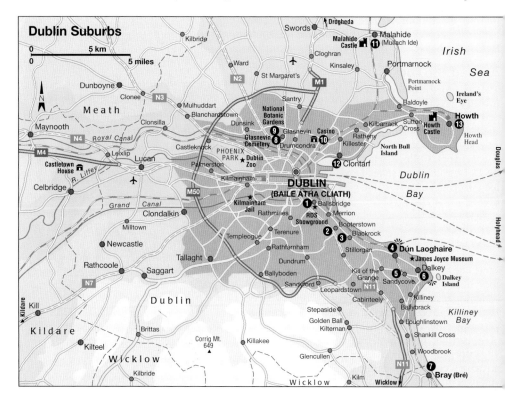

Dublin Suburbs

by the patriot Wolfe Tone, which turned back from Bantry Bay in 1796. Other memorabilia include the effects of Captain Robert Halpin, the Wicklow man who laid the first transatlantic telegraph cable in 1866 from his ship, the *Great Eastern* (of which there is a model). One of the most eye-catching exhibits is the Baily Optic, the clockwork-driven lens which beamed the light from the Baily Lighthouse at Howth on the north side of Dublin Bay until 1972.

On 20 July 1898, Guglielmo Marconi made the first radio transmissions from Dun Laoghaire, from Moran House at Moran Park. This has recently opened as the **Marconi Museum and Business Centre** (tel: 01-236 0815).

James Joyce Museum

The next promontory, within easy walking distance, is that of **Sandycove** ❺, where James Joyce lived for a short time in 1904 in the Martello Tower (one of a series built along Ireland's south and east coasts at the turn of the 19th century to deter Napoleonic invasion). It is the setting for the opening scene of *Ulysses*, and in 1962 the book's original publisher, Sylvia Beach, opened it as a **James Joyce Museum** (April to October, Monday to Saturday 10am–1pm and 2–5pm, Sunday 2–6pm; fee). Exhibits include letters, photographs and rare editions (including a *Ulysses* illustrated by Henri Matisse), the writer's death mask, and various personal belongings such as his walking stick and guitar.

The rocky cove just in front of the tower, known as the **Forty Foot** because the 40th Regiment of Foot used to be stationed nearby, was for generations a spartan haven of nude bathing for men, but is now used by both sexes. Enthusiasts swim here even on Christmas Day in what Joyce described as the "snot-green, scrotum-tightening sea".

Map on page 198

MARITIME MUSEUM →

BELOW: Dun Laoghaire, a main terminal for sea routes to Britain.

BELOW: Killiney, which has been likened to the Bay of Naples.

Dalkey

About a mile further on is **Dalkey ❻** (DART: Dalkey; pronunciation *Dawky*), a meandering old village of great charm and some cachet. A thriving port as early as Norman times, it was known as the Town of Seven Castles, and two of these – 15th and 16th-century fortified mansions – still survive in the main street, along with a ruined church, St Begnet's, dedicated to a local virgin saint.

One of these, Goat Castle, has been converted into the **Dalkey Castle and Heritage Centre** (April to December, Monday to Friday 9.30am–5pm, year-round Saturday and Sunday 11am–5pm; admission fee). Apart from viewing the castle's curious medieval features such as the murder hole and garderobe, and climbing up to the battlements, you can see models of medieval Dalkey when it served as Dublin's main port, and models of the funicular railways and trams. There are also exhibits on the town's folklore, customs and literary history.

From nearby Coliemore Harbour there are boat trips in summer to **Dalkey Island**, a stone's throw offshore, which contains another Martello tower and the ruins of a Benedictine church. The island is a bird sanctuary.

Torca Cottage, George Bernard Shaw's boyhood home between 1866 and 1874, is on **Dalkey Hill**, which affords superb views of Dublin Bay and some of the most beautiful stretches of Ireland's east coast. The excavation on the side of the hill marks the spot where the granite for Dun Laoghaire harbour was quarried.

This stretch of coast, with its winding roads and grand secluded villas, has a decidedly Continental air, and many of the roads are named accordingly. A few hundred metres west of **Killiney Strand**, one of Dublin's finest suburban beaches, are the ruins of **Killiney Church**, near which is a curious collection of stones known as the **Druid's Chair**. From Vico Road, which continues along

the coast, you can enter **Killiney Hill Park**; motorists should drive instead up Dalkey Avenue, where there is a car park. At the park's summit is a Victorian obelisk, built in 1742 as a famine relief work project after a very harsh winter when even the River Liffey froze. The spot commands splendid views of the broad sweep of **Killiney Bay** (often likened to the Bay of Naples), **Bray Head** – the hump-backed promontory at its far side – and Sugar Loaf mountain.

Killiney became especially fashionable in the 1990s when Hollywood stars such as Mel Gibson and Tom Cruise bought property there, joining local celebrities such as U2 singers Bono and The Edge and best-selling novelist Maeve Binchy.

Bray

DART travellers can easily continue on to **Bray ❼**, where James Joyce lived from 1888 to 1891. The trouble is that a lot of Dubliners took advantage of the rapid rail link to move to the beautifully situated seaside resort and a great deal of the town's character has been lost in the expansion. The promenade is lined with tacky amusement arcades and fast-food joints.

The **National Sea-Life Centre** (daily 10am– 5pm, tel: 286 4688; admission fee), on the seafront, is a popular Irish-oriented aquarium.

Bray Head offers bracing walks, especially the 8-km (5-mile) walk between Bray and Greystones, and fine views further southwards along the coast. Bray is also a convenient base for exploring Wicklow beauty spots such as Powerscourt, Enniskerry, the Devil's Glen, Glendalough and Avoca.

In August a lively international festival of music and dance is held in Bray, and an Oscar Wilde Autumn School celebrates and examines the life and work of the Dublin-born playwright. ❑

Map on page 198

Enjoying the outdoors at Bray Head.

BELOW: a seaside kiosk at Bray.

WHY DUBLIN ISN'T A ONE-HORSE TOWN

The Dublin Horse Show is a highlight of the social calendar. But it isn't just an excuse for seeing and being seen – the Irish have a real love for horses

Horses are said to thrive in Ireland because of the moist climate, which produces some of the world's lushest pastures, and the limestone subsoil, which makes the grass rich in bone-building calcium. Certainly, whether they're breeding them, racing them, exporting them or betting on them, the Irish, have always had an extraordinary affinity with horses. The Red Branch Knights of pre-Christian Ireland raced each other, and racing was an essential part of fairs since the earliest times. The greatest of these fairs was held at the Curragh, a wide, grassy plain in what is now in County Kildare, southwest of Dublin, across which a horse can gallop to exhaustion.

Summer visitors to such top-class tracks as Leopardstown, in the southern suburb of Foxrock, and the Curragh are likely to see runners entered by Ireland's leading trainers. Most promising two-year-olds experience the rigours of racing life here before they are sent across the Irish Sea in search of a big race win to set them on their planned careers as classic victors and, later, top-priced stallions. But their odds are likely to be rather short and, as the experienced denizens of Dublin's many betting shops know to their cost favourites don't always win.

△ **THE STAKES ARE HIGH**
The winner of a great flat race like the Irish Derby may be worth tens of millions of dollars in breeding fees.

△ **THE WAITING GAME**
The stables at Dublin Horse Show. The Royal Dublin Society, which runs the show, began its life in 1731 as The Dublin Society for improving Husbandry, Manufactures and other useful Arts, and it helped create the National Library, the National Gallery and the Botanic Gardens.

HOW TO MAKE MONEY ON HORSES

Putting your money on a fancied filly at Leopardstown is unlikely to make you rich. Investing in the bloodstock industry is a much better bet.

Each spring there's a migration of hundreds of mares (mainly from the US, Britain and France) to be mated with the many former leading males of the turf who have retired to stallion duties in Ireland.

The health of this bloodstock business owes much to a 1969 government concession under which fees received for the services of thoroughbred stallions are fully exempt from tax. But it also owes a lot to the natural ability of many Irish people to handle. train and understand horses.

◁ **BIG MONEY AT STAKE**
The Curragh is the setting for all the Irish classic races. Prizes at the Derby in June exceed £750,000.

△ **DUBLIN SPRING SHOW**
The Royal Dublin Society's Spring Show is held each May at the society's grand grounds at Ballsbridge, a southern suburb. It has an agricultural emphasis.

▷ **ON SHOW**
Since 100,000 people can attend the Dublin Horse Show, it's wise to book ahead. The telephone number is 668 0866.

◁ **ON THE BEACH**
Laytown, a resort about 30 miles (50 km) north of Dublin, hosts Europe's only official race held on a beach.

△ **THE MELTING POT**
The wealthy in their finery, bowler-hatted remnants of the old gentry, down-at-heel city dwellers… all are here.

GLASNEVIN CEMETERY AND THE BOTANIC GARDENS

Map on page 198

Ireland's national necropolis keeps alive the memory of the country's generations of martyrs but accommodates artists and writers too

Like many Catholic countries, Ireland does not try to conceal the fact that life ends in death, and the traditional wake is more likely to be a bibulous celebration of the deceased's existence than an occasion for long-faced mourning. So it's not inappropriate that Ireland's largest burial ground, **Glasnevin Cemetery ❽** (open daily 8.30am to 5pm, admission free), should be deemed worth a visit. Situated on the Finglas Road (take bus no. 40 or 40A from Parnell Street or no. 19 from O'Connell Street), it is the resting place of some of the most famous names in the country's political and cultural pantheon.

Originally called Prospect Cemetery, it was opened in 1832 following the success of Daniel O'Connell's Catholic Emancipation campaign. At that time it was difficult and expensive for Roman Catholics to have burials conducted according to their own religious rites. A burial in that year cost two shillings and sixpence (12½p in today's money) and the size of the cemetery was just 3.6 hectares (9 acres). The cemetery has since grown to cover nearly 50 hectares (120 acres) and contains 1 million burials. In keeping with the traditions in which it was established, it caters for all denominations.

LEFT: the Botanic Gardens.
BELOW: Parnell's burial place at Glasnevin Cemetery.

The first resident of Glasnevin cemetery was Michael Carey from Francis Street in Dublin's Liberties. The inscription on his tombstone bears witness to the historic occasion: "Michael Carey the first ever interred in this cemetery. 22nd February 1832".

Illustrious corpses

Among those who subsequently joined him are **Michael Collins** (1890–1922), the eponymous subject of Neil Jordan's 1996 epic movie. Collins is one of the most romantic figures in Irish history. He fought in the GPO during the 1916 rising against the British and went on to be the director-general of the IRA, setting up an elite squad to hunt down British spies and informers. After being the most wanted man in Ireland for many years, he was ambushed and shot dead in County Cork, not by the British but by fellow Irishmen during the civil war which followed the signing of the Treaty of Independence; they saw his signing as a betrayal.

Eamon de Valera (1881–1975), who fought with Collins during the war against the British and later became his opponent, is also buried in Glasnevin. De Valera, by virtue of his American parent-

BELOW: Glasnevin Cemetery.

age, had his death sentence rescinded and went on to become Prime Minister and President of Ireland.

Other famous political figures buried here include **Charles Stewart Parnell** (1846–1891), the champion of Ireland's oppressed peasants and leader of the Home Rule party, **Kevin O'Higgins**, founder of the Irish police force, **Countess Constance Markievicz**, revolutionary and the first woman elected to Britain's parliament, and **Roger Casement** (1864–1916), hanged by the English for treason after trying to import arms for the Irish revolutionaries.

Glasnevin is also the resting place of many artists and writers including the playwright **Brendan Behan** (1923–64), well-known roisterer and author of *Borstal Boy*, *The Quare Fellow*, and *The Hostage*. **Christy Brown**, author of the biographical novel *My Left Foot*, is buried here, as is the celebrated English poet **Gerard Manley Hopkins** (1844–89), who was appointed to the chair of Greek and Latin at University College Dublin in 1884 but became increasingly depressed and eventually died of typhoid.

The architecture in and around the cemetery is worth noting. The most striking piece is the **round tower** in memory of Daniel O'Connell. It was completed in 1861, 14 years after his death, and is the tallest such structure in Ireland at 51 metres (168 ft). The influence of Celtic motifs, in particular celtic crosses, is very noticeable throughout the cemetery. Occasionally good taste lapses into Celtic kitsch, as on John Keegan Casey's memorial which shows a wolfhound guarding a manuscript of his most famous song.

One of the the earliest difficulties to beset Glasnevin was the problem of bodysnatching. Most of the people who engaged in this business were eager medical students who needed bodies to practise dissection

Map on page 198

because of the shortage of suitable corpses at the medical schools. Some of the methods employed were particularly ingenious. One bodysnatcher made a practice of joining relatives watching over a new grave and passing round a drugged bottle of whiskey until everyone had lost consciousness. Another grave robber used to dress up disinterred corpses and walk out with them through the cemetery gates.

In an effort to deter body-snatchers, a high wall was built around the perimeter of the cemetery with five watch towers which are all still intact. Cuban bloodhounds were kept as an extra deterrent but were subsequently removed in 1853 after they attacked the city coroner who barely escaped with his life.

The National Botanic Gardens

Close to the dead, life flourishes. The **National Botanic Gardens** ❾ are directly behind the cemetery and contain over 20,000 species of plants. The gardens (summer 9am–6pm Mon–Sat, 11am–6pm Sun; winter 10.30am–4.30pm Mon–Sat, 11am–4.30pm Sun; free) were founded by direction of the Irish parliament in 1795, when the Royal Dublin Society acquired 11 hectares (27 acres) of land at the site in Glasnevin, and subsequent acquisitions of land have seen them grow to their present size of 19 hectares (47 acres).

The man who originally laid out the Botanic Gardens was Dr Walter Wade, Professor of Botany to the Dublin Society but only the Yew Walk, also known as Addison's Walk, remains from the original planting. Richard Turner, the creator of the conservatories between 1843 and 1876, turned his skills as a maker of Dublin fanlights to good use, ingeniously designing cornices to act as gutters, columns as drainpipes and palmettes as wind deflectors. He also built the Palm House at London's Kew Gardens.

The glasshouses include the Fern House, the Aquatic House, which contains the giant amazon waterlily (*victoria amazonia*), the Orchid House and the Great Palm House.

Depending on time available, a variety of walks can be taken. A short tour might include – as the information leaflet and map available at the entrance suggests – "a visit to the rose garden, the rhododendron and heather collections and the rockery, returning to the main entrance via the main herbaceous border."

If more time is available, the visitor might go on from the rockery to see the conifers and return by the yew collection, the Chinese shrubbery, seasonal display beds, the herb garden and the native plant collection. The rose garden is particularly fine, especially in the summer when the roses are in bloom It is secluded in the corner of the Gardens and is accessed via a bridge.

Spring and autumn are the most interesting times to visit for gardeners but, thanks to Ireland's generally mild climate and abundance of rain, there are plenty of blooms to see at any time of year. The river Tolka, which runs through the Gardens, adds significantly to the aesthetic beauty. ❑

TIP

Bus no 19, which can be picked up on Upper O'Connell Street, will take you to the Botanic Gardens. Ask the driver to let you know when it is time to get off.

BELOW: the Botanic Gardens.

MALAHIDE AND HOWTH

The DART rapid-transit system has make it easy for both commuters and visitors to reach the attractive seaside towns to the northeast of Dublin

Map on page 198

East of Glasnevin, just off Malahide Road in the suburb of **Marino** (buses 20A, 20B,27,27B,42) is the 18th-century folly known as the **Casino** (Feb–Mar & Nov, Sun & Thurs noon–4pm, Apr–May daily 10am–5pm, Jun–Sept daily 10am–6pm; Oct daily 10am–5pm. Tel: 833 1618; fee). Designed in 1758 as a summer house for the 27-year-old Lord Charlemont, whose town residence is now the Municipal Gallery of Modern Art, it stands incongruously, bordered by lawns and a wire fence, next to a housing estate and deprived of its parent mansion, Marino House, demolished in the 1920s. It is a small Palladian villa, a gem of its kind, with several ingenious features: the roof urns are actually chimneys and the columns are hollow, serving as drains.

The exterior gives the impression through *trompe l'oeil* effects – such as a large, but bogus, front door – of a single space within. In fact the Casino contains a complex of many rooms around a central staircase, including a saloon with beautiful parquet flooring. Odd artefacts include an extendable child's bed.

Malahide

Car drivers can continue out along Malahide Road to reach the coastal town of **Malahide** , about 14 km (9 miles) north of Dublin. (It can also be reached by buses 42 and 32A, or by northbound trains from Connolly and Pearse stations). If driving, watch out on the left, just as you reach the open countryside, for **St Doulagh's Church**, claimed to be the oldest still in use in Ireland. Built on the site of a 7th-century hermit's cell, its remarkable high-pitched stone roof is 12th-century. The larger nave attached alongside is 19th-century. The grounds contain a stone-roofed holy well. In summer, a member of the congregation is on duty from 3pm to 5pm to show visitors around.

Malahide itself is a pretty seaside resort and dormitory town well-stocked with restaurants and stylish shops, but the main attraction is **Malahide Castle and Demesne** on the outskirts of the town. The castle, which stands in 100 hectares (250 acres) of parkland, was occupied continuously by the Norman-Irish Talbot family from 1185 until 1976, except for a short period in Cromwell's time. The result is a charming mixture of architectural styles. The rambling interior (Apr–Oct, Mon–Sat 10am–5pm, Sun and holidays 11.30am–6pm; Nov–Mar, Mon–Fri 10am–5pm, Sat–Sun 2–5pm; admission fee) is furnished with many antiques and a collection of portraits from the National Gallery. The most impressive room is the oak-beamed Great Hall, one wall of which is dominated by a huge painting of the Battle of the Boyne (1690).

Beside the castle, in its former corn store, is the **Fry Model Railway**, a working miniature impression

PRECEDING PAGES: the fishing port of Howth. **LEFT:** boys on the beach. **BELOW:** a good catch at Howth.

The Fry Model Railway.

TIP

Dublin Bus operates a Coast and Castle open-top tour of Malahide and Howth. Tel: 873 4222.

BELOW: Malahide Castle.

of Ireland's rail system, complete with stations, viaducts, tunnels, trains, barges and even a car ferry (Apr–Oct, Mon–Sat 10am–5pm, Saturday 10am–1pm & 2–5pm, Sun 2–6pm; closed lunch 1–2pm; Nov–Mar, Sat and Sun 2–5pm; admission fee).

Clontarf

Drivers can return to Dublin via Howth, but really it is worth a separate outing and can also be reached by DART or bus. The coast road north from the city passes the attractive suburb of **Clontarf** ⑫, site of the battle in 1014 in which King Brian Ború defeated the Danes, ending their expansion in Ireland.

Just past Clontarf, the **North Bull Wall** extends into Dublin Bay. It was built early in the 19th century on the recommendation of Captain Bligh (of the *Bounty*) to prevent silting in Dublin port. It also caused the gradual build-up of sand that formed the still-growing **North Bull Island**, where plants and animals thrive among the sand dunes and salt marshes. The most celebrated inhabitants are seabirds – up to 40,000 of them, for at high tide all the birds in Dublin Bay come to roost here. On a good day in winter, you may see 5,000 ducks, 800 geese and 30,000 waders roosting on the island, part of which was designated a UNESCO Biosphere Reserve.

The island has two golf courses, the Royal Dublin and St Anne's.

Howth

The road continues via the isthmus at Sutton to reach **Howth** ⑬ village (it rhymes with *both*), at the foot of rugged **Howth Head**, which overlooks the northern entrance to Dublin Bay. With its steep streets, attractive fishing harbour and wild hinterland, Howth attracts affluent residents who commute to the city by DART.

The cliff walk around the headland offers a view (weather permitting) described by the novelist H. G. Wells as "one of the most beautiful in the world." You can go directly to Howth village, then walk around the headland to Howth Summit, but it's probably better to start at the Summit (bus 31B from Lower Abbey Street, or DART to Sutton, then bus 31B), and walk to the village via the cliff path, which descends steeply to Howth harbour.

Ireland's Eye, the quartzite island just offshore, was the site of a 7th-century monastery, and is now a bird sanctuary. You can get there on weekend afternoons by motorboat from Howth harbour. The privately owned **Lambay Island**, which can be seen beyond, is of even more interest to sea bird lovers.

Apart from being a picturesque resort, Howth is one of Ireland's most important fishing ports and a major yachting centre. The ruins of the parish church of **St Mary's Abbey** (1235) overlook the harbour.

A short walk west of the village (follow signs for Deer Park Hotel) is **Howth Castle**, originally Norman but much rebuilt, notably by the British architect Sir Edwin Lutyens in 1910. The castle, which has been owned by the St Lawrence family since 1177, is closed to the public, but there's a **Transport Museum** (Sat & Sun all year 2–5pm and Jun–Aug Mon–Fri 10am–5pm; fee) with almost 100 exhibits, including the old Hill of Howth tram. The gardens can also be visited; they are famous for their countless varieties of rhododendrons and azaleas which are in full bloom from April to June. Previous strollers through the gardens included Leopold and Molly Bloom in James Joyce's *Ulysses*.

Above the castle is a portal dolmen with a massive capstone which archaeologists believe to be the remains of a 4,500-year-old burial chamber. Beyond the castle is a hotel and public golf course commanding glorious sea views. ❏

Map
on page
198

Howth Abbey.

BELOW: the Bull
Wall at Clontarf.

THE WICKLOW MOUNTAINS

Here is spectacular mountain and moorland terrain, as well as splendid gardens and the monastic ruins of Glendalough, one of early Christian Ireland's most important relics

Map on page 218

The **Wicklow Mountains** are rich in magnificent scenery and fascinating antiquities and, being just half an hour south of the city, wonderfully accessible. In London terms, it's like having the Lake District just beyond Golders Green – or, in New York terms, like having Maine begin not far beyond Harlem. The region is sparsely inhabited – just a few villages, scattered farms and cottages, and the occasional large mansion.

Wicklow county takes its name from the Norse words *Wyking alo*, meaning Viking meadow. Perhaps when they named it the Vikings had not travelled far south of Dublin, for although Wicklow has some lush meadowland much of the county is covered by the great granite outcrops thrown up by ancient earth movements. In the Ice Age, glaciers smoothed and rounded their peaks and carved deep, dark, steep-sided glens whose wide floors glitter with rivers and lakes.

Powerscourt Estate and Gardens

Leave Dublin by the main N11 route towards Wicklow and Wexford. Shortly after the exit for Bray, turn right for the picturesque village of **Enniskerry ❶**, which lies in the glen of the Cookstown or Glencullen river and much of whose history revolved around the nearby Powerscourt demesne. The Roman Catholic church by Patrick Byrne (1843) was one of Ireland's first Gothic Revival churches. Many of the battle scenes in Laurence Olivier's film version of *Henry V* (made in neutral Ireland during World War II) were shot around Enniskerry.

Just beside the village are the **Powerscourt Estate and Gardens ❷** (open daily 9.30am– 5.30pm, times vary in winter; fee), which have magnificent views across a deep valley to the 506-metre (1,660-ft) Sugar Loaf Mountain – which is not volcanic, as popular opinion would have it, but an eroded lump of quartize. Powerscourt House, designed by Richard Cassels around 1730, was gutted by fire in 1974. After years of uncertainty about its future, its owners, the Slazenger family, reopened it in 1997, re-roofed and reglazed, with the interior converted to house a restaurant, a visitor centre and stylish shops. The gardens (begun in 1745) descend to the lake in five terraces. A Japanese garden dates from 1908, and there's a pets' cemetery. The arboretum includes a sitka spruce said to be Ireland's tallest tree.

Also in the demesne is the highest **waterfall** (122 metres/400 ft) in the British Isles, the subject of many 19th-century paintings. The Chevalier de Latocnaye, author of *A Frenchman's Walk Through Ireland* (1796–97) thought it resembled "the wind-blown, snowy hair of a venerable old man."

Leaving the estate near the waterfall, follow signs for **Glencree**. The narrow, winding road through this

PRECEDING PAGES: the Vale of Avoca. **LEFT** and **BELOW:** Powerscourt House and Gardens.

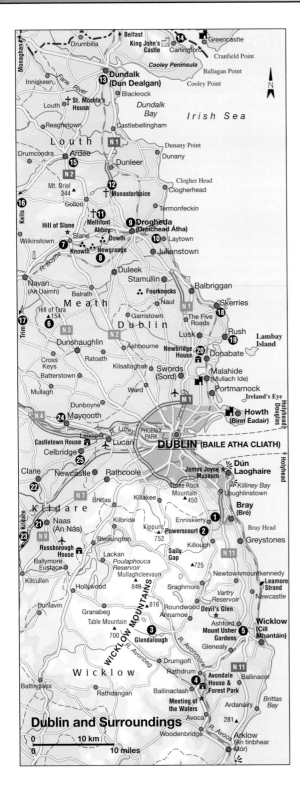

Dublin and Surroundings

wooded valley – once covered with oak forests, later preserved as a royal park and now clothed mainly in spruce – passes a gaunt old British military barracks built after the 1798 rebellion, subsequently used as a boys' reformatory, and more recently converted to a "reconciliation centre" for promoting understanding between the divided communities of Northern Ireland. Nearby is a small **German Cemetery** for servicemen (mainly airmen and sailors) who died in or near Ireland during the two world wars.

Glendalough

At the top of Glencree the road rises to a T-junction; turn left for **Sally Gap**, one of two high passes through the Wicklow Mountains. You are now travelling along the "Military Road", built after the 1798 Rebellion as part of a campaign to bring this wild region, a haven for insurgents, under the control of Dublin Castle. Today the road's main value lies in the

series of panoramic views which it offers (weather permitting). At Sally Gap, carry straight on through the heathery heart of the mountains, descending via **Glenmacnass**, a lovely narrow valley with a fine **waterfall**, to the village of Lara.

Map
on page
218

From here it is just a mile into **Glendalough** ❸ ("Glen of Two Lakes"), a secluded wooded valley containing the evocative remains of a monastic city founded in 545 by St Kevin. Religious life continued here, despite Viking and English raids, until the 16th-century suppression of the monasteries. In the Visitor Centre (open Jun–Aug daily 9am–6.30pm, Sept–mid-Oct and mid-Mar–May 9.30am–6pm, mid-Oct–mid-March 9.30am–5pm; admission fee) there is an exhibition on Glendalough's history and an interesting film of about Irish monastic sites.

There is no charge to enter the grounds. The ruins include a **cathedral**, dating from about the 9th century; **St Kevin's Church**, a good example of an early Irish oratory, with a pitched stone roof; and the dominant, 133-metre (110-ft) round tower, into which the monks could retreat if attacked. **St Kevins's Cross**, made of granite and about 3.3 metres (nearly 11 ft) tall, dates from about 1150.

It is well worth taking the path to the upper lake where, amid smaller, even older ruins, you can sense the deep longing for peace and solitude that was central to the ancient monks' idea of sanctity. The small cave carved into the cliff above the southern shore of the lake is called **St Kevin's Bed**. This is where the hermit is said to have hidden from the attentions of a beautiful, naked young woman; when she tracked him down, he is said to have pushed her into the lake.

ABOVE:
St Kevin's Church
at Glendalough.
LEFT: 11th-century
tower, Glendalough.
BELOW: the
Georgian elegance
of Avondale.

Where Parnell was born

Driving south through Rathdrum, you reach **Avondale** ❹, the Georgian birthplace and home of the 19th-century Irish leader Charles Stewart Parnell. Built

Traditional horse-drawn caravans are popular with many holidaymakers – but they're harder work than at first appears.

in 1779 for Samuel Hayes, an amateur architect who may have designed it himself, the house passed to Parnell's grandfather. Parnell himself lived there for most of his life. Despite his Protestant, land-owning background, he espoused the cause of Irish nationalism and land reform. His great parliamentary gifts, allied to a streak of ruthless pragmatism – he invented the technique of boy-cotting – made his party a powerful force at Westminster and gave him great leverage with Britain's prime minister, William Ewart Gladstone.

But his reign as the "uncrowned king of Ireland" was ended by the public scandal of his affair with Kitty O'Shea, a married woman. Parnell, broken-hearted, died soon afterwards, aged 45. His house, surrounded by Thuja (western red cedar) trees, is now a museum on public parkland owned by the Forest and Wildlife Service – appropriately enough, for Parnell encouraged afforestation as an industry.

The Vale of Avoca

A couple of miles further on is the celebrated **Vale of Avoca**, where the Avonmore and Avonbeg rivers join and which was supposedly described in Thomas Moore's song *The Meeting of the Waters*:

There is not in the wild world a valley so sweet
As that vale in whose bosom the bright waters meet...

Controversy, however, surrounds the sentiment: some people claim that Moore (1779–1852) was actually describing the meeting of the Aughrim and Avoca rivers at Woodenbridge, 3 km (2 miles) south of Avoca village. When asked, Moore is supposed to have said that he couldn't remember.

BELOW: the meeting of the Avondale and Avonbeg rivers.

At Avoca village, you can turn northwards again and drive, via the unremarkable county town of Wicklow, to the village of **Ashford**, beautifully situ-

ated by the Vartry river and a convenient point from which to explore the eastern Wicklow Mountains as well as the local demesnes. Shortly before reaching Ashford you pass the **Devil's Glen**, a deep chasm along the river with craggy sides shrouded in vegetation and spectacular walks beside tumbling waters. The glen gave refuge to insurgents after the abortive rebellion of 1798.

Map on page 218

Mount Usher Gardens

On arrival in Ashford, turn right to visit the **Mount Usher Gardens** ❺ (open 15 March to 31 October, 10.30am–6pm; fee), which contain over 4,000 different species of exotic and rare trees, shrubs and plants collected by generations of the Walpole family. About a mile from Ashford, on the road to Rathnew, is **Hunter's Hotel**, an old coaching inn whose delightful riverside gardens are ideal for afternoon tea. You can return to Dublin on the main N11 route.

The Wicklow Way

The easiest way to see Wicklow is by car, though its chief attractions are served by coach tours from Dublin. But perhaps the best way to see it is to walk it. The **Wicklow Way** is a 130-km (80-mile) waymarked long-distance walking route running along the eastern flanks of the Dublin and Wicklow mountains – said to be the largest unbroken area of high ground in the country, and scarcely inhabited.

The Wicklow Way begins in Marlay Park, Rathfarnham, on the outskirts of Dublin, and wends its way over spurs and tracks, by forest walks and country lanes, to the southern end of County Wicklow. Much of the route is for the serious walker; youth hostels provide accommodation. Come prepared with wet weather gear, compass and good map – conditions can turn treacherous. ❏

Bus Eireann runs guided tours to Wicklow attractions from its Busaras terminus in Store Street, Dublin. Tel: 836 6111.

BELOW: climbing is popular in the Wicklow Mountains.

EXCURSIONS NORTH

Map on page 218

History is inescapable here, from the ancient burial mounds at Brú na Bóinne to the seat of the High Kings at Tara, from St Patrick's early ministry to the Battle of the Boyne

L eave Dublin by the N3 route running northwest across the fertile farmlands of County Meath. About 6 km (4 miles) past the village of Dunshaughlin, a small signpost points left to **Tara ❻**. This broad, grassy hill was the residence of the High Kings of ancient Ireland and the country's main cultural and religious centre in the first five centuries AD. A great assembly (*feis*) was held there every three years to pass laws and settle disputes, and you can still see a pillar-stone said to have been used in the coronation of the ancient kings. The statue of St Patrick on top of the hill is jarringly modern to some eyes.

To help make sense of the site, it's best to take a tour from the Visitor Centre (open mid-June to October, daily 10am–6pm; admission fee); there's also a film about the history of Tara. A signboard explains the various earthworks – the Fort of the Synods, the banqueting Hall, the Fort of the Kings, and so on – though there is little worthy of prolonged inspection. But the view across the plains from the central "Mound of the Hostages" (actually a passage grave from the 3rd century BC) is very impressive and the place is undeniably atmospheric.

Although Tara's influence declined soon after Christianity took root in the country, it has remained a powerful symbol of Irish unity, expressed in the Thomas Moore (1779–1825) song *The Harp that Once Through Tara's Halls*, and Daniel O'Connell chose it in 1843 as the venue for one of his "monster meetings" to demand repeal of the union with Britain. A million people attended, according to *The Times*.

PRECEDING PAGES: Trim Castle by the River Boyne. **LEFT:** entrance to the passage grave at Newgrange. **BELOW:** Slane Abbey.

Slane and its castle

Rejoin the N3 and drive to **Navan**, skirting the town and following signs for Drogheda (N51) to the old village of **Slane ❼**. Turn left up the steep main street, then left again to the **Hill of Slane**, where St Patrick is said to have proclaimed the Christian message to Ireland by lighting a bonfire that could be seen by the High King from his royal seat on the Hill of Tara. Patrick founded a church here, but the hilltop ruins are of a 16th-century **Franciscan abbey**.

A faint circular ditch marks the boundary of a monastery associated with St Erc, a local man converted to Christianity by St Patrick. St Erc is said to have mortified himself by standing all day in the river, immersed up to his armpits, reciting psalms. The view from the Hill of Slane is splendid, on a clear day: to the east, the River Boyne meets the sea at the smoky port of Drogheda; to the south, the Wicklow Mountains, blue in the distance; to the west, the pastures of the central plain roll away into the great bog of the Midlands.

West of Slane, on a commanding site among lush woodland by the river, is **Slane Castle**, a mock-medieval

TIP

Tours of Knowth and
Newgrange are
directed from the Brú
na Bóinne Visitors'
Centre: Jun–mid-Sept
9am–7pm, mid-Sept
& May 9am–6.30pm,
Oct, Mar & Apr
9.30am– 5.30pm,
Nov–Feb 9.30am–
5pm. Admission fee.
Arrive early as tour
numbers are limited
and sites are busy.

edifice erected late in the 18th century for the Marquess of Conyngham. It now contains a restaurant, but the rest is closed to the public. The castle grounds have been used to stage rock concerts by the Rolling Stones and Bob Dylan.

At the mid-point of Slane's main street, four matching greystone houses stand at each corner of a crossroads, facing each other diagonally like sentries. At this central crossroads, take the N51 again towards Drogheda. About a kilometre from the village you pass the home of the poet Francis Ledwidge (1891–1917), who was killed in Flanders in World War I. His stone-built cottage is now a small museum to his memory. His poetry dealt chiefly with the countryside and with Irish mythology and folklore.

A few minutes' drive further on, a turn to the right leads into an area known as **Brú na Bóinne** (Dwelling Place of the Boyne), a burial site for Stone Age kings, and one of the most important prehistoric sites in Europe. The whole necropolis, dating from the 3rd millennium BC, extends for several kilometres on a low rise over a broad curve in the River Boyne. It contains three great man-made mounds (tumuli), each containing central burial chambers. There are also many smaller remains, though most have been disturbed at some time and others are overgrown. The three principal tumuli, standing about 1.5km apart from each other, are called Dowth, Knowth and Newgrange.

Newgrange's secrets

Dowth, which was badly plundered by 19th-century souvenir seekers, has not been thoroughly excavated and is not open to the public. **Knowth**, which contains two passages, is surrounded by 15 satellite tombs and ornate kerbstones have been discovered there. But **Newgrange ❽**, a passage grave of Stone Age

BELOW: small-town
shopfront in Navan.

kings, is one of the most important prehistoric sites in Europe. It has been fully excavated and restored to resemble its original state.

It is a huge, circular, mound of white and black boulders, largely covered with earth and grass, about 90 metres across and 15 metres high (300 ft by 50 ft). A narrow passage leads 20 metres (65 ft) into the interior to a central domed chamber almost 6 metres (20 ft) high. The great stones here are decorated with intricate abstract designs. A small aperture over the entrance is precisely aligned so that the sun's rays illuminate the chamber only at the winter solstice on 21 December – a powerful symbol of rebirth and renewal. (The waiting list to view the real event is years long, but the effect is re-created for visitors using electricity.) This construction suggests that its creators were aware of the calendar and may well have been sun worshippers.

One archaeologist has estimated that it must have taken a million man-days to build Newgrange. Another put forward a figure of 40 years. As well as the positioning of nearly 100 large stones, each weighing between 4 and 8 tons, thousands of tons of pebbles had to be carried from the banks of the Boyne and then interleaved with a huge number of sods dug from forest clearings.

Some have supposed that the tombs were inspired by the megaliths in Brittany, another Celtic culture, but the more ornate decoration found in Ireland suggests that they derived from local folk customs and beliefs.

If Newgrange is too crowded, there's an alternative. About 90 km (55 miles) northwest of Slane, close to the remote ancient village of **Oldcastle** on the Meath–Cavan border, are the less visited **Loughcrew cairns**, the remains of 30 Stone Age passage graves. Cairn T has impressive examples of prehistoric art. The site is open all year; there are tours from mid-Jun to mid-Sept (10am–6pm).

Map on page 218

TIP

Those without a car can take advantage of Bus Eireann's daily services to Slane, leaving from Dublin's Busaras terminus. The journey is 45 minutes.

BELOW: Newgrange.

King William at the Battle of the Boyne.

The Battle of the Boyne

The road from Newgrange to Drogheda, by the quiet, leafy riverside and old canal cuttings, passes the signposted site of the **Battle of the Boyne** (1690), an event – still celebrated with much drum-beating by the Orangemen of Ulster – in which a Dutchman, William of Orange, defeated a Scotsman, James II, for the throne of England. The real losers were Ireland's Catholics, who entered the long nightmare of the discriminatory Penal Laws.

The accession of the Catholic James to the English throne in 1685 had given Irish Catholics some hope of recovering some of the vast tracts of land seized from them by Oliver Cromwell three decades earlier and of being admitted to government and administration. But their hopes were dashed when James was toppled in England's "Glorious Revolution" of 1688 and fled to France. In 1689 he landed at Kinsale, in County Cork, with French troops, planning to rally his followers and regain his throne.

The main engagement at the Boyne took place on 1 July 1690. James, a poor general, had taken up an exposed position on the hill of Donore, just south of the river. His army was composed of about 18,000 poorly armed Irish irregulars and 7,000 Frenchmen. William bombarded them from the hill of Tullyallen, directly across the Boyne, and sent 10,000 men west to Rosnaree and Slane to cross the river and attack the flank of James's army. William's main force then began to cross the Boyne by Oldbridge, and James was soon in retreat. He fled south through Dublin to Waterford and escaped to France. So began a long period when Catholics in Ireland were automatically treated as second-class citizens.

You can now continue into Drogheda directly, or turn left to follow sign-posts to Mellifont and its Cistercian abbey (*see page 230*).

Drogheda

The port of **Drogheda** ❾ dates from Viking and Norman times and was a frontier outpost of the Pale, that strip of land around Dublin still under the control of the conquerors in the late Middle Ages. Its main features are: the Millmount, a prehistoric mound surmounted by an 18th-century barracks, now including a museum; St Lawrence's Gate, one of the best-preserved town gates in Ireland; the ruins of several medieval churches; the 18th-century Tholsel (town hall), now a bank; and the 19th-century St Peter's Church, which contains the preserved head of St Oliver Plunkett, a Meath man who became Roman Catholic archbishop of Armagh and was martyred in 1681 at Tyburn, now Marble Arch, in London. He was canonised in 1975.

The name of Oliver Cromwell is still an accursed one here: during his campaign of suppression in 1649, he slaughtered 2,000 of the garrison and inhabitants – "a righteous judgment of God upon those barbarous wretches". Others were transported to the West Indies.

Racing on the beach

You have now crossed into **Louth**, Ireland's smallest county. But, before seeing more of it, you may enjoy a brief coastal detour south of Drogheda to the nearby small resorts of Bettystown and **Laytown** ❿, which stand by a 10-km (6-mile) sandy beach. At Laytown, horse-racing is staged annually on the sands, the date – in July or August – being determined largely by the tidal calendar. It is a crazy, colourful event, well worth catching if you're around at the right time. But it is a *bona fide* race meeting, part of the European Racing Calendar.

Ten km (6 miles) northwest of Drogheda, the evocative ruins of **Mellifont**

Map on page 218

Oliver Plunkett's preserved head in St Peter's Church.

BELOW: Laytown races.

Mellifont Abbey.

The coastal strip north of Dublin now promotes itself as "Fair Fingal", and claims to be Ireland's most populated golf area (28 courses).

BELOW:
market day in Trim.

Abbey (1142) ⑪ (May–Oct 10am–6pm), the first Cistercian foundation in Ireland, stand by a small, murmuring river, the Mattock. Its creation marked the beginning of a monastic reform set in train by St Malachy, Archbishop of Armagh. The remains include those of a square tower, a large church, and a lavabo, an octagonal building where the monks used to wash.

At **Monasterboice** ⑫, a few miles to the northeast, are the remnants of a 5th-century monastic settlement founded by St Buithe, a disciple of St Patrick; they consist of a round tower, two churches, three sculptured High Crosses (two of which are among the finest of their kind), two early graveslabs and a sundial. High Crosses, like round towers, are found at monastic ruins all over Ireland. Their decorated panels in deep relief – originally brightly painted – depict scriptural scenes; they were probably used for religious instruction.

You can now join the main N1 route north to **Dundalk** ⑬, a busy but visually undistinguished border town and a good centre for exploring the picturesque **Cooley Peninsula**. This area features prominently in the great epic legends of ancient Ireland, particularly those concerning Cuchulainn, hero of the Red Branch Knights. **Carlingford** ⑭ village, today a sleepy place, was once a vital northern outpost of the Pale. King John's Castle, built by John de Courcy in 1210, commands the entrance to the sea inlet, **Carlingford Lough**. A corkscrew road through the nearby forest park climbs to a viewing point near the summit of Carlingford Mountain, providing splendid views of the Mourne Mountains to the north. You may also enjoy browsing the small resorts of **Greenore** and **Omeath**.

The N52 road southwest from Dundalk leads to **Ardee** ⑮ (in Irish, *Baile Atha Fhirdiadh*, "the Town of Ferdia's Ford"). According to legend, it was here, at a ford on the River Dee, that Cuchulainn slew his friend Ferdia, the champion of Queen Maeve, in the great epic story of the Cattle Raid of Cooley.

Continue southwest on the N52 to **Kells** ⑯, where St Colmcille founded a monastery in the 6th century. The extant remains are more recent: a round tower and a high-roofed 9th-century building known as St Colmcille's house are the most interesting.

The traveller may now be feeling rather antiquity-drunk, but **Trim**, another pleasant town 24 km (16 miles) further southwest, can claim the largest Anglo-Norman fortress in Ireland (mid-Jun–Oct, daily 10am–6pm; fee), built by Hugh de Lacy in 1173. The Mel Gibson movie *Braveheart* was shot here. Its well-preserved remains cover 0.8 hectares (2 acres) and the surrounding moat could be filled from the River Boyne. The tour of the keep is worth taking for an inside look at the four interconnecting towers which retain their original features, and for the splendid view from the top. The ragged outline of the Yellow Steeple (1358), part of a collapsed abbey, stands on a ridge opposite the castle.

En route to Dublin

If you take the coastal route back to Dublin, you may wish to detour at Balbriggan to see the quiet resorts of Skerries and Rush. **Skerries** ⑰ has a sandy beach, a small pier and an active sailing community. St Patrick is said to have made his first landing on one of the

Map on page 218

rocky offshore islands, now **St Patrick's Island**, and spent time on **Red Island**, where footprint shapes are cut into the solid rock to mark the spot where he supposedly stood. **Shenick's Island**, to the south and connected to the mainland at low tide, has one of the Martello towers erected in the 19th century.

Rush ⓲, which traditionally supplied early potatoes and vegetables to the Dublin market, has a fine bathing strand and a good view of **Lambay Island**, 5 km (3 miles) offshore. The remnant of an ancient volcano, it has cliffs over 120 metres (400 ft) high and is an important seabird sanctuary. Its medieval castle was restored by the celebrated architect Sir Edward Lutyens.

A bracing cliff walk to the south of Skerries takes you to the fishing village of **Loughshinny**, which is very much off the beaten tourist track, but has a pleasant little harbour and beach and cave-riddled cliffs.

Also off the N1, closer to Dublin (follow signs for Donabate) is **Newbridge House ⓳**, a country manor built in 1737 for Charles Cobbe, the Archbishop of Dublin, to a design by Richard Cassels (Apr–Sept, Tues–Sat 10am–5pm, Sun 2–6pm; Oct–Mar, Sat & Sun 2–5pm; fee). The house stands in 140 hectares (350 acres) of parkland, and its interior, largely untouched for more than a century, has elaborate plasterwork. Its laundry and kitchen exhibit early examples of labour-saving devices such as a washing machine and a vacuum cleaner, and the family's Museum of Curiosities throws together a collection of odd souvenirs ranging from shells to the mummified ear of a sacred Egyptian bull.

The courtyard is flanked by a dairy, an estate worker's house, a carpenter's shop and a blacksmith's forge, all with 19th-century implements. The stables house the Lord Chancellor's ornate coach, dating from 1790. In the grounds is a farm with some rare breeds such as the Kerry cow and Connemara pony. ❏

The coastline north of Loughshinny.

BELOW: the harbour at Loughshinny.

EXCURSIONS WEST

Map on page 218

Horses dominate in Kildare, with the grassy limestone plain of the Curragh producing some of the world's top racehorses. Then there's Maynooth, a leading producer of priests

Kildare county, with its rich flatlands of the Liffey and Barrow river basins and the vast peatlands of the Bog of Allen, is the "horsiest" part of Ireland. It is also speckled with the stately homes of the Protestant Ascendancy. **Naas ⓴**, its principal town, is about 34 km (21 miles) west of Dublin; you can drive there quickly over one of the Republic's few modern highways.

As its Irish name, *Nas na Riogh,* implies, it was in early times one of the seats of the Kings of Leinster. Its Church of Ireland is supposed to occupy the site used for St Patrick's camp when he visited on one of his missionary journeys. Although uninteresting architecturally, Naas, as a popular centre for hunting and horse-racing, has a distinctly racy atmosphere. Naas **racecourse,** on the Dublin side of the town, stages races both on the flat and over jumps. **Punchestown,** 5 km (3 miles) to the southeast, is one of the country's most characterful local courses; all races here are "over the sticks". The April meeting here, when the gorse around the course is in bloom, is particularly colourful.

Just outside the town on the Newbridge road, stand the ruins of **Jiginstown House**, a 17th-century Stuart mansion and one of the first brick buildings in Ireland. It was built by Thomas Wentworth, Earl of Strafford and Viceroy to Charles I, as a residence fit to lodge the king, but before it could be completed Wentworth was recalled to London. He died on the scaffold in 1641, a victim of the faction-fighting that preceded the English Civil War.

Near the village of **Clane ㉑**, 8 km (5 miles) north of Naas, are the ruins of a 13th-century Franciscan friary founded by Sir Gerald Fitzmaurice, and also **Bodenstown Churchyard**, burial place of Wolfe Tone, leader of the 1798 rebellion. Annual republican commemoration ceremonies are held here.

PRECEDING PAGES: barging through Newcastle, Co. Dublin. **LEFT:** cutting turf in Co. Kildare. **BELOW:** horse racing in Kildare.

Where Joyce studied

About 3 km (2 miles) north of Clane is **Clongoweswood**, a Jesuit boarding college founded in 1814. James Joyce, who was a pupil there, described the place evocatively in *A Portrait of the Artist as a Young Man:* "The wide playgrounds were swarming with boys. All were shouting and the prefects urged them on with strong cries. The evening air was pale and chilly and after every charge and thud of the footballers the greasy leather orb flew like a heavy bird through the grey light." The college chapel contains interesting work by modern Irish artists: stations of the cross by Sean Keating, stained glass by Evie Hone and Michael Healy.

The Curragh

From Naas you can drive on the main road southwest through Newbridge to the Curragh, a great unfenced expanse of grassy limestone plain and the centre of Irish horse-racing. The origins of the sport here are lost in prehistory. The Red Branch Knights of pre-Christian Ireland raced each other on horseback and horse-races were an essential part of public assemblies or fairs in the early centuries AD.

According to John Welcome's history, *Irish Horseracing,* "these fairs were held for the purpose of transacting all sorts of business – marriages were celebrated, deaths recorded, laws debated and defined, methods of defence agreed; but always they were followed by sports and games and of these sports and games the most popular was horse-racing." The greatest of these fairs was held at the Curragh; and the present-day equivalent, the Irish Derby, is held there also, as are all the Irish classic races.

Apart from the racecourse, and numerous training stables, the Curragh contains an important military camp, established in 1646. This was the scene of the "Curragh Mutiny" of 1914, when British officers stationed there threatened to disobey if ordered to fire on Edward Carson's Ulster Volunteers, who had armed illegally to oppose Home Rule. Near the road south to Kilcullen is a depression known as Donnelly's Hollow, where a small obelisk commemorates an 1815 prize fight in which Dan Donnelly, the giant Irish boxing champion, defeated George Cooper of England.

Kildare ㉒, 20 km (12 miles) west of Newbridge, takes its name *(Cill Dara)* from the "church of the oak" – a monastery founded in the 5th century by St Brigid, the most revered Irish saint after Patrick. Her attributes

BELOW: Jigginstown Castle in Naas.

have been reinforced by others borrowed from the great pagan goddess of the same name, who was venerated also in Britain and Europe. Her monastery became the principal church of the kingdom of Leinster, and was remarkable for being organised for both monks and nuns.

The **Cathedral of St Brigid**, begun in 1229, was devastated in the 16th century and given a new chancel in the 1680s: it has served since as a Protestant cathedral of the diocese. After 1680, it was allowed to deteriorate until 1875, when G. E. Street oversaw its restoration. He was also in charge of the restoration of Christ Church in Dublin, deemed by some to be disastrous. To the southwest of the cathedral is a 33-metre (108-ft) medieval round tower with a crenellated 19th-century cap. The view from the top is worth the climb.

The National Stud

Just south of Kildare is the **National Stud**, a state-run bloodstock farm. The original establishment was founded at the beginning of the 20th century by Colonel Hall-Walker, an eccentric English breeder who consulted the horoscopes of his horses to determine which he should train for important races. The animals' boxes had skylights to permit the stars to do their work. The system seems to have worked: Hall-Walker's horses won many classic races in Britain and Ireland, In 1915, he presented the estate and horses to the Crown as a national stud and the British Government handed it over to the Irish authorities in 1943. In summer, there are guided tours of the extensive stables and the adjoining **Irish Horse Museum.**

Attached to the stud are the **Japanese Gardens**, laid out in 1906 by Eito, a Japanese gardener brought here by Colonel Hill-Walker. The gardens

Map on page 218

You can buy a joint ticket for the National Stud and the Japanese Gardens. They are open Feb–Nov daily 9.30am–6pm.

BELOW: putting the breeding to the test.

A figure in the Japanese Gardens.

BELOW: painting the farm red at Athy.

represent the seven ages of man and are well worth a visit, if only to experience passing through the Gateway of Oblivion, beyond Temptation and across the Hill of Ambition.

On the road to Monasterevan, once the home of John McCormack, the great tenor, there is a well-known landmark at Kyle Railway Bridge. It is the **Shell House,** a single-storey farmhouse, the walls of which are covered with multi-coloured sea-shells, stones, pieces of glass and bottle-tops, arranged decoratively by the late owner, Miss Elizabeth O'Beime, who died in 1967. The shells were collected over 15 years on Irish and European beaches, and the many designs include the Ardagh Chalice and the Irish Harp.

At **Athy,** 26 km (16 miles) south of Kildare, a 16th-century tower, now a private house, overlooks a fine old bridge over the River Barrow, once an important commercial waterway to Dublin. But the town's main attraction, just beyond the bridge, is modern: the striking, fan-shaped **Dominican Church** (1963–65). The dramatic, theatrical interior has stained glass and stations of the cross by the painter George Campbell.

The priests of Maynooth

Returning to Dublin via Naas, it is worth diverting to **Maynooth ㉓,** a university "village" beside the Royal Canal on the main Dublin–Galway road. "The miserable village of Maynooth" was the novelist William Makepeace Thackeray's comment after his brief stay, but today it has a lively air, thanks to the 3,400 students attending **St Patrick's College.** Originally devoted entirely to the training of Ireland's diocesan Catholic clergy, the college is now part of the National University (along with the University Colleges of Dublin, Cork

Map on page 218

and Galway) and only about 10 percent of students are training for the priesthood.

"Maynooth", as the seminary is generally known, has supplied priests and bishops to all parts of the world. It was founded in 1795, when the British decided that it was not in their interests that Irish priests were trained in continental Europe. There are two quadrangles, the first from 1795, the second, by the English Gothic-Revival architect, A. W. Pugin, from 1845.

The college chapel, with its tall spire, was designed in 1875 by J. McCarthy, who died before its completion. The library has a large collection of manuscripts and early printed books in Irish, while the museum contains a collection of mainly ecclesiastical works of art. There is also some early electrical apparatus, invented and used by Father Nicholas Callan, a pioneer in electrical research who was professor of science at Maynooth from 1826 until 1864. To the right of the college gates are the massive ruins of a medieval keep, once a stronghold of the FitzGeralds, the Earls of Kildare.

A short drive to the southeast is the attractive village of **Celbridge ㉔**, home of Esther Vanhomrigh, the "Vanessa" who competed with "Stella" (Esther Johnson) for the affections of Jonathan Swift (*see page 162*). He often came here to visit her and you can see the seat by the river where they sat and talked. Her unrequited love for him may have caused her early death.

Northeast of the village is **Castletown House** (Jun–Sept Mon–Fri 10am–6pm, Sat–Sun 1–6pm; Oct Mon–Fri 10am–5pm, Sun 1–5pm; Nov Sun 1–5pm; Apr–May Sun 1–6pm; fee), the largest private house in Ireland, built by William Connolly, the Speaker of the Irish House of Commons, in 1722. It was designed by Alessandro Galilei, who was responsible for the facade of St John Lateran's in Rome, and is a fine example of Palladian architecture. ❑

The playwright Sean O'Casey, condemning the influence of Maynooth, described the spire of its church as being "like a dagger through the heart of Ireland".

BELOW:
Castletown House.
OVERLEAF: Dublin's Ha'penny Bridge.

INSIGHT GUIDES
Travel Tips

Insight FlexiMaps

Maps in Insight Guides are tailored to complement the text. But when you're on the road you sometimes need the big picture that only a large-scale map can provide. This new range of durable Insight Fleximaps has been designed to meet just that need.

Detailed, clear cartography
makes the comprehensive route and city maps easy to follow, highlights all the major tourist sites and provides valuable motoring information plus a full index.

Informative and easy to use
with additional text and photographs covering a destination's top 10 essential sites, plus useful addresses, facts about the destination and handy tips on getting around.

Laminated finish
allows you to mark your route on the map using a non-permanent marker pen, and wipe it off. It makes the maps more durable and easier to fold than traditional maps.

The world's most popular destinations
are covered by the 125 titles in the series – and new destinations are being added all the time. They include Alaska, Amsterdam, Bangkok, Barbados, Beijing, Brussels, Dallas/Fort Worth, Florence, Hong Kong, Ireland, Madrid, New York, Orlando, Peru, Prague, Rio, Rome, San Francisco, Sydney, Thailand, Turkey, Venice, and Vienna.

☆ INSIGHT GUIDES
The world's largest collection of visual travel guides

CONTENTS

Getting Acquainted

Note: The international dialling code for the Republic of Ireland is 353, followed by 1 for Dublin.

The Place

The first thing that strikes nearly all visitors to Dublin is its superb setting on the estuary of the River Liffey, overlooked by hills and headlands which reach out to embrace a broad, sweeping bay. The city stands at roughly the mid-point of Ireland's east coast, at a latitude of 53° 23'N – equivalent to northern Newfoundland – and a longtitude of 6° 9'W.

The Climate

Although all of the country is relatively moist, the Dublin area is the driest part, with rainfall of about 94 cm (37 inches) a year.

Average air temperatures in the coldest months, January and February, are between 4°C and 7°C (39–45°F). The warmest months, July and August, have average temperatures between 14°C and 16°C (57–61°F), but occasionally reaching as high as 25°C (77°F). The sunniest months are May and June, with an average 5½ to 6½ hours of sunshine a day, although even in these months dry weather shouldn't be taken for granted.

Population

Just over 1 million people live in Dublin city and county – almost one in three of the entire population of the Irish Republic. The city has been swollen greatly in recent decades by an influx of returning emigrants with the economic boom and by a marked population drift from country to capital. This means that many Dubliners have very recent rural roots, even though they are likely to profess a disdain for "culchies" (country people). And another demographic statistic is even more striking: 41 percent of the population is under 25. Dublin is a young city – and this fact has been an important element in the rapid social and economic changes of recent years.

Time Zone

Ireland follows Greenwich Mean Time. In late March, the clock moves one hour ahead for Summer Time to give extra daylight in the evening; in late October it moves back again to GMT.

At noon according to GMT, it is 4am in Los Angeles; 7am in New York; 1pm in western Europe; 8pm in Singapore; 10pm in Sydney; and midnight in New Zealand.

Many visitors find that time passes more slowly in Ireland. As the old joke has it, a visitor once asked if the Irish attitude to time could be expressed by the word *mañana*. He was told: "Oh, we've nothing as urgent as that here."

The Economy

The Republic's gross national product is €98.5 billion and its principal trading partner is Britain, followed by Germany, France and the US. Racehorses, whiskey, hand-woven tweed, handcut crystal glass and agricultural products are among the best-known exports.

The country imports more goods than it sells, but the gap in the balance of trade is closed by its substantial earnings from tourism and foreign investments. Tourism continues to grow: the Republic's 3.7 million people welcome over 6 million visitors a year.

Factfile: The Irish Sea

The Irish Sea (*Muir Éireann* in Irish) is 130 miles (210 km) long and 150 miles (240 km) wide. Its total area is roughly 40,000 sq. miles (100,000 sq. km) and its deepest point is 576 ft (175 metres).

Government

The 26-county Republic is a parliamentary democracy, with two Houses of Parliament, an elected president who is head of state and a prime minister (Taoiseach, literally "leader") who is head of government. In 1998 the Republic abandoned its constitutional claim to the six counties of Northern Ireland, which is part of the UK.

The national symbol is the shamrock, a three-leafed plant which is worn on the national holiday, 17 March, to honour Ireland's patron saint, St Patrick – hence the expression "the wearing of the green".

The Language

The Republic of Ireland has two official languages, English and Irish (Gaelic). English is spoken everywhere, but while many people throughout the country know Irish, it is the everyday language of fewer than 100,000 people in remote areas known as Gaeltachts, mainly in the far west.

Intrepid linguists may wish to wrap their tongues round the following Gaelic phrases:

Dia dhuit/God be with you.
To which the reply is:
Muire dhuit/God and Mary be with you.
Conas atá tú/How are you?
To which the hoped-for reply is:
Tá mé go maith, go raibh maith agat/I am well, thank you.
Slán leat/Goodbye.
To which the desirable reply is:
Slán leat agus go n-éirí an bóthar leat/Goodbye and may the road rise to meet you.

Planning the Trip

Visas and Passports

Passports are required by everyone visiting the Republic except British citizens. Visas are not required by citizens of European Union countries, Australia, Canada or the United States.

What To Wear

Casual clothing is acceptable almost everywhere in Dublin, including smart hotels and restaurants. Because of the unpredictability of the weather, pack an umbrella, some rainproof clothing and a warm sweater, even in summer.

Electricity

220 volts AC (50 cycles) is standard. Hotels usually have dual 220/110 voltage sockets for electric razors only. To use their own small appliances, visitors may need a plug adaptor (best purchased in their home country) to fit Ireland's 3-pin flat or 2-pin round wall sockets.

Money

On 1 January 2002 the Euro (€) became the official currency of the Republic of Ireland. (Northern Ireland has not yet adopted the Euro and retains the pound sterling). Although the old Irish pounds (punts) are no longer legal tender, the Central Bank of Ireland will continue to exchange the old notes for Euros.

One Euro is divided into 100 cents. There are seven Euro banknotes in denominations of €5, 10, 20, 50, 100, 200 and 500. These have the same design throughout the European Union. There are eight coins in denominations of 1, 2, 5, 10, 20 and 50 cents or €1 and €2. They vary in size, colour and thickness according to their value. One side of each coin has an individual design related to the member state where it was minted. All Irish coins bear the traditional symbol of Ireland, the Celtic harp, and the word 'Eire', the Irish name for the nation. Euro coins can be used anywhere in any Euro country regardless of their country of origin.

Banks are open 10am–4pm, Monday–Friday, with many staying open until 5pm on Thursday.

Travellers' cheques are accepted at all banks, money-change kiosks and many hotels. MasterCard and Visa are the most commonly acceptable credit cards, followed by American Express and Diners Club.

Health

There are no particular health concerns to consider when visiting Dublin. Citizens of European Union countries are eligible for free medical treatment *(see Practical Tips, page 244)*. Other nationalities will have to pay and are advised to take out private medical insurance.

Getting There

By Air

Dublin International Airport (tel: 844 4900) is, not surprisingly, Ireland's busiest. It lies 12 km (7½ miles) north of the city centre. It handles flights from the UK, Europe and North America. There is considerable competition between the airlines, including Irish carriers Aer Lingus and Ryanair. It is well worth shopping around for low-cost fares and fly/drive packages.

There is a regular bus service from Dublin Airport (tel: 873 4222 for general transport information) to the main bus station in the city centre, taking about 30 minutes. Aircoach buses depart every 15 minutes for various city locations. A taxi from Dublin Airport to the city centre will cost about €16–20.

Aerdart (tel: 862 5363) provides a shuttle bus service between the airport and Howth Junction DART station, with onward links to the city centre and suburbs via the DART network. Tickets €5 adults, €3.15 children.

The main airlines connecting Dublin to the UK and the European mainland are Aer Lingus, Ryanair and British Airways. To contact **Aer Lingus**: tel: 0818 365 000 (local rate within Ireland), 0845-973 7747 from the North, 020 8899 4747 in London, 1800-474 7424 in the US, 069-133 85410 in Frankfurt, 01-553 83855 in Paris, 06 481 8518 in Rome, or go to www.aerlingus.ie. There are also flights from Malaga, Barcelona and Nice.

Ryanair can be contacted on 01-609 7800 in Dublin and 0541-569 569 in Britain, or visit www.ryanair.com.

British Airways flies from Heathrow, Gatwick and various provincial airports in England and Scotland to Dublin, and can be contacted in Dublin on 1800 626747 and (BA Express) 08457 733 377 in the UK or go to www.british-airways.com.

British Midland (tel: 0870 607 0555 or visit www.flybmi.com) has daily flights from London Heathrow and East Midlands.

Air Wales (tel: 8700 133 151; www.air-wales.co.uk) operates a Dublin–Swansea route, with three flights daily Monday– Friday, and twice daily Sunday.

Student/youth fares operate all

Public Holidays

- **January** New Year's Day (1)
- **March** St Patrick's Day (17)
- **March/April** Good Friday, Easter Monday
- **May** May Day (first Monday)
- **June** First Monday
- **August** Summer Bank Holiday (first Monday)
- **October** Last Monday
- **December** Christmas Day (25), St Stephen's Day (26)

year round between Britain and Ireland. Contact: STA Travel, London (tel: 020-7361 6161).

By Sea

Details of services and operators are liable to change, so check with the following operators in the UK.
Irish Ferries, Reliance House, Water Street, Liverpool L2 8TP, tel: 08705 171 717; book online: www.irishferries.com. Services: Holyhead–Dublin North Wall (3 hours 15 minutes); two departures daily. Holyhead–Dublin fast service (1 hour 49 minutes) three crossings daily; Pembroke–Rosslare (4 hours). Also sailings every second day between Rosslare and the French ports of Roscoff and Cherbourg (tel: Dublin 638 3333).
Stena Line, Charter House, Park Street, Ashford, Kent TN24 8EX, tel: 01233-647022/0990-707070. www.stenaline.com. Dublin, tel: 204 7700. Services: Holyhead–Dublin (3 hours 45 minutes); Holyhead–Dun Laoghaire high-speed service (1 hour 39 minutes) five sailings daily; Fishguard–Rosslare (3 hours 30 minutes or 1 hour 30 minutes); Stranraer–Belfast (3 hours 15 minutes or 1 hour 45 minutes by HSS).
P&O Irish Sea, Larne Harbour, Larne BT40 1AQ, tel: 0870 242 4777; www.poirishsea.com. One to two sailings per day between Liverpool and Dublin (8–9 hours).
Isle of Man Steam Packet Company, P.O. Box 5, Imperial Buildings, Douglas, Isle of Man IM99 1AF, tel: 01624-661661. Dublin, tel: 944 1010; www.steam-packet.com. Services: Isle of Man–Dublin (2 hours 45 minutes). Liverpool–Dublin (4 hours) April–October. Tel: 0870 552 3523.

By Bus

Bus companies run services from various points in England and Wales via the ferries. Contacts: **National Express/Irish Bus**, tel: 836 6111 in Dublin and 08705 808 080 in England. For times, fares and bookings to Dublin, call Victoria Coach Station in London on 020-7824 0041.

Practical Tips

Emergencies

For emergency services, such as police, ambulance, fire service, lifeboat and coastal rescue, tel: 999 and ask for the service you need.

The Samaritans, who help lonely, depressed and suicidal people, can be contacted on 850 609090.

Medical Treatment

With the exception of UK citizens, visitors for EU states should obtain form E111 from their own national social security office. These forms entitle the holders to free treatment by a doctor and free medicines on prescription. If hospital treatment is necessary, this will be given free in a public ward. UK visitors need only go to a doctor (or, in an emergency, a hospital), present some proof of identity (e.g. driving licence) and request treatment under EU health agreement. All other nationalities will be expected to pay for treatment.

In the case of a medical emergency, go to the Accident and Emergency Deparment in a major hospital. A & E departments are on 24-hour call in most large hospitals.

Hospitals

Adelaide and Meath Hospital, Tallaght, Dublin 24, tel: 453 6555.
St. James Hospital, 1 James Street, Dublin 8, tel: 453 7941.
Beaumont Hospital, Beaumont Road, Dublin 9, tel: 837 7755.
Mater Hospital, Eccles Street, Dublin 7, tel: 803 2000.

Late-night Pharmacies:

O'Connell's Pharmacy, late-night branches are located at O' Connell Street, tel: 873 0427 (until 10pm Monday–Sunday); 310 Harolds X Road, tel: 492 3977 (until 10pm Monday–Sunday); 85 Terenure Road North, tel: 490 7179 (until 10pm Monday–Saturday). Other branches at 17 Westmoreland Street, tel: 677 8440; Grafton Street, tel: 679 0467; Henry Street, tel: 873 1077.
Boots Late-night Pharmacy, The Square, Town Centre, Tallaght, tel: 950 6111 (until 11pm).

Other Useful Numbers:

Poisons Information Service. Tel: 837 9964/837 9966.
Alcoholics Anonymous. Tel: 453 8998.
Family Planning: Well Woman Centre, 67 Pembroke Road, Dublin 4, tel: 660 9860.
Rape Crisis Centre. Tel: 661 4911 or 1800 778888.
Aids Helpline. Tel: 872 4277, Monday–Friday 7–9pm, Saturday 3–5pm.
Gay Switchboard. Tel: 872 1055, Sunday–Friday 8–10pm, Saturday 3.30–6pm.
Lesbian Line. Tel: 872 9911, Thursday 7–9pm.

Media

Newspapers

The Irish devour newspapers, and have no fewer than five morning newspapers to serve the island's population of 5 million. The *Irish Times* and the *Irish Independent* are Dublin's two morning papers.

The *Times*, the most serious and comprehensive, is best for foreign news, arts and business, and has a great letters page. It avoids political affiliations, but has a broadly liberal bias, and is part of a syndicating group that includes *The Guardian* in the UK, *Le Monde* in France and *El País* in Spain. The *Independent* broadly supports the Fine Gael party and aims for a hard-hitting style.

The Herald group publishes the *Evening Herald* on weekday afternoons. It is strong on sport, gossip and showbiz.

The *Independent* and the *Times* both have Sunday versions; in addition, there is the *Sunday*

Tribune, which aims to be a serious paper of political analysis, arts reviews, etc; the *Sunday World*, a lurid tabloid (pin-ups, scares, scandals, etc); and the *Sunday Business Post*, which concentrates on business and politics.

Since all the British dailies and Sundays are readily obtainable on both sides of the border, even the most news-hungry visitor should be satisfied. However, UK readers can expect an "Irish edition" of their favourite paper, with a focus on Irish topics. The London *Sunday Times*, for example, maintains a Dublin office and includes a lot of local news and cultural coverage.

Magazines

Hot Press is a lively local pop culture paper. *In Dublin* is useful for telling you what's on at the theatre, cinema, etc, as is the free *Event Guide*; both are published fortnightly.

Radio and Television

The national broadcasting service, Radio Telefis Eireann (RTE) has three TV channels (one of them, TG4 broadcasting exclusively in the Irish language) and three radio stations. TV3, Ireland's first independent television network, was launched in 1998 to provide an alternative to RTE – "a middle-of-the-road service aimed at Middle Ireland". In addition, the British TV channels (both BBC and commercial channels) can be received – which accounts for the unsightly height of television aerials. Several satellite channels, including Sky and Screensport, are widely available via cable.

On radio, RTE1 (Radio 1) is the main station for news, current affairs and drama; RTE2 (2 FM) has a staple output of pop music, while Lyric FM is for lovers of classical music. There are also a number of independent local radio stations.

Tracing your Roots

The number of visitors to Ireland who want to uncover half-forgotten roots in the "ould sod" has mushroomed. A good starting point is the Genealogy Service in the **National Library** of Ireland, which is staffed by professional genealogists and experienced library staff. They give free advice on how to go about tracing your ancestry (Monday–Friday 10am– 5pm and Saturday 10am– 12.30pm). Visitors are offered expert advice on their research and access to reference material, information leaflets, etc. Although library staff do not carry out research for individuals themselves, they have a list of professional researchers who can be hired for a fee. They can also put you in touch with Genealogy centres operating in each country, under the auspices of the Irish Genealogical Project. The National Library is located at Kildare Street, Dublin 2, tel: 606 0200, fax: 676 6690, website: www.nli.ie, e-mail: info@nli.ie.

Another source for researchers is the Association of Professional Genealogists in Ireland, c/o The Honorary Secretary, 30 Harlech Crescent, Clonskeagh, Dublin 14, website: http//indigo.ie/~apgi/

Whether you intend to do your own research or hire a professional, it is important to gather as much information as possible in your home country. Try to find out the name of your emigrant ancestor; his or her place of origin in Ireland, as precisely as possible; approximate dates of birth, marriage and death; religion; occupation and social background; and names of children. Look for old diaries, letters or family bibles.

In the US National Archives, Irish-Americans can often find their ancestor date and port of arrival in the New World. Immigrant records and shipping lists show the country, age and trade of the immigrant and the port of departure. Australian records are helpful because many immigrants arrived on state "assisted passage" schemes.

In Ireland, all centralised records for the 26 counties of the Republic are stored in Dublin. The main sources are as follows:

The Reading Room of the National Library, Kildare Street, has an extensive collection of journals of local historical societies, trade directories, old newspapers, private papers and letters. It also houses the Genealogical Office (formerly in the Heraldic Museum) on the first floor *(see above)*.

The National Archives (formerly the Public Record Office), in the Four Courts, was damaged badly in a fire in 1922 at the outbreak of the Civil War and many invaluable documents were lost (but, contrary to rumour, not all).

The General Register Office, Joyce House, Lombard Street, has the civil registrations of all births, marriages and deaths since 1864.

The Register of Deeds, Henrietta Street, has deeds relating to property and marriage settlements dating from 1708. Most of these concern the gentry of the time.

The State Paper Office, Dublin Castle, is of special interest to Australians because it houses records of people who were sentenced to be transported there. There is no stigma attached to this, because the crime concerned was often petty or notional, or was simply nothing more than supporting the rebel cause.

An annual Family History Conference sponsored by the Ulster Historical Foundation, focusing on practical research in Ireland's main archives takes place in September in Belfast and Dublin. For details, tel: 028 9033 2288; fax 028 9023 9885, e-mail: enquiry@uhf.org.uk. Or visit www.uhf.org.uk.

Postal Services

Most post offices are open Monday–Friday 9am–5.30pm and some are open on Saturday 9am–1pm. The General Post Office on O'Connell Street is open Monday–Saturday 8am–8pm, and on Sunday and holidays 10am–6.30pm for limited services including selling stamps and changing money. Among the other city centre post offices is one at the corner of Anne and Grafton streets. **Philatelists** can obtain information on Irish stamps from the Controller, Philatelic Section, GPO, Dublin 1.

Telecommunications

The international dialling code for the Republic of Ireland is 353. (Northern Ireland is 44). The Dublin city code (area code) is 01. When dialling from abroad, drop the initial '0' from the area code.

There are public phone boxes throughout Dublin, as well as pay phones in pubs, restaurants, shops and hotels. They take either coins or phone cards. A three-minute local call costs €.25 (25 cents). A three-minute long-distance call is around €1. About half of the public phones are card phones. You can buy phone cards ('callcards') at post offices, supermarkets and newsagents. They are sold in denominations of 10, 20 and 50 units, starting at €2.54.

To make a long-distance call within the Republic, dial the area code and then the number. To call Northern Ireland, dial 048 or 4428, followed by the eight-digit local number. Local area codes are listed in the front of the telephone directories.

You can make international calls from most phones. It is best to direct dial, as operator-assisted calls are much more expensive. Avoid making calls from your hotel room, as phone charges are often double or even triple the price.

When phoning abroad, first dial the international prefix '00' followed by the country code, then the number. For operator assistance on international calls, dial 114. Dial 10 for operator assistance within Ireland and the UK.

For directory enquires within the Republic and Northern Ireland, dial 1190; for UK numbers dial 1197; for international numbers dial 1198.

The long-distance services of AT&T, Sprint and MCI are also available. For the weather forecast in the republic tel: 1550 122 111.

Internet Cafés

Internet cafés can be found throughout Dublin. Some of the most central ones include Planet Cybercafé at 13 St Andrew Street and at 23 South Great George's Street, and the Global Internet Café at 6 Grafton Street and 8 Lower O'Connell Street.

Tourist Offices

General postal enquiries should be directed to Irish Tourist Board (Bord Fáilte), Baggot Street Bridge, Baggot Street, Dublin 2, tel: 1850 230330, fax: 602 4100, website: www.ireland.travel.ie

The main **Dublin Tourism Centre** (open July and August, Monday–Saturday 9am–6.30pm, Sunday and holidays 10.30am–3pm; September–June, Monday–Saturday 9am–5.30pm) is located inside St Andrew's Church, Suffolk Street, Dublin 2; email: information@dublintourism.ie; website: www.visitdublin.com. For accommodation and ticket reservations only, tel: 605 7777; email: reservations@dublintourism.ie. As well as obtaining leaflets and information, you can book accommodation, transport, car rentals, tours and theatre tickets, change money and buy guide books and souvenirs. There is a numbered queuing system, and assistants will help direct you when you enter. This office and the branch at **O'Connell Street** do not have telephone information lines. Other branches are at **Dublin Airport**

arrivals hall (tel: 844 5387), **Dún Laoghaire** ferry terminal (tel: 284 6361) and The Square, Tallaght, Dublin 24 (tel: 462 0671).

For information in Ireland, tel: 1850 230 330; in UK, tel: 08000 397 000; elsewhere, tel: 00 353 66979 2083. For reservations in Ireland, tel: 1800 668 668; in UK tel: 00800 668 66866 (Gulliver); elsewhere tel: 00353 66979 2082.

For general information before departure, contact the **UK office** of the Irish Tourist Board, 150 New Bond Street, London W1S 2AQ, tel: 020-7518 0800, or fax: 020-7493 9065; email: info@irishtouristboard.co.uk. The **US office** is at 345 Park Avenue, New York, NY 10154, tel: (212) 418 0800 or fax: (212) 371 9052; email: infony@irishtouristboard.com.

Embassies

Australia: Fitzwilton House, Fitzwilton Terrace, Dublin 2. Tel: 676 1517.
Britain: 29 Merrion Rd, Dublin 4. Tel: 205 3700.
Canada: 65 St. Stephen's Green, Dublin 2. Tel: 478 1988.
Israel: Carrisbrook House, 122 Pembroke Rd, Dublin 4. Tel: 230 9400.
United States: 43 Elgin Rd, Dublin 4. Tel: 668 8777.

Disabled Travellers

For people with mobility problems, the **National Rehabilitation Board** publishes a booklet, *Dublin: A Guide for Disabled Travellers*. It is full of practical information and available from the NRB, 25 Clyde Road, Dublin 4, tel: 608 0400, fax: 660 9935 or the tourist board.

Getting Around

The state transport authority, CIE, is the umbrella body for three companies: Dublin Bus (serving the city), Bus Eireann (serving provincial areas from Dublin) and Iarnród Éireann (Irish Rail; operating inter-city trains as well as the DART, the Dublin Area Rapid Transit system). Timetables for bus and train services, including details of money-saving tourist tickets, are sold in newsagents.

For information: Dublin Bus tel: 873 4222; Bus Eireann tel: 836 6111; Iarnród Éireann tel: 1850 366 222 in Ireland only. You can dial a recorded timetable for most mainline rail destinations (look in the telephone directory under Iarnród Éireann). Tickets and information are also available from the **Irish Rail Travel Centre**, 35 Lower Abbey Street, tel: 836 6222, www.irishrail.ie

In Dublin city, the DART rail service is the most efficient way to travel, but it runs only along the coastal strip from Howth to Bray. The DART operates Monday–Saturday 7am–11.30pm and Sunday 9.30am–11.30pm. Timetables and maps are available at main stations and tourist information offices. There is a minimum fare for a single journey, depending on the distance; day passes, family cards and four-day passes combining DART and buses are also available. For information contact DART (tel: 703 3504).

The Dublin Bus service operates throughout the city, but buses can be crowded and slow, due to the heavy traffic. They are a convenient way of getting to attractions slightly out of the city centre and not on the DART, such as Phoenix Park or the National Botanical Gardens.

Most services run about every 15 minutes, and operate from 6am–11.30pm, although there are also suburban night buses till 3am on Thursday, Friday and Saturday nights. Bus stops cluster in places such as O'Connell Street, Eden Quay and Aston Quay. Stops give the numbers and routes of buses. Fares vary according to the number of stops travelled: ask the driver when you board. Have plenty of coins ready as you often need to have the exact fare. For information call Dublin Bus (tel: 873 4222).

A variety of travel passes are available, ranging from one-day tickets covering bus, DART and suburban rail, to family tickets covering bus and rail, to Rambler bus tickets for one, three, five or seven days. Tickets can be bought from any bus or train station in the Republic, or through a travel agent abroad.

Eurailpasses are not valid for cities, but can be used for intercity bus and train travel elsewhere in the Republic. A free ferrylink is provided by Irish Continental Line from Le Havre and Cherbourg in France to Rosslare. These tickets must be bought in advance from offices of the participating railways.

Driving in Dublin is no pleasure, with ill-policed parking regulations adding to the general traffic congestion. Outside the city, things are much better and hiring a car will make it much easier to undertake some of the excursions described in this book.

At the height of summer, though, hire cars can be harder to find than gold at the end of the rainbow, so book in advance. If you're heading west, the smaller the car, the better – the most alluring lanes are the narrowest. It pays to shop around – a recent survey revealed that rental prices were significantly lower outside the Dublin area. You must be over 23 with two years' full

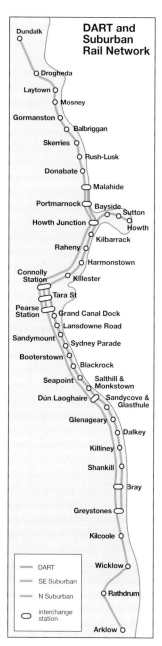

DART and Suburban Rail Network

Dundalk
Drogheda
Laytown
Mosney
Gormanston
Balbriggan
Skerries
Rush-Lusk
Donabate
Malahide
Portmarnock
Bayside
Howth Junction
Sutton
Howth
Kilbarrack
Raheny
Harmonstown
Connolly Station
Killester
Tara St
Pearse Station
Grand Canal Dock
Lansdowne Road
Sandymount
Sydney Parade
Booterstown
Blackrock
Seapoint
Salthill & Monkstown
Dún Laoghaire
Sandycove & Glasthule
Glenageary
Dalkey
Killiney
Shankill
Bray
Greystones
Kilcoole
Wicklow
DART
SE Suburban
N Suburban
interchange station
Rathdrum
Arklow

● The above map covers destinations mentioned in several chapters: Southern Suburbs (pages 197–201), Malahide and Howth (pages 211–213), and Excursions North (pages 225–231).

licence and under 70 to hire a car in the Irish Republic.

All the companies listed here are members of the Car Rental Council and operate a code of practice drawn up by the council and the Irish Tourist Board.

Car Rentals

Argus Rent A Car, Terenure, Dublin 6, tel: 490 4444. Also an office at Dublin Airport. Delivers to ferry ports and hotels.

Atlas Car Rentals, arrivals hall Dublin Airport, tel: 844 4859.

Avis, Dublin Airport, tel: 605 7555.

Budget Rent-a-Car, Dublin City, tel: 837 9611. Dublin Airport, tel: 844 5150.

Dan Dooley Rent-a-Car, Dublin Airport, tel: 842 8355. Dublin City, tel: 677 2723.

Hamill's Rent-a-Car, Mullingar, tel: 044 48682/44500. Delivery to Dublin Airport and Dublin ferry terminals.

Hertz Rent-a-Car, Leeson Street Bridge, Dublin 4, tel: 660 2255. Dublin Airport, tel: 844 5466.

Murrays Europcar Rent-a-Car, Baggot Street Bridge, Dublin 4, tel: 614 2888. Dublin Airport, tel: 812 0410.

National Alamo Car Rental, Arrivals Hall, Dublin Airport, tel: 844 4162.

Thrifty Car Rentals, Herberton Bridge, Rialto, Dublin 8, tel: 872 6401; Dublin Airport, tel: 840 0800.

Windsor Car and Van Rentals, Howth Road, Raheny, Dublin 5, tel: 831 1944.

Taxis

City centre taxi ranks are located at St. Stephen's Green, at O'Connell Street, on Dame Street and on Aston Quay. Taxis can be hailed on the street provided you are not standing near a taxi rank.

Many taxi companies cover the entire city and most will give you a fairly accurate estimate of the cost of a journey when you ring to book a taxi. Individual drivers are also very helpful. It is advisable to price the cost of long journeys as prices can jump significantly when you travel

further than 40 km (25 miles) from the city centre.

Dublin taxi drivers live up to their reputation for talking a lot. Stay off the subjects of politics, sports and the weather unless you're in the mood for a long chat.

Access Cabs, 20 Upper Baggott Street, Dublin 4, tel: 668 3333.

Airport Express, 241 Swords Road, Santry, Dublin 9, tel: 836 1111; 46 Mountjoy Square, Dublin 1, tel: 855 3333.

Alpha Taxi Cabs, Lower Dorset Street, Dublin 1, tel: 856 0777.

Blue Cabs, 41 Westland Row, Dublin 2, tel: 676 1111.

Cab Charge, Citywide, tel. 677 2222.

City Group, City House, New Market, Dublin 8, tel: 872 7272.

The Dublin Cab Company, 6 Temple Road, Blackrock, tel: 288 8300.

Southside Cabs, Dublin, tel: 283 6622.

Taxi Radio Link, 1b St. Margaret's Road, Finglas, Dublin 11, tel: 478 1111.

Where to Stay

The Choice

As soon as it became clear that Dublin's new-found status as the trendy European capital of the 1990s might be more than a flash in the pan, the city's hoteliers started building feverishly, adding several dozen new hotels in the last three years of the century. The boom also prompted renovations and improvements in many long-established hotels. Despite this, it hasn't kept pace with the influx of visitors. It is always recommended to book ahead, especially if you want to stay in a particular part of the city centre, where there is a particular shortage of accommodation in the cheaper price bracket. More budget accommodation can be found in B&Bs in the inner suburbs such as Ballsbridge. If you stay outside the centre, try to find accommodation near a DART station for a quicker journey into town.

It is possible to pay as much as €158 or more for a room in a top-rated hotel, or as little as €12 to bunk down in a hostel. Dearer is not necessarily better, of course – but, generally speaking, the more you pay, the more facilities are on offer.

Apart from what you can afford to pay, you may decide that you prefer small, family-run guesthouses with a bit more character. Most serve a full Irish breakfast (sausages, bacon, eggs, tomatoes, black pudding), which is very filling and, depending on the size of your appetite, could keep you going until early evening.

Holiday villas beyond indulgence.

BALEARICS ~ CARIBBEAN ~ FRANCE ~ GREECE ~ ITALY ~ MAURITIUS
MOROCCO ~ PORTUGAL ~ SCOTLAND ~ SPAIN

If you enjoy the really good things in life, we offer the highest quality holiday villas with the utmost privacy, style and true luxury. You'll find each with maid service and most have swimming pools.

For 18 years, we've gone to great lengths to select the very best villas at all of our locations around the world.

Contact us for a brochure on the destination of your choice and experience what most only dream of.

INTERNATIONAL
CHAPTERS

INSIGHT GUIDES

The classic series that puts you in the picture

Alaska
Amazon Wildlife
American Southwest
Amsterdam
Argentina
Arizona & Grand Canyon
Asia, East
Asia, Southeast
Australia
Austria
Bahamas
Bali
Baltic States
Bangkok
Barbados
Barcelona
Beijing
Belgium
Belize
Berlin
Bermuda
Boston
Brazil
Brittany
Brussels
Buenos Aires
Burgundy
Burma (Myanmar)
Cairo
California
California, Southern
Canada
Caribbean
Channel Islands
Chicago
Chile
China
Continental Europe
Corsica
Costa Rica
Crete
Cuba
Cyprus
Czech & Slovak Republics
Delhi, Jaipur & Agra
Denmark
Dominican Rep. & Haiti

Dublin
East African Wildlife
Eastern Europe
Ecuador
Edinburgh
Egypt
England
Finland
Florence
Florida
France
France, Southwest
French Riviera
Gambia & Senegal
Germany
Glasgow
Gran Canaria
Great Britain
Great Railway Journeys
  of Europe
Greece
Greek Islands
Guatemala, Belize
  & Yucatán
Hawaii
Hong Kong
Hungary
Iceland
India
India, South
Indonesia
Ireland
Israel
Istanbul
Italy
Italy, Northern
Italy, Southern
Jamaica
Japan
Jerusalem
Jordan
Kenya
Korea
Laos & Cambodia
Lisbon
London
Los Angeles

Madeira
Madrid
Malaysia
Mallorca & Ibiza
Malta
Mauritius, Réunion
  & Seychelles
Melbourne
Mexico
Miami
Montreal
Morocco
Moscow
Namibia
Nepal
Netherlands
New England
New Orleans
New York City
New York State
New Zealand
Nile
Normandy
Norway
Oman & The UAE
Oxford
Pacific Northwest
Pakistan
Paris
Peru
Philadelphia
Philippines
Poland
Portugal
Prague
Provence
Puerto Rico
Rajasthan
Rio de Janeiro

Rome
Russia
St Petersburg
San Francisco
Sardinia
Scandinavia
Scotland
Seattle
Sicily
Singapore
South Africa
South America
Spain
Spain, Northern
Spain, Southern
Sri Lanka
Sweden
Switzerland
Sydney
Syria & Lebanon
Taiwan
Tenerife
Texas
Thailand
Tokyo
Trinidad & Tobago
Tunisia
Turkey
Tuscany
Umbria
USA: On The Road
USA: Western States
US National Parks: West
Venezuela
Venice
Vienna
Vietnam
Wales

*The world's largest collection of
visual travel guides & maps*

What Prices Include

Prices are based on an average price for two people sharing a double room in the hotel or guesthouse indicated including VAT and service. Rooms can vary from standard to luxury in top hotels and specific requirements should always be indicated when booking. For example, you may have to pay extra for breakfast. Single rooms are hard to find and carry a premium, or single person supplement.

€€€€ (over €200 a night for a double room).

Berkeley Court Hotel
Lansdowne Road, Dublin 4.
Tel: 660 1711, fax: 661 7238.
Email: berkeleycourt@jurysdoyle.com
Website: www.jurysdoyle.com
Don't be put off by the concrete-shoebox exterior, there is five-star luxury inside. Sited in Ballsbridge near the famous Lansdowne Road international rugby ground.

The Burlington
Upper Leeson Street, Dublin 4.
Tel: 660 5222, fax: 660 8496.
Email: burlington@jurysdoyle.com
Website: www.jurys.com/ireland/doyle_burlington.htm
Ireland's largest hotel and conference centre. Located near "The Strip", although the number of nightclubs on the once legendary Leeson Street is now dwindling. The bar is a popular spot for après-rugby match knees-ups.

Camden Court Hotel
Camden Street, Dublin 2.
Tel: 475 9666, fax: 475 9677.
Email: sales@camdencourthotel.com
Website: www.tyrconnell-group.com/camden_court.html
Large hotel located 10 minutes' walk from the city centre. Modern interior with a leisure centre and swimming pool. Parking available.

The Clarence
6–8 Wellington Quay, Dublin 2.
Tel: 407 0800, fax: 407 0820.
Email: reservations@theclarence.ie
Website: www.theclarence.ie
City-centre, riverside location, backing onto Temple Bar. Redesigned with stylish restraint,

this place delights the eye as well as the stomach (the restaurant is first-class). Owners include members of the U2 rock group, clientele is self-consciously hip.

Conrad International Hotel
Earlsfort Terrace, Dublin 2.
Tel: 602 8900, fax: 676 5424.
Email: info@conraddublin.com
Website: www.conrad–international.ie
Luxurious, American-style, gleaming five-star hotel across the street from the National Concert Hall and just a few metres from St. Stephen's Green. Telephones even in the bathrooms.

The Davenport Hotel
Merrion Square, Dublin 2.
Tel: 607 3500, fax: 661 5663.
Email: davenportres@ocallaghan hotels.ie
Website: www.ocallaghanhotels.ie/davenport
Luxurious hotel in the heart of Georgian Dublin. Sited near the National Gallery of Ireland, Trinity College and Grafton Street.

Gresham Hotel
23 Upper O'Connell Street, Dublin 1.
Tel: 874 6881, fax: 878 7175.
Email: info@thegresham.com
Website: www.ryan-hotels.com
Once rivalled the Shelbourne as Dublin's grandest hotel. Still characterful and atmospheric.

The Morgan Hotel
10 Fleet Street, Temple Bar, Dublin 2.
Tel: 679 3939, fax: 679 3946.
Email: reservations@themorgan.com
Website: www.themorgan.com
Modern hotel in the heart of Temple Bar. High-tech facilities; all rooms have hi-fi systems and video players, ISDN lines and Internet access.

Shelbourne Hotel
27 St. Stephen's Green, Dublin 2.
Tel: 663 4500, fax: 661 6006.
Email: shelbourneinfo@lemeridien-hotels.com
Website: www.shelbourne.ie
Long established as Dublin's most prestigious hotel, with plenty of old-world atmosphere. The lounge is a great place for afternoon tea, the Horseshoe Bar is popular with some of the city's "heavy hitters".

Westbury Hotel
Balfe Street, off Grafton Street,

Dublin 2.
Tel: 679 1122, fax: 679 7078.
Email: westbury@jurysdoyle.com
Website: www.jurysdoyle.com
Modern, luxury hotel right in the city centre with a shopping mall next door. First-class food.

€€€ (from €140 a night for a double room).

Hibernian Hotel
Eastmoreland Place, Dublin 4.
Tel: 668 7666, fax: 660 2655.
Email: hibernian@slh.com
Website: www.slh.com/ireland/dublin/hotel_ianire.html
Luxurious old house in Ballsbridge offering a high level of personal service. First-rate food.

Longfield's Hotel
9–10 Lower Fitzwilliam Street, Dublin 2.
Tel: 676 1367, fax: 676 1542.
Email: info@longfields.ie
Website: www.longfields.ie
Charming small hotel in the heart of southside Georgian Dublin. Good food in basement restaurant.

Mont Clare Hotel
Clare Street, Dublin 2.
Tel: 607 3800, fax: 661 5663.
Email: montclareres@ocallaghan hotels.ie
Website: www.ocallaghanhotels.ie/montclare
Excellent location on the corner of Merrion Square, close to the National Gallery and main southside shopping areas.

Number 31
31 Leeson Close, Dublin 2.
Tel: 676 5011, fax: 676 2929.
Email: number31@iol.ie
Website: www.number31.ie
Interesting, friendly guesthouse based in two houses, one modern, one Georgian. Just off Leeson Street, known for its basement nightclubs.

€€ (from €80 a night for a double room).

Aberdeen Lodge
53 Park Avenue, Dublin 4.
Tel: 283 8155, fax: 283 7877.
Email: aberdeen@iol.ie
Well-equipped guesthouse in pair of Edwardian houses on elegant road.

Albany House
84 Harcourt Street, Dublin 2.
Tel: 475 1092, fax: 475 1093.
Email: albany@indigo.ie
Website: www.byrne-hotels-
ireland.com/albany-house.htm
Elegant house in the heart of
Georgian Dublin. Bedrooms are
decorated with period prints and
antiques.

Anglesea Town House
63 Anglesea Road, Dublin 4.
Tel: 668 3877, fax: 668 3461.
Privately run guesthouse in
Edwardian villa in Ballsbridge.
Famous for its breakfasts.

The Arlington Hotel
23–25 Bachelors Walk, O'Connell
Bridge, Dublin 1.
Tel: 804 9100, fax: 804 9112.
Email: arlington@tinet.ie
Website: www.arlington.ie
Modern rooms and suites in a
pleasant hotel with medieval-style
public rooms. Front rooms overlook
the Liffey. Great bar with live music
and Irish dancing. Underground
parking.

Bewley's Principal Hotel
19–20 Fleet Street, Temple Bar,
Dublin 2.
Tel: 670 8122, fax: 670 8103.
Email: bewleyshotel@eircom.net
Website: www.bewleysprincipal
hotel.com
The legendary café group has
branched into the accommodation
market. An old-fashioned intimate
hotel with every modern facility.
Plus fresh Bewley's coffee.

Buswell's Hotel
25 Molesworth Street, Dublin 2.
Tel: 614 6500, fax: 676 2090.
Email: buswells@quinn-hotels.com
Former Georgian townhouses used
as a hotel since the 1920s. A haunt
of politicians because of its
proximity to Leinster House.

Central Hotel
1–5 Exchequer Street, Dublin 2.
Tel: 679 7302, fax: 679 7303.
Email: reservationa@centralhotel.ie
Website: www.cenratlhotel.ie
Arguably has more character than
some of the bigger, pricier places,
with interesting paintings on the
walls. Close to Grafton Street.

Drury Court Hotel
28–30 Lower Stephen's Street,
Dublin 2.
Tel: 475 1988, fax: 478 5730.
Email: druryct@indigo.ie
Popular 3-star hotel with large
comfortable rooms, near St
Stephen's Green and central Dublin
attractions.

Hotel Isaacs
Store Street, Dublin 1.
Tel: 855 0067, fax: 836 5390.
Email: hotel@isaacs.ie
Website: www.isaacs.ie/hoteld
Small, efficient, friendly place
handily situated close to Connolly
Station and Busaras (central bus
stations).

Jurys Christchurch Inn
Christchurch Place, Dublin 8.
Tel: 454 0000, fax: 454 0012.
Email: bookings@jurys.com
Website: www.jurys.com/ireland/
jurys_christchurch.htm
Less expensive addition to a long-
established chain of hotels. Well
located for the old city and Temple
Bar.

Merrion Hall
56 Merrion Road, Dublin 4.
Tel: 668 1426, fax: 668 4280.
Email: merrionhall@iol.ie
Rambling, cosy Victorian
guesthouse near the Royal Dublin
Society grounds. Good breakfasts.

Mount Herbert Hotel
Herbert Road, Lansdowne Road,
Dublin 4.
Tel: 668 4321, fax: 660 7077.
Email: info@mountherberthotel.ie
Website: www.mountherberthotel.ie
Family-run guesthouse in an
extended Victorian house near
Lansdowne Road stadium.
Children's playground.

Othello Guesthouse
74 Lower Gardiner Street, Dublin 1.
Tel: 855 5442, fax: 855 7460.
Handy, inner north-city location near
the principal rail and bus stations.
Well equipped.

River House Hotel
23–24 Eustace Street, Temple Bar,
Dublin 2.
Tel: 670 7655, fax: 670 7650.
Email: riverhousehotel@
compuserve.com
Close to the action in the hip
Temple Bar area. Opposite the Irish
Film Centre, and near art and
photographic galleries, pubs and
restaurants.

St. Aiden's Guesthouse
32 Brighton Road, Dublin 6.
Tel: 490 2011, fax: 492 0234.
Email: staidens@eircom.net
Good guesthouse in a pleasant
south-side suburb of Rathgar.

Hotel St. George
7 Parnell Square, Dublin 1.
Tel: 874 5611, fax: 874 5582.
Email: hotels@indigo.ie
Website: http://indigo.ie/~hotels/
george.htm
Comfortable hotel in two converted
Georgian houses. Close to the Hugh
Lane Municipal Art Gallery, Gate
Theatre, and O'Connell Street.

Temple Bar Hotel
Fleet Street, Dublin 2.
Tel: 677 3333, fax: 677 3088.
Email: templeb@iol.ie
Website: www.towerhotelgroup.ie/
templebar
Sited in trendy Temple Bar area with
its bustling night-life. Great location
if you're not a light sleeper.

**€ (under €80 a night for a
double room).**

Avalon House
55 Aungier Street, Dublin 2.
Tel: 475 0001, fax: 475 0303.
Email: info@avalon–house.ie
Website: www.avalon–house.ie
Well-located hostel near Grafton
Street and Temple Bar. Single
rooms, double rooms, family rooms,
dorms. Cheap.

The Cumberland Lodge Town House
54 York Road, Dun Laoghaire,
Co. Dublin.
Tel: 280 9665, fax: 284 3227.
Email: cumberlandlodge@tinent.ie
Beautifully restored Georgian house
situated in a scenic suburb south of
the city centre. Elegant rooms and
extensive parking.

Dorchester House
69 North Circular Road, Dublin 7.
Tel: 838 5204, no fax.
Two restored Georgian houses in
central northside location.

Gogarty's Temple Bar Hostel
18–21 Anglesea Street, Temple
Bar, Dublin 2.
Tel: 671 1822, fax: 671 7637.
Email: info@olivergogartys.com
Website: www.olivergogartys.com
Bright and airy private en-suite

rooms and dorm rooms in the heart of trendy Temple Bar.

Kinlay House
2–12 Lower Edward Street, Dublin 2.
Tel: 679 6644, fax: 679 7437.
Email: kinlay.dublin@usitworld.com
Website: www.iol.ie/usitaccm/khdublin.htm
Close to Christchurch Cathedral, backing onto Temple Bar. Singles, doubles, 4–6 bedded rooms, dorms. Cheap.

Trinity College Accommodation
Accommodation Office, West Chapel, Trinity College, Dublin 2.
Tel: 608 1177, fax: 671 1267.
Email: reservations@tcd.ie
Simple, cheap accommodation in student rooms, some en-suite, and apartments. Lovely setting on campus. Available June to September.

Where to Eat

The Choice

You will find many superb natural ingredients on offer in Dublin restaurants – fresh and smoked salmon, trout, prawns and oysters; succulent beef, pork and lamb – above all, perhaps, delicious and chewy wholemeal and soda bread. But you will find few dishes that are specifically Irish, partly because the country has no tradition of haute cuisine and partly because the people tend to associate traditional fare such as Irish stew of boiled bacon and cabbage with the poor old days. These may be humble dishes, but they are also wholesome and delicious. Keep an eye out, too, for the ever-growing range of Irish cheeses, many of which are first-class.

Eating out in Ireland is not cheap, though it is getting cheaper. There is no shortage of fast-food places offering everything from hamburgers to fish-and-chips or sweet-and-sour chicken. At the other end of the scale there are plush, expensive restaurants. A welcome new development is the increasing trend towards bar food at lunch time and in the early evening. The meal will be served at your bar room table featuring a substantial but moderately priced main course (around €8) and a limited choice of starters and desserts.

The restaurant scene has undergone a revolution for the better in the past decade. Many young cooks who have trained in the best kitchens of Europe and America have returned home determined to make the best of Ireland's wonderful raw ingredients. They have opened restaurants where you will eat succulent, fresh produce cooked simply and well, and you will find that the fresh Irish air gives you the appetite of a lifetime.

But you can still be unlucky enough to pay inflated prices to eat overcooked and over-dressed food (probably from a menu with misspelt French names) in pretentious surroundings. If this happens, complain. Many Irish people hate to make a fuss, and bad restaurants survive as a result.

Price Guide

Prices are based on the average cost of a three-course evening meal, excluding wine:
€ = less than €20 per head
€€ = between €20 and €35 per head
€€€ = €35-plus per head.
Lunch is usually cheaper.

€€€ (€35-plus per head).

The Commons
86 St. Stephens Green, Dublin 2.
Tel: 475 2597.
Old-world atmosphere in the former dining room of University College. Superb, imaginative cuisine has earned it a Michelin-star.

Cooke's Café
14 South William Street, Dublin 2.
Tel: 679 0536.
Atmospheric restaurant serving Mediterranean/Californian cuisine. Pleasantly close to a range of good pubs around Grafton Street.

Dobbins Wine Bistro
15 Stephen's Lane, Dublin 2.
Tel: 676 4679.
First choice of movers and shakers for power lunches. Dinner tends to be a boisterous affair; the louder the dinner the more successful the evening is the policy of management. Excellent food.

Eden
Meeting House Square, Temple Bar, Dublin 2.
Tel: 670 5373.
Minimalist decor and well-defined flavours combine to make this restaurant a very sophisticated experience.

Ernies
Mulberry Gardens, Donnybrook,
Dublin 4.
Tel: 269 3300.
A restaurant beloved of socialites
and name-droppers. But don't hold
that against this dining insitution
whose reputation is also built on
magnificent food. Intimate
atmosphere.

King Sitric
East Pier, Howth, Co. Dublin.
Tel: 832 5235.
Seafood restaurant with no excuse
for not having fresh fish. It's
positioned beside one of the most
scenic harbours in Dublin, with a
view of Ireland's Eye.

Le Coq Hardi
35 Pembroke Road, Ballsbridge,
Dublin 4.
Tel: 668 9070.
Swish French restaurant with huge
snob value. The place to be seen
indulging in delicately prepared food
complimented by a prestigious wine
list.

L'Ecrivain
109a Lower Baggot Street,
Dublin 2.
Tel: 661 1919.
Excellent New Irish cuisine cooked
with a classic French flair. Famous
for fish dishes, with fresh catches
of the day from around the island.

Les Frères Jacques
74 Dame Street, Dublin 2.
Tel: 679 4555.
Quality French food at affordable
prices – provided you don't go mad
with the tempting wine list – ensure
that this restaurant has an enduring
appeal to locals who keep going
back.

Lobster Pot
9 Ballsbridge Terrace, Dublin 4.
Tel: 668 0025.
Long-established seafood
restaurant near the city centre in
which you'll feel immediately at
home. Fresh seafood served in
mouth-watering sauces.

Locks Restaurant
1 Windsor Terrace, Portobello,
Dublin 8.
Tel: 454 3391.
Full of atmosphere, set alongside
the canal – excellent food. Favourite
haunt of theatregoers.

Lord Edward
23 Christchurch Place, Dublin 8.
Tel: 454 2420.
Dublin's oldest seafood restaurant,
with intimate rooms on three floors.
Traditional decor and a great range
of seafood dishes from sole to
Dublin Bay prawns, along with a few
other options.

Patrick Guilbaud
21 Upper Merrion Street, Dublin 2.
Tel: 677 3363.
Dublin's best-known French
restaurant, producing classic
cuisine with immense attention to
detail. The prices are
commensurably high.

Peacock Alley
Fitzwilliam Hotel, St. Stephen's
Green, Dublin 2.
Tel: 677 0708.
Without doubt the "hottest"
restaurant in Dublin. Chef Conrad
Gallagher is the darling of food
critics besotted by his experimental
Mediterranean cooking.

Siam Thai Restaurant
Gasyard Lane, Malahide,
Co. Dublin.
Tel: 845 4698.
Popular restaurant in a pretty
seaside village. Excellent Thai food.

The Tea Room
The Clarence Hotel, Wellington
Quay, Dublin 2.
Tel: 670 9000.
International celebrities head to this
restaurant part-owned by members
of the U2 pop group. You can
expect a lot of gossip columnists to
turn up in tow. More refined than
rock 'n' roll, this restaurant was
awarded the Beck's Taste of Temple
Bar Award.

Thornton's
1 Portobello Road, Dublin 8.
Tel: 454 9067.
High-class cooking from top chef
Kevin Thornton, served in a formal
but contemporary candle-lit dining
room. The six-course 'Surprise'
menu is a treat.

**€€ (between €20 and €35
per head).**
Belgo
17–19 Sycamore Street, Dublin 2.
Tel: 672 7555.
Spacious Temple Bar branch of the

popular Belgo chain, specialising in
mussels and Belgian beers.
Lunchtime bargain menus.

Cafe En Seine
40 Dawson Street, Dublin 2.
Tel: 677 4369.
Stylish hangout for over a decade.
Salads, steaks, pasta and simple
dishes. Live jazz brunch on Sunday.

Café Mao
2 Chatham Row, Dublin 2.
Tel: 670 4899.
Favourite among top models who
have made something of a second
home out of this groovy Indonesian
restaurant. Great green curry
washed down with an Indonesian
beer.

Cedar Tree
11A St. Andrew Street, Dublin 2.
Tel: 677 2121.
Lebanese restaurant popular with
serious foodies and late-night
revellers. Ultra-relaxed atmosphere
– don't be surprised if the diners
start dancing on the tables.

Da Pino
38–40 Parliament Street, Dublin 2.
Tel: 671 9308.
Classic Italian dishes and fantastic
pizzas, prepared in front of your
eyes. Friendly and very popular spot
opposite Dublin Castle, so you may
want to book.

Fitzer's Café
51 Dawson Street, Dublin 2.
Tel: 677 1155.
Also: 40 Temple Bar Square, Dublin 2.
Tel: 679 0440.
Also: National Gallery of Ireland,
Merrion Square, Dublin 2.
Tel: 661 4496.
This restaurant chain offers a
variety of attractive locations, each
serving the same cosmopolitan and
delicious dishes.

Gotham Café
8 South Anne Street, Dublin 2.
Tel: 679 5266.
Bright, trendy café-restaurant with
Rolling Stone covers on the walls.
Great range of pizzas and delicious
dishes such as honey-roasted pork
with basil mash. Very busy
evenings, so book ahead.

Mermaid Café
69 Dame Street, Dublin 2.
Tel: 670 8236.
Recent arrival which is fast

becoming the hippest place in town. A stylish restaurant with nothing in common with a truckers' stop-over.

Mongolian Barbeque
7 Anglesea Street, Dublin 2.
Tel: 670 4154.
Groovy American franchise in trendy Temple Bar. Choose your own stir fry ingredients which are cooked on a public hot plate. A boisterous, "cool" restaurant. Not for the self-conscious.

Nico's
53 Dame Street, Dublin 2.
Tel: 677 3062.
Old-fashioned romantic restaurant for when you've proposed marriage on the Ha'penny Bridge. Tasty Italian dishes by candlelight. Plush setting.

Pizza Stop
6 Chatham Lane, Dublin 2.
Tel: 679 6712.
Authentic Italian restaurant located in the heart of the shopping district. Popular any time of the day or night.

Rajdoot Tandoori
26 Clarendon Street, Dublin 2.
Tel: 679 4274.
Excellent Tandoori dishes in the restaurant which set the standard for authentic Indian cooking in Dublin. Good atmosphere.

Roly's Bistro
7 Ballsbridge Terrace, Dublin 4.
Tel: 668 2611.
Lively bistro with imaginative and affordable Irish-French cuisine, such as Clonakilty black pudding in brioche. Good wine list, irresistible desserts.

Sassi's Mediterranean Restaurant
146 Leeson Street, Dublin 4.
Tel: 668 4544.
Reasonably priced Mediterranean dishes in a brasserie-style restaurant.

Shalimar
17 South Great Georges Street, Dublin 2.
Tel: 671 0738.
Relaxed and inexpensive Balti House downstairs; upstairs offers a more upmarket and extensive Indian menu. Very reliable.

101 Talbot
100–102 Talbot Street, Dublin 1.
Tel: 874 5011.
Italian/Continental fare in a

convivial restaurant. The pre-theatre dinner menu is great value if you are heading to the Abbey Theatre, located around the corner.

Yamamori Noodles
71 South Great Georges Street, Dublin 2.
Tel: 475 5001.
Japanese restaurant, and probably the best place for noodles in Dublin. Predominantly cool clientele.

€ (less than €20 per head).

Acapulco
7 South Great George's Street, Dublin 2.
Tel: 677 1085.
Tasty Tex-Mex dishes and killer margaritas by the pitcher, served amidst colourful Mexican decor. Friendly service.

Bad Ass Café
9–11 Crown Alley, Dublin 2.
Tel: 671 2596.
Always busy, serving good pizzas, pasta, burgers and salads.

Busyfeet and Coco
42 South William Street, Dublin 2.
Tel: 671 9514.
Small, relaxing local spot serving from breakfast to early evening. Homemade soups, salads and light meals, and a large choice of coffees, teas and fruit cocktails.

Cornucopia
19 Wicklow Street, Dublin 2.
Tel: 677 7583.
Vegetarian restaurant which makes the best use of fresh produce. Arrive early for lunch to guarantee a seat.

Gallagher's Boxty House
20–21 Temple Bar, Dublin 2.
Tel: 677 2762.
A good place to try Irish dishes such as *boxty* (potato pancakes). Always busy and popular with tourists. You may share a table.

Juice
9 Castle House, 73 South Great George's Street Dublin 2.
Tel: 475 7856.
Tasty vegetarian dishes, organically produced wines, juice bar.

Kilkenny Restaurant and Café
6 Nassau Street, Dublin 2.
Tel: 677 7066.
On the first floor of the Kilkenny

Design Shop, overlooking Trinity College. Large, bright cafeteria-style place, serving freshly prepared stews, quiches, salads, light meals and cakes.

Little Caesar's Palace
5 Balfe Street, Dublin 2.
Tel: 671 8714.
There's usually a queue for this popular pizza parlour, where you can watch the chef at work.

Pasta Fresca
2–4 Chatham Street, Dublin 2.
Tel: 679 2402.
Delicious homemade pastas and good-value pizzas, served all day. Lively atmosphere, and brisk service keeps the queue moving in this popular spot.

The Winding Stair Bookshop and Cafe
40 Lower Ormond Quay, Dublin 1.
Tel: 873 3292.
Cheap wholesome food, books to browse through, and soothing jazz sounds. Open 9.30am–6pm.

Pubs

Dublin's pubs are among the best in the world, largely because their clients regard the drink – still overwhelmingly Guinness stout – as a lubricant to the conversation. But what a lubricant – smooth, dark, creamy-collared and incomparably tastier when drunk in its home city, where the skilful bar staff know just how to pour it slowly and respectfully, waiting judiciously before topping it off. English visitors should note, incidentally, that while it is all right to call for "a pint", the correct terminology for a half-pint is "a glass". If you stay long enough in Dublin, you may acquire the local knack of communicating your order with a mere twitch of an eyelid.

Where to Drink

The Brazen Head
20 Lower Bridge Street, Dublin 8.
Dublin's oldest pub is conveniently close to the Guinness Brewery at St James Gate. Recently revamped and a live music venue, popular with the young crowd.

Davy Byrne's
21 Duke Street, Dublin 2.
Hugely popular city centre pub, and the pub in which James Joyce's literary hero Leopold Bloom enjoys a glass of burgundy and a gorgonzola sandwich with a dab of mustard in *Ulysses*. You'll be lucky to get a seat on Bloomsday (16 June), a celebration of James Joyce and his great novel *(see pages 86–87)*. Tasty lunches go down well with the Art Deco surroundings including murals by Cecil French Salkeld, the father-in-law of writer Brendan Behan.

Doheny and Nesbitt's
5 Lower Baggot Street, Dublin 2.
Atmospheric pub with a dark, faded interior and a favourite haunt of many of the city's leading opinion makers from nearby Government buildings, hence the media description "The Doheny and Nesbitt School of Economics". It's also popular with the media, especially journalists from the nearby *Sunday Tribune*.

The Duke
9 Duke Street, Dublin 2.
A pub with more than a hint of history – dating back 200 years to the 18th century and the second-oldest surviving public house in this part of Dublin. Literary connections include past regulars Brendan Behan and Patrick Kavanagh. Today's regulars are a mixed crowd, especially on Saturdays with the pub being close to Dublin's premier shopping boulevard, Grafton Street.

The Grave Diggers
Prospect Square, Glasnevin, Dublin 9.
With its low ceilings, bench seats and sawdust-covered floors, this low-key establishment offers an old-style Irish pub experience. Located near Dublin's largest cemetery, it takes its name from the profession of many of its clientele.

Grogan's
15 South William Street, Dublin 2.
Dublin's young bohemian set are devoted to this seriously laid-back pub. The unpretentious decor is a perfect backdrop for the fantastic collection of contemporary art on the walls, and which are also on sale should one take your fancy. The place where young aspiring artists love to be seen.

Horseshoe Bar
Shelbourne Hotel, St. Stephen's Green, Dublin 2.
Watering hole of the city's movers and shakers. Posh hotel bar where it's okay to stagger out of but not into the swish foyer.

Kehoe's
9 South Anne Street, Dublin 2.
Pub renovations are rampant in Dublin. Unlike many, Kehoe's managed to pull it off without losing the integrity of the place. Kehoe's is a hero for drinkers who like a pint without being blinded by trendy mahogany veneer and polished brass. Charming low-key atmosphere and at times a seriously bohemian clientele.

The Long Hall
51 South Great George's Street, Dublin 2.
One of Dublin's great old Victorian pubs, with an ornate wood-and-glass interior and a hand-carved bar, said to be the longest in the city. Sparkly antique chandeliers, a wooden arch and other details add to the atmosphere. It's a laid-back local during the day, a fashionable pre-club hang-out for the younger crowd in the evenings.

McDaid's
3 Harry Street, Dublin 2.
Enjoy a pint in this Gothic-style pub which was once the city morgue. Today it's difficult to find a more lively drinking spot and the mainly young clientele don't seem to mind the squeeze in the small pub.

Mulligans
8 Poolbeg Street, Dublin 2.
Dublin pubs have the knack of being associated with famous people but they rarely come more colourful than President John F. Kennedy and Bing Crosby who stopped off here to check out the legendary Guinness. An authentic pub which places more value on a good pint of plain than fussy decor.

Nancy Hands
30–32 Parkgate Street, Dublin 8.
Named for a legendary brothel owner, this popular bar serves over 500 whiskies and vodkas, as well as champagne cocktails. There is live music some evenings, as well as a bar menu and a good restaurant upstairs. Good for refreshment after a visit to Phoenix Park.

Neary's
1 Chatham Street, Dublin 2.
A beautiful example of Victorian public house design featuring cast-iron arms bearing lamps to light your way to the main entrance. Once inside, the pub's faded elegance in plush red upholstery and dark mahogany provides a genteel ambience for the theatrical and showbiz types who regularly drop in.

A Who's Who of Irish Whiskies

The comparative affluence and sophisticated tastes of recent years have stimulated the demand for Ireland's more traditional whiskies as well as Scotland's rarer malts. There are 15 or so different whiskies on sale in Ireland. John Power's Gold Label is by far the most popular. Next come Jameson, Bushmills, Coleraine (which sells in Northern Ireland), Paddy, Hewitt's and Dunphy's. Murphy's sells mainly in the United States, and Tullamore Dew, a particularly light brand, does well in Europe.

Two popular premium brands are Black Bush (from Bushmills in County Antrim, the world's oldest distillery) and Crested Ten, matured for 10 years in the Jameson stable. At the top of the range are liqueur whiskies, among the most exceptional drinks on earth. Bushmills Malt is a single 10-year-old; Jameson 1780 is aged for 12 years; and Redbreast, also 12 years old, is matured in wood by the house of Gilbey, renowned for its wines, ports and sherries. To put ice in these last three whiskies is an act of sacrilege to an Irishman.

O'Neill's
2 Suffolk Street, Dublin 2.
The warren of rooms inside this popular pub, opposite the Tourist Information Centre, is frequented by visitors and students from nearby Trinity College. Dubliners come here for the famous carvery at lunchtime, and bar food is available well into the evening.

Ryan's
28 Parkgate Street, Dublin 8.
Old-fashioned gem of a pub, with a mahogany bar, brass fittings, mirrors and snugs (enclosed private booths) that recall the traditional ambience. Food served at lunchtime and evenings till 9pm, and a good Sunday carvery. Near the entrance to Phoenix Park.

The Stag's Head
1 Dame Court, Dublin 2.
The first pub in Dublin to install electricity but the industrial revolution seems to have stopped with light bulbs in this pleasantly old-fashioned place. Good spot for back-packers to meet a local student crowd.

Culture

Art Galleries

Anyone interested in the visual arts should visit the National Gallery, the Hugh Lane Municipal Gallery, the Irish Museum of Modern Art, and the Gallery of Oriental Art (Chester Beatty). There are also many smaller exhibition centres and commercial galleries which often contain interesting work.

Arthouse Multimedia Centre for the Arts, Curved Street, Temple Bar, Dublin 2, tel: 605 6800. Tuesday–Friday 10am–6pm, Saturday 10am–5pm. Avant-garde multimedia exhibitions, installations, "living art". Café open till 9.30pm.

Bank of Ireland Arts Centre, Foster Place, Dublin 2, tel: 671 1488. Tuesday–Friday 10am–4pm; admission fee. Puts on both modern Irish and international exhibitions.

Bridge Gallery, 8 Upper Ormond Quay, Dublin 7, tel: 872 9702. Monday–Saturday 10am–6pm, Sunday 2pm–5pm. Painting, print and applied arts. Mainly Irish work.

Chester Beatty Library, tel: 407 0750. Monday–Friday 10am–5pm, Saturday 11am–5pm, Sunday 1–5pm, closed Monday (October–April); free. This superb collection of Oriental art and manuscripts is housed in a new exhibition gallery in the gardens at Dublin Castle.

Combridge Fine Arts, 17 South William Street, Dublin 2, tel: 677 4652. Monday–Saturday 9.30am–5.30pm. Conventional landscapes in oil and watercolour.

Douglas Hyde Gallery, Trinity College, Dublin 2, tel: 608 1116. Tel: 677 2941 ext: 1116.

Monday–Friday 11am–6pm, Thursday 11am–7pm, Saturday, 11am–4.45pm. Contemporary Irish and international painting, sculpture and photography.

Gallery of Photography, Meeting House Square, Temple Bar, Dublin 2, tel: 671 4654. Tuesday–Saturday 11am–6pm, Sunday 1–6pm; free. Changing exhibitions of international photography.

Green on Red Gallery, 26–28 Lombard Street East, Dublin 2, tel: 671 3414. Monday–Friday 10am–6pm; Saturday 11am–5pm. Cutting-edge contemporary art.

Hugh Lane Municipal Gallery of Modern Art, Parnell Square, tel: 874 1903. Tuesday–Thursday 9.30am–6pm, Friday–Saturday 9.30–5pm, Sunday 11am–5pm; free to permanent collection, admission fee to Francis Bacon Studio.

Irish Museum of Modern Art, Royal Hospital, Kilmainham, tel: 612 9900. Tuesday–Saturday 10am–5.30pm, Sunday noon–5.30pm; free. Irish and international art of the 20th century.

Kerlin Gallery, Anne's Lane, South Anne Street, Dublin 2, tel: 670 9093. Monday–Friday 10am–5.45pm, Saturday 11am–4.30pm. Contemporary European and Irish artists.

Malahide Castle, Malahide, Co. Dublin, tel: 846 2184. Monday–Saturday 10am–5pm, Sunday and bank holidays 11am–6pm (April–October), Monday–Friday 10am–5pm, weekends and bank holidays 2–5pm and closed for lunch (November–March); admission fee. Houses a selection from the National Portrait Gallery.

National Gallery of Ireland, Merrion Square West, Dublin 2, tel: 661 5133. Monday–Saturday 9.30am–5.30pm (Thursday to 8.30pm), Sunday 2pm–5pm; free. Old masters, Irish and international art from the 16th to the 19th century. Permanent Yeats exhibition, mainly dedicated to the work of Jack B. Yeats.

National Photographic Archive, Meeting House Square, Temple Bar, Dublin 2, tel: 603 0200.

Monday–Friday 10am–5pm, Saturday 10am–2pm; free. Changing themed exhibitions from the National Library of Ireland's collection of over 300,000 photographs.

Oriel Gallery, 17 Clare Street, Dublin 2, tel: 676 3410. Monday–Friday 10am–5.30pm, Saturday 10am–1pm. Has 19th and 20th-century Irish paintings, mostly landscapes. Established names such as Paul Henry, Jack B. Yeats, "AE".

Paul Kane Gallery, 53 South William Street, Dublin 2, tel: 670 3141. Tuesday–Saturday 11am–6pm. Showcase for Irish artists, with solo shows and new works by a range of artists in the Summer Gallery Show.

RHA Gallagher Gallery, 15 Ely Place, Dublin 2, tel: 661 2558. Tuesday–Saturday 11am–5pm; Thursday 11am–8pm; Sunday 2–5pm; free. Exhibitons by Irish and international artists in spacious modern gallery.

Rubicon Gallery, 10 St. Stephen's Green, Dublin 2, tel: 670 8055. Monday–Saturday 11am–5.30pm. Contemporary Irish and international art.

Solomon Gallery, Powerscourt Townhouse Centre, South William Street, Dublin 2, tel: 679 4237. Monday–Saturday 10am–5.30pm. Contemporary Irish and international art.

Taylor Galleries, 16 Kildare Street, Dublin 2, tel: 676 6055. Monday–Friday 10am–5.30pm, Saturday 11am–1pm. Contemporary Irish painting and sculpture by leading artists.

Temple Bar Gallery and Studios, 5–7 Temple Bar, Dublin 2, tel: 671 0073. Monday–Saturday 11am–6pm, Thursday 11am–7pm, Sunday 2–6pm. Avant garde contemporary Irish and international art.

Tower Craft Design Centre, Pearse Street, Dublin 2, tel: 677 5655. Monday–Friday 9.30am–5pm. Permanent collection of contemporary Irish craft design.

Theatres

For a city of its size, Dublin has an excellent range of theatre, as befits its strong tradition in the art, and performance and production standards are high. In October virtually all the venues in the city participate in the Dublin Theatre Festival, which features both mainstream and fringe Irish and international performances.

Abbey Theatre, Lower Abbey Street, Dublin, tel: 878 7222. Ireland's national theatre. Founded in the early years of the century by W. B. Yeats, Lady Gregory and their collaborators, it quickly won a world reputation with some outstanding plays and a unique style of acting. Many Irish classics feature in its programme. The Abbey's sister theatre, the **Peacock**, is used to try out new, experimental work.

Andrews Lane Theatre, 9–17 Andrews Lane, Dublin 2, tel: 679 5720. Opened in 1989 in a converted warehouse and a popular smaller venue.

City Arts Centre, 23–25 Moss Street, Dublin 2, tel: 677 0643. Arts centre based in a renovated warehouse. Fringe theatre, comedy, and community-based drama groups. Also art and photographic exhibitions.

Crypt Arts Centre, Dublin Castle, Dublin 2, tel: 671 3387. Small, intimate theatre in historical setting offering a mix of mainstream theatre and experimental work. Popular for theatre festivals.

Focus Theatre, 6 Pembroke Place, Dublin 2, tel: 676 3071. Long-established small theatre off the beaten track and offering quality drama.

Gaiety Theatre, South King Street, tel: 677 1717. A fine Victorian building, recently restored. The programme includes opera, ballet, pantomime, variety concerts and serious drama.

Gate Theatre, Cavendish Row, Parnell Square, tel: 874 4045. Founded by Micheál MacLiammóir. New Irish drama premieres and productions of 20th-century dramatists such as Harold Pinter and Noël Coward.

New Theatre in the Connolly Books shop, 43 East Essex Street, Dublin 2, tel: 670 3361. Opened in 1998 as a venue for the work of young emerging playwrights.

Olympia Theatre, 72 Dame Street, Dublin 2, tel: 677 7744. Similar shows to the Gaiety. Once a Victorian music hall.

Players Theatre, Front Square, Trinity College, Dublin, tel: 608 2242. Based in the university which produced such dramatists as Goldsmith, Synge and Beckett. Trinity College Dublin also has the Samuel Beckett Arts Centre. Both stage college drama productions and small independent companies.

Project, 39 East Essex Street, Temple Bar, Dublin 2, tel: 679 6622. Offers new work, often experimental, and innovative revivals from mainly Dublin-based independent companies.

Film

Irish Film Centre, 6 Eustace Street, Temple Bar, Dublin 2, tel: 679 3477. The city's top art-house cinema. Two screens showing Irish-made independent films, and international works. Good atrium café and bookshop.

Music

Ireland has some of the most vital traditional music in the world. You can hear it in pubs almost everywhere in the country, but visitors who want to be sure of hearing some good stuff are best advised to attend an organised session, such as one of those presented on Friday and Saturday nights at Culturlann na hEireann, the headquarters of Comhaltas Ceoltóirí Eireann (the traditional music association). The address is 32 Belgrave Square, Monkstown, Co. Dublin, tel: 280 0295. Buses 7, 7A and 8 from Dublin city centre stop nearby and the Monkstown and Seapoint DART station is only a short walk away.

The biggest change in Irish

popular music over the past few years, particularly among the young, is the advent of "club" music as the dominant means of expression. Dublin's new-found reputation as a "clubbing capital" has been enhanced by venues like POD (Place of Dance) and The Kitchen (the nightclub owned by U2), which are still two of the best places in the city. Local DJs are now bringing out records on their own labels and dabbling in genres such as Garage, Drum 'n' Bass and Trance.

Traditional folk music abounds throughout the city. Details of sessions and other venues appear in *In Dublin* magazine.

In Dublin also carries details of jazz, rock and classical music events. The top venue for the latter is the **National Concert Hall** in Earlsfort Terrace, just south of St. Stephen's Green,

The Hot Press Irish Music Hall of Fame in Middle Abbey Street is an interpretive centre of traditional and contemporary Irish music.

Classical Concerts
Bank of Ireland Arts Centre, Foster Place, Dublin 2, tel: 671 1488. Lunchtime concerts during summer months.
Hugh Lane Municipal Gallery of Modern Art, Charlemont House, Parnell Square North, Dublin 1, tel: 874 1903. Lunchtime classical concerts during summer months.
National Concert Hall, Earlsfort Terrace, Dublin 2, tel: 475 1572. Evening and lunchtime concerts.

Rock and Live Music
Break for the Border, Lower Stephen St Dublin 2, tel: 478 0300.
Bruxelles, 7 Harry Street, Dublin 2, tel: 677 5362.
The Mean Fiddler, 26 Wexford Street, Dublin 2, tel: 475 8555.
Olympia Theatre, 72 Dame Street, Dublin 2, tel: 677 7744.
The Point, East Link Bridge, North Wall Quay, Dublin 1, tel: 836 3633.
Red Box, Old Harcourt Street Train Station, Harcourt Street, Dublin 2, tel: 478 0225.

Vicar Street, 58–59 Thomas Street, Dublin 8, tel: 890 925 150, website: www.vicarstreet.com. Concert venue.
Whelan's, 25 Wexford Street, Dublin 2, tel: 478 0766.

Traditional Music
Clifton Court Hotel, O'Connell Bridge, Dublin 1, tel: 874 9869.
The Cobblestone, 77 North King Street, Dublin 1, tel: 872 1799
Comhaltas Ceoltóirí Eireann, 32 Belgrave Square, Monkstown, Co. Dublin, tel: 280 0295, fax: 280 3759. www.comhaltas.com. Music sessions on Friday and Saturday nights, and a free informal session on Wednesday nights. A *céilídh* (dance) is held on Friday nights throughout the year.
Fitzsimons, 21–22 Wellington Quay, Temple Bar, Dublin 2, tel: 677 9315.
Harcourt Hotel, 60 Harcourt Street, Dublin 2, tel: 478 3677.
Knightsbridge Bar, The Arlington Hotel, Bachelor's Walk, Dublin 1, tel: 804 9100.
Mother Redcaps, Back Lane, Christchurch, Dublin 8, tel: 453 8306.
Mulligans, 18 Stoneybatter, Dublin 7, tel: 677 9249.
O'Donoghue's, 15 Merrion Row, Dublin 2, tel: 661 4303.
Oliver St. John Gogarty's, 58–59 Fleet Street, Temple Bar, Dublin 2, tel: 671 1822.

Jazz & Blues
J.J. Smyths, 12 Aungier Street, Dublin 2, tel: 475 2565.
Sach's Hotel, 19–29 Morehampton Road, Dublin 2, tel: 6680995. Wednesday night and Sunday afternoon.
Sheehans, 17 Chatham Street, Dublin 2. Monday, tel: 677 1914
Tá Sé Mohogani Gaspipes, Manor Street, Dublin 7, tel: 679 8138.

Museums

Casino, Marino, off the Malahide Road, North Dublin, tel: 833 1618. Designed by celebrated architect Sir William Chambers in 1759, the Casino is considered one of the finest neo-classical buildings in

Europe and has a unique position in Irish architecture. Open daily June–September 10am–6pm, daily May and October 10am–5pm, November, December and February to March Saturday and Sunday noon–4pm, April Saturday and Sunday noon–5pm; admission fee. Access is by guided tour only. Relevant bus routes are 20A, 20B, 27, 27A, 27B, 42 and 42C from city centre bus stops located close to Busarus, and the 123 Imp Bus from O'Connell Street.
Dublin Writers Museum, 18 Parnell Square, Dublin 1, tel: 872 2077. An insight into literary Dublin with an exhibition of photographs, paintings, busts, letters, manuscripts, first editions and others memorabilia relating to writers such as Swift, Shaw, Yeats, O'Casey, Beckett, and Behan. Open Monday–Saturday 10am–5pm, Sunday 11am–5pm; admission fee.
The Findlater Museum, The Harcourt Street Vaults, 10 Upper Hatch Street, Dublin 2, tel: 475 1699. Situated in granite vaults, the museum traces the history of a Dublin merchant family over the past 170 years. Established by Alexander Findlater in 1823 as a wine and spirit merchant. Old Dublin is vividly recalled in photographs, labels, packaging, advertisements, and assorted memorabilia. Open Monday–Friday 9am–6pm, Saturday 10.30am–5.30pm.
Irish Jewish Museum, 4 Walworth Road, Portobello, Dublin 8, tel: 453 1797. Exhibition which traces the Jewish community in Dublin from 1890 to the present day; including memorabilia, books, photos and a selection of holocaust letters. A restored synagogue from the early 20th century is on view to visitors. Open May–September Sunday, Tuesday, Thursday 11am–3.30pm, October–April Sunday only 10.30am–2.30pm; free admission.
Marsh's Library, St. Patrick's Close, Dublin 8, tel: 454 3511. The first public library in Ireland was built in 1701 by Archbishop Narcissus Marsh (1638–1713) and designed by Sir William Robinson who also gave Dublin the Royal

Hospital Kilmainham. A magnificent example of a 17th-century scholar's library, the interior remains unchanged with dark oak bookcases and elegant wired alcoves where readers were locked in with rare books. Over 25,000 books relate to the 16th, 17th and early 18th centuries. Open Monday and Wednesday–Friday 10am–12.45pm and 2–5pm, Saturday 10.30am–12.45pm; admission fee.

National Museum of Ireland, Archaeology and History, Kildare Street, Dublin 2, tel: 677 7444. Collections consist of the Treasury, displaying artefacts from the Christian period; Viking Age Ireland, which traces the Vikings from their arrival in 795 AD; Or, which displays a fine collection of prehistoric gold in Europe. Other exhibitions include Ancient Egypt and The Road to Independence dealing with Irish history from 1916 to 1921. Open Tuesday–Saturday 10am–5pm, Sunday 2–5pm; free.

National Museum of Ireland, Decorative Arts and History, Collins Barracks, Benburb Street, Dublin 7, tel: 677 7444. Extension of the National Museum and located five minutes from Heuston Station. It houses the decorative arts collection of the National Museum and artefacts illustrating the economic, social, political, and military history of Ireland. Open Tuesday–Saturday 10am–5pm, Sunday 2–5pm; free.

National Print Museum, Garrison Chapel, Beggars Bush, Haddington Road, Dublin 4, tel: 660 3770. Located in a former soldiers' chapel and housing a unique colletion of implements, artefacts, and machines from all sectors of the print industry. Visitors can view the changes in printing from when each letter was assembled by hand to the development of Linotype machines which were operated by keyboard, up to present-day operation. Open Monday–Friday 10am–5pm, Saturday, Sunday and bank holidays noon–5pm; admission fee.

Natural History Museum, Merrion Street, Dublin 2, tel: 677 7444.

Zoological museum containing collections illustrating the wildlife of Ireland. There is also an extensive African and Asian exhibition. Open Tuesday–Saturday 10am–5pm, Sunday 2–5pm; free.

Newbridge House, Donabate, Co. Dublin, tel: 843 6534. Magnificent 18th-century manor set in 140 hectares (350 acres) of park land and featuring one of the finest Georgian interiors in Ireland. Open April–September Tuesday–Saturday 10am–5pm, Sunday and public holidays 2–6pm. October–March Saturday and Sunday only 2–5pm; admission fee.

Pearse Museum, St Enda's Park, Grange Road, Rathfarnham, Dublin 16, tel: 493 4208. Museum dedicated to the memory of Patrick Pearse (1879–1916), nationalist and educator who ran a school here from 1910 to 1916, the year he was executed for his part in the Easter Rising. Facilities include audio-visual show, self-guiding outdoor trail, nature study centre, and car/coach park. Open daily all year 10am–1pm and November–January 2–4pm, February–April and September–October 2–5pm, May–August 2–5.30pm; free admission.

Rathfarnham Castle, Rathfarnham, Dublin 14, tel: 493 9462. Conservation works are ongoing at this castle which was built around 1583 by Yorkshireman Adam Loftus. The castle has a colourful history and features 18th-century interiors by Sir William Chambers and James "Athenian" Stuart, and was declared a national monument in the mid-1980s. Open late spring–autumn 10am–5pm, summer 10am–6pm. Access by guided tour only; admission fee.

Shaw Birthplace, 33 Synge Street, Dublin 8, tel: 475 0854. The first home of Nobel prizewinner and celebrated playwright George Bernard Shaw has been restored to its Victorian elegance. On view is the parlour room, drawing room, maid's room, Bernard Shaw's bedroom and the nursery. Open May–September Monday–Saturday 10am–5pm, Sundays and bank holidays 2–6pm; admission fee.

Dublin for Children

Dublinia, St. Michael's Hill, Christ Church, Dublin 8, tel: 679 4611. Experience medievel Dublin in a reconstruction of life long ago in the restored Synod Hall. Attractions include tableaux, a merchant's house, a medieval pillory, a scale model of medieval Dublin with commentary, and a 17th-century tower offering a panoramic view of modern Dublin. Open April–September 10am–5pm daily; admission fee.

Dublin's Viking Adventure, Essex Street West, off Fishamble Street, Temple Bar, Dublin 8, tel: 679 6040. Explore Dublin's historical past aboard a Viking longship or by visiting Gioll Iosa's new stone church as he struggles to convert the Vikings to Christianity. Reconstruction of Viking Dublin featuring professional actors. Open April–September Tuesday–Saturday 10am–4.30pm; admission fee.

Dublin Zoo, Phoenix Park, Dublin 8, tel: 677 1425. Dublin's most popular children's attraction. The animals live in re-created natural habitats, with the African Plains spread over 12.5 hectares (30 acres). Exhibits include World of Cats, World of Primates and Fringes of the Arctic. The City Farm, where children can pet the animals, is a favourite. The zoo's conservation programme focuses on endangered species and returning them to the wild. Open March–October, Monday–Saturday 9.30am–6pm, Sunday 10.30am–6pm; November–February Monday–Saturday 9.30am–5pm, Sunday 10.30–5pm; admission fee.

Lambert Puppet Theatre, Clifton Lane, Monkstown, tel: 280 0974. A variety of shows to suit all ages. Regular Saturday and Sunday performances year-round at 3.30pm. Ring to confirm shows and times.

National Wax Museum, Granby Row, Parnell Square, Dublin 1. Tel: 872 6340. Over 200 figures, a hall of megastars, chamber of horrors, and adventure tunnels. Open Monday–Saturday 10am–5.30pm, Sunday noon–5.30pm; admission fee.

Activities

Walks and Tours

Bus Tours. Several companies operate hop-on, hop-off bus tours of the city on open-topped double-decker buses, which run at 15-minute intervals and link many of the main attractions. The ticket is valid for a full day, and is a good way to get around if you want to fit in several attractions, particularly outlying ones. These include The Dublin City Tour, operated by **Dublin Bus**, tel: 873 4222; The Dublin Tour, operated by **Irish City Tours**, tel: 401 1092, Website: www.irishcitytours.com; and **Guide Friday's** Dublin City Tour, tel: 676 5377. Tickets from Dublin Tourism Centre.

These companies also do tours to destinations further afield, such as County Wicklow and the north and south Dublin coast.

Cultur Beo on the Heritage Trail. Organised walks through the Dublin mountains and County Wicklow. Days, times and pick-up points differ according to the walks. For further information and bookings contact 459 9159, extension 134, 10am–5pm Monday–Friday.

Dublin Bike Tours. Three-hour guided bicycle tours of the city on quiet streets. Leisurely pace and lots of stops for places of interest. Meets at the front gate of Christchurch. Tours April–October, daily at 10am and 2pm. Tel: 679 0899, Email: dublinbiketours@connect.ie

Historical Walking Tours of Dublin. History graduates of Trinity College take you on a 2-hour tour of Irish history, from Dublin's beginnings through the War of Independence to the present day. Tours leave from Trinity College Front Gates. May–September, daily at 11am, noon

and 3pm; October–April, Friday–Sunday at noon. Tel: 878 0227, Website: www.historicalinsights.ie

Musical Pub Crawl. Led by two professional musicians, this 2½-hour tour visits famous pubs and bars in the Temple Bar area where you learn the story of Irish music and its influence in modern times. Tel: 478 0193, Website: www.musicalpubcrawl.com.

1916 Rebellion Walking Tour. Two-hour guided walk through the streets of Dublin which played a part in the Easter Rebellion of 1916 and the formation of the Irish Free State. Departs the International Bar, Wicklow Street, late April–September Monday–Saturday at 11.30am and Sunday 1pm. The tour returns to the bar for a few pints and a chat. Tel: 676 2493, Email: 1916@indigo.ie, Website: www.1916rising.com.

Viking Splash Tours. A land and water tour of Dublin in re-vamped World War II amphibious military vehicles. Tours leave from the gardens beside St. Patrick's Cathedral, and end in the Grand Canal Basin. Tours run every half hour from 10am–5pm, daily except Tuesdays from March–October (daily from mid-June–August), weekends only in November. Tel: 855 3000, Website: www.vikingsplashtours.com

The Zozimus Ghostly Experience. A walking tour of Medieval Dublin, as the ageing blind storyteller Zozimus leads you past the scenes of murders, great escapes and mythical events in the old city. Tours leave outside the main gate of Dublin Castle, every evening by appointment. Bookings essential, through the Dublin Tourism Centre or tel: 661 8646.

Literary Tours

Jameson Literary Pub Crawl. Find out which famous writer drank in which pub on this award-winning pub crawl run by professional actors who perform from the works of Irish writers. Takes place April–October nightly at 7.30pm, November–March Thursday, Friday and Saturday at 7.30pm, and on Sunday at noon and 7.30pm, starting from

the Duke Pub on Duke Street. Tickets available at the pub from half an hour before the tour. For more information, tel: 670 5602, Website: www.dublinpubcrawl.com.

Joycean Walking Tour. Tour of James Joyce's Dublin led by a member of staff of the James Joyce Centre. Tours leave at varying times from the centre at 35 North Great Georges Street, Dublin 1. There is a special Bloomsday tour on 16 June. Booking essential on 878 8547.

Literary Georgian Walking Tour. Run by the Dublin Footsteps Co-operative, this two-hour walk passes places associated with famous Irish writers such as Joyce, Yeats and Wilde, and also looks at the architecture and origins of Dublin's Georgian squares. Tours leave from the James Joyce room at Bewleys, Grafton Street, from June to September at 10.30am Monday, Wednesday, Friday and Saturday. No need to book. Price includes a cup of tea or coffee. Tel: 496 0641.

Calendar of Events

January
Races at Leopardstown, Dublin: top-class National Hunt (jumping) meeting.

Opening of Point-to-Point season: races run at different venues every Sunday over unfenced courses.

Aer Lingus Young Scientists Exhibition, RDS Showgrounds, Ballsbridge, Dublin.

Six Nations Rugby Championship (Ireland versus England, Wales, Scotland, France and Italy). Home matches at Lansdowne Road stadium (January/February).

February
Irish Motor Show, RDS, Ballsbridge, Dublin.

March
St Patrick's Day (17th), parades, street theatre, fireworks and funfairs are among the cultural and sporting events to mark Ireland's national day. Traditionally also a time to break the Lenten abstention from alcohol and "drown the shamrock".**March/April:** Dublin

Film Festival. Irish premieres of a selection of Irish and international cinema (March/April).

Opera Ireland Spring Season, grand opera performances, Gaiety Theatre (Easter).

The Irish Grand National (steeplechase) is held at Fairyhouse on Easter Monday. The Circuit of Ireland Car Rally takes place over Easter weekend.

April

Feis Ceoil, classical music festival competitions held at various venues, principally the RDS, Ballsbridge.

Messiah in the Street, Our Lady's Choral Society, one of Ireland's leading choirs, performs choruses from Handel's masterpiece on the anniversary – and at the site – of its 1742 première in Fishamble Street (13th).

June

Bloomsday, a celebration of James Joyce's greatest novel, *Ulysses*, held on the day on which it takes place, with readings, lectures, pub talks, picnics and outings in period costume (16th).

July

James Joyce Summer School, lectures and seminars in Newman House, St Stephen's Green, where Joyce studied as an undergraduate.

Laytown Races, horse racing on a County Meath beach, about 50 km (30 miles) from Dublin (July or August – the exact date depends on the tidal calendar.

August

Temple Bar Blues Festival, a weekend of music in the street.

Dublin Horse Show, RDS. Ireland's premier equestrian event, also an important social occasion.

Bray International Festival of Music and Dance. Three-day festival of Irish music and dance (early August).

September

Hurling and Gaelic Football: All-Ireland finals, Croke Park, Dublin

Dublin Fringe Festival. The Irish answer to the famous Edinburgh Fringe, with theatre, music, dance and other arts, for three weeks (late September).

October

Dublin Theatre Festival, mainstream and fringe Irish and international drama in venues all over the city.

Dublin City Marathon, international mass masochism.

Dublin Cat Show, RDS, Ballsbridge.

November/December

Opera Ireland Winter Season, grand opera performances, Gaiety Theatre.

Nightlife

Late Spots

The Irish have always had their priorities in the right order when it comes to having a good time and their fun-loving attitude can't help but rub off. The recent changes in the city's nightlife reflect the upbeat mood of a city experiencing an economic boom.

If you're under 30 years old and believe in having a good time, the chances are you've heard of Dublin's club scene. Much has been written internationally about how the city has begun to rival groovy European cities for exciting clubs. The reality behind the hype is improving all the time.

You don't have to dance till dawn. Visitors more sophisticated in years can enjoy late-night bars, cabarets, or smart nightclubs where tables positioned away from the dance floor allow for meaningful conversations.

Nightclubs

The Ballroom Nightclub, 21–22 Wellington Quay, Dublin 2, tel: 677 9315. One of Dublin's top clubs, located underneath Fitzsimons in Temple Bar. Guest DJs play a mix of pop, dance and chart music nightly.

Club M, Blooms Hotel, 6 Anglesea Street, Temple Bar, Dublin 2, tel: 671 5622. If you don't feel like posing and just want to bop the night away. City centre disco playing classic '70s and '80s sounds. Smart dress recommended.

Gaiety Theatre, South King Street, Dublin 2, tel: 677 1717. There's plenty of room to groove after midnight when this theatre turns into a nightclub. DJs and live music ranging from salsa to soul to swing,

Fridays and Saturdays from 12.30am until late.

The George, 89 South Great Georges Street, Dublin 2, tel: 478 2983. Probably the city's most popular gay club. The George pub from which the club gets it name is a favourite meeting place among gay men. Stylish dress.

The Globe, South Great Georges Street, Dublin 2, tel: 671 1220. Airy pub with modern decor. Laid-back during the day, when regulars come to play chess and read newspapers, but it becomes lively in the evening with good DJs keeping the beat going until it transforms itself into a nightclub after hours.

Howl At The Moon, O'Dwyer's, Lower Mount Street, Dublin 2, tel: 676 1717. Attached to a popular pub. Attracts punters who decide to keep the night alive as well as people on a serious night out. Classic sounds. Casual dress.

HQ at the Irish Music Hall of Fame, 57 Middle Abbey Street, Dublin 1, tel: 878 3345. Intimate venue that attracts an older crowd with classic rock and pop. There is a Soul Clinic on Friday nights; Viva! on Saturday nights is a salsa spectacular that features live music.

The Kitchen, The Clarence Hotel, East Essex Street, Dublin 2, tel: 677 6635. Attached to the Clarence Hotel, this is a cool hangout whose door policy isn't as strict as you might expect. Hip-hop, heavy rock sounds are enjoyed by a mainly young and trendy clientele. Trendy gear a must. Doors open 11pm.

La Cave, 28 South Anne Street, Dublin 2, tel: 679 4409. Cosy and compelling late-night venue which falls somewhere between a restaurant, wine bar and nightclub, although there's no dance floor as such. The soothing Latino sounds and intimate atmosphere mean this is a winner with thirty-somethings wanting to kick back. Smart dress.

The PoD, Harcourt Street, Dublin 2, tel: 478 0225. Ultra-hip club where everyone who is anyone in rock music, the media, and the world of modelling congregate. You probably already know to wear hip clothes.

Ri-Ra, Dame Court, Dublin 2, tel:

677 4835. Groovy club for babes with attitude and cool dudes. Funk, hip-hop, and audio-visual shows. As for clothes, the hipper the better.

Switch, Eustace Street, Dublin 2, tel: 670 7655. Powerhouse music and techno at this popular dance club beneath the Riverhouse Hotel in Temple Bar.

Temple Bar Music Centre, Curved Street, Dublin 2, tel: 670 9202. Live music seven nights a week and themed clubs, appealing mainly to a younger, teenybopper crowd. Screamadelica ranges from indie to metal to hip-hop, Salsa Villa on Tuesday nights, Soul Riot on Wednesdays.

Temple Theatre, Temple Street, Dublin 1, tel: 874 5088. Hip young club with student nights every Wednesday, R 'n' B spectacular every Friday at the Rhythm Corporation, house music in The Crypt, and top international guest DJs at sp@ce.

Late Bars

Late-night bars are a new phenomenon in Dublin thanks to revised – though still not exactly liberal – licensing laws. The following pubs are open on various nights, mainly weekends, until the crazy hour of 1.30am.

Bleeding Horse, 24 Upper Camden Street, Dublin 2, tel: 475 2705.

Conways, 70 Parnell Street, Dublin 1, tel: 873 2687.

Foggy Dew, 1 Upper Fowne's Street, Dublin 2, tel: 677 9328.

Hogans, 35 Great South Georges Street, Dublin 2, tel: 677 5904.

Mercantile Bar, 28 Dame Street, Dublin 2, tel: 679 8497.

Reynards, Setanta Centre, South Frederick Street, Dublin 2, tel: 677 5876.

Sinnotts, South King Street, Dublin 2. Tel: 478 4698.

Thomas Reads, 1 Parliament Street, Dublin 1, tel: 671 7283.

Turks Head Chop House, Parliament Street, Temple Bar, Dublin 2, tel: 679 2606.

Whelans, 25 Wexford Street, Dublin 2, tel: 478 0766.

Cabaret

Doyles Cabaret, Burlington Hotel, Upper Leeson Street, Dublin 4, tel: 660 5222. Cabaret inspired by the postcard image of Ireland; lots of pretty *cailins* doing Irish jigs and handsome men singing Celtic songs. A show with a certain charm for the mature and sentimental. Dinner can be included if you wish. Summer season Monday–Saturday.

Fonntrai, Culturlann na hEireann, Belgrave Square, Monkstown, Co. Dublin, tel: 280 0295. Show with a strong Irish flavour. Musicans, singers, storytellers and dancers entertain in the comfortable folk theatre. Runs during July and August Monday–Thursday. Also a *ceílídh* on Friday nights.

Jurys Irish Cabaret, Jurys Hotel, Pembroke Road, Ballsbridge, Dublin 4, tel: 660 5000. A strong accent on traditional Irish culture with dancers, singers and comedians. Likely to offer a good performance of *Danny Boy* before the night is over. Dinner included. Summer season, Tuesday to Sunday.

The Sugar Club, 8 Lower Leeson Street, Dublin 2, tel: 478 0012, Website: www.thesugarclub.com. A new multimedia theatre geared towards the over 25s with a vast range of entertainment from classic and cult cinema screening to international live music, comedy, live theatre, cabaret, burlesque etc. Check the programme before you go. Open 7 nights a week with a bar licensed until 2.30am.

Comedy

The Comedy Cellar, 23 Wicklow Street, Dublin 2, tel: 677 9250. Arrive promptly, as this small venue fills up early and the routines pull no punches.

The Ha'penny Bridge Inn, Wellington Quay, Dublin 2, tel: 677 0616. Comedy nights, along with some music and drama, on Tuesday nights from 9pm.

Murphy's Laughter Lounge, Eden Quay, Dublin 1, tel: 1-800-266 339. Dublin's first full-time comedy venue is proving successful since opening in 1998 in a disused cinema along the Liffey's northside quay. Top Irish comedians and international comics compete for the loudest laughs. Performances Thursday to Sunday inclusive.

Late-night Food

Beshoff's, 7 Upper O'Connell Street, Dublin 1. This cheerful fish-and-chip shop is a Dublin institution, and serves up the fresh catch of the day daily until 3am. Another branch at 14 Westmoreland Street is open until 3am on Friday and Saturday.

Bewley's Oriental Café, 78 Grafton Street, Dublin 2, tel: 635 5470. This branch of Dublin's famous coffee shop is open until 1am daily, and until 4am on Friday and Saturday. Although the late-night menu is limited, it's popular with clubbers.

Burdocks, 2 Werburgh Street, Dublin 8, tel: 454 0306. They're not called the best chips in town for nothing. Particulalry popular with the after-pub crowd. Open daily from noon–midnight.

Eddie Rockets, 77 Dame Street, Dublin 2, tel: 670 3893. Late-night revellers don't mind sharing a booth with strangers in this American-style diner. It's either that or queue even longer for the tasty barbecue chicken wings, hot dogs, chilli and burgers. Open till 4am.

Jury's Coffee Dock, Jury's Hotel, Pembroke Road, Ballsbridge, Dublin 4, tel: 660 5000. You'll never go hungry with this 24-hour coffee dock which despite its name serves an extensive menu in pleasant hotel surroundings. Friendly staff have the perfect indulgent touch for customers who are the worse for wear. Open around the clock.

McDonald's, 9 Grafton Street, Dublin 2, tel: 677 8393. Well-situated branch of the fast food outlet. Open daily till 4am.

Spar, 28 Westmoreland Street, Dublin 2, tel: 671 5923. Twenty-four hour convenience store offering everything from pastries, milk and fresh fruit, to magazines and toiletries

Shopping

What to Buy

Traditional crafts still flourish in Ireland, partly as a source of merchandise but partly out of a very Irish sense that the excellence cultivated by past generations is worth nurturing. Cut crystal, a craft which had just about died out, was resurrected in the 1960s and today flourishes in Waterford and elsewhere.

Ireland's internationally renowned wool textile industry has moved its emphasis from the old homespun, handwoven tweed to very finely woven scarves, stoles and dress fabrics. Linen and lace remain remarkably delicate.

Pottery has been fast developing as a craft industry, and new studios are opening all the time. Basket-weaving remains widespread and provides such souvenirs as table mats and St Brigid crosses.

While Irish crafts have always been well-made, they have not always been particularly fashionable. This is changing, with design improving by leaps and bounds. Whether buying for the wardrobe or for the home, the fashion-conscious will be pleasantly surprised at the variety of styles available nowadays in Irish tweeds, knitwear and linen.

The two main areas for shopping in Dublin are Grafton Street and its tributaries; and – less stylish but often better value – the Henry Street area, off O'Connell Street. Recent years have seen a major invasion of the city by British-based multiples such as Marks and Spencer, Boots, Debenhams and Habitat, and Dublin now retains only three indigenous department stores: Brown Thomas, on Grafton

Street; Arnott's, on Henry Street; and Clery's, on O'Connell Street.

Don't miss the Powerscourt Townhouse Centre, just off Grafton Street, an 18th-century mansion and courtyard converted into a stylish shopping complex with many crafts and antiques shops and several restaurants. The Kilkenny Shop on Nassau Street, a showcase for Irish crafts and clothes, is also worth a browse. On the same street, the Celtic Note record shop specialises in Irish music, and Blarney Woollen Mills and Kevin & Howlin stock classic Irish knitwear and tweeds. Just on the north side of the Ha'penny Bridge, Dublin Woollen Mills, stocks similar items at more reasonable prices. DESIGNyard, Temple Bar, sells innovative Irish and international jewellery and artefacts.

The antiques quarter can be found around Francis Street in the Liberties, but there are many other antiques traders, especially around the Liffey quays and on the small streets off Grafton Street.

If you're looking for food, there's an excellent range of Irish cheeses at The Big Cheese Company in Trinity Street; hard cheeses travel best. The Kilkenny Shop in Nassau Street has a selection of Irish-made jams, chutneys, cakes, biscuits and confectionery. Bewley's cafés sell attractive gift-packs of cakes, brack (a fruity loaf traditionally eaten around Hallowe'en), fudge, tea and coffee. Butler's Irish Chocolates in Grafton Street offers many delights for the sweet-toothed.

If you're interested in taking some Irish food home with you, smoked salmon is a good bet (but be sure it's labelled "smoked Irish salmon" as opposed to "Irish smoked salmon"). Air travellers can buy some at the Wrights of Howth shop in Dublin Airport.

VAT Refunds

Sales tax is included in the price of goods. Visitors from outside the European Union can claim a VAT (value added tax) refund on all goods bought in Ireland. Ask for a special VAT receipt when you purchase the goods, as a regular cash-register receipt may not be sufficient. This needs to be stamped at Customs in the airport and a cash refund will be given. The amount of VAT varies for different goods. Look for the Cashback logo in participating shops.

Shopping Hours

Most shops open Monday–Saturday 9am–6pm. City centre shops are open until 8pm on Thursday, while Friday is the late shopping night for suburban areas. Most shopping centres stay open late on other nights as well, and are also open on Sunday from noon to 6pm. Some city centre shops also have Sunday trading. Many small grocery stores are open until late at night and there are a few 24-hour shops.

Department Stores

Arnotts, 12 Henry Street, tel: 805 0400. A multi-million pound renovation has made this one of the most stylish stores in the heart of the city. Restaurants and children's play area.

Brown Thomas, Grafton Street, tel: 605 6666/679 5666. By far Dublin's poshest department store, stocking designer wear for both women and men, and with a children's department. Everything under one roof (except food) if you're in the mood to splash out.

Clery's, O'Connell Street, tel: 878 6000. One of the few remaining Irish-owned department stores in Dublin. Slightly old-fashioned, but with a wide range of Irish and international goods.

Debenhams, Jervis Street Shopping Centre, Mary Street, tel: 878 1222. Spanking new branch of the British chain store in the centre of Dublin. Excellent range of designer wear and household goods.

Dunnes Stores, St. Stephen's Green, tel: 478 0188 and Henry Street. Tel: 872 3911. Department store which prides itself as being within everybody's budget.

Marks & Spencer, 24 Mary Street, tel: 872 8833 and 28 Grafton Street, tel: 679 7855. Wide range of own-brand clothes in this high-street department store. Wonderful food hall.

Shopping Centres

Ilac Centre, Henry Street and the **Jervis Centre**, Mary Street, are two shopping enclaves north of the Liffey, with a range of shops selling clothing and home wares.

Old City Shopping District, Cow's Lane/Essex Street West. A new retail and commercial area in Temple Bar, with high-quality shops selling fashion, interiors, arts and crafts, etc.

Powerscourt Centre, William Street South. A stylish shopping complex built in a renovated townhouse, set around a spacious indoor courtyard. Three floors of boutiques, galleries and antiques shops, and several restaurants.

Royal Hibernian Way. A small outdoor arcade off Grafton Street, with upmarket shops selling menswear, women's fashions and chocolates.

St. Stephen's Green Shopping Centre, at the bottom end of Grafton Street, opposite St. Stephen's Green. Large modern indoor mall on three levels, with a vast range of clothing and gift shops.

The Westbury Centre, Harry Street. A smaller complex of shops adjoining the Westbury Hotel, selling clothes, lingerie and carpets.

Delicatessens

The Big Cheese Company, 14–15 Trinity Street, Dublin 2, tel: 671 1399. Exciting Dublin delicatessen offering a selection of amazing cheeses complemented by equally enticing wines. The type of delicatessen where you leave with olive oil and chocolate bars.

Caviston's, 59 Glasthule Road, Sandycove, Dublin 4, tel: 280 9120. Visit this seafood deli on an empty stomach and you'll end up in a state of dizzy confusion; the overwhelming temptations include a fresh fish and seafood counter, a cheese display, and any type of cooked meat you'd like to devour.

The Douglas Food Company, 53 Main Street, Donnybrook, Dublin 4, tel: 269 4066. Swanky deli offering freshly prepared meals to fit any occasion.

The Epicurean Food Hall, entrances at Lower Liffey Street opposite Ha'penny Bridge and at Middle Abbey Street opposite Arnott's. A galaxy of food, wine and coffee outlets, showcasing the best of Irish produce. Open 8am–8pm.

Magill's, 14 Clarendon Street, Dublin 2, tel: 671 3830. Offering produce from every corner of Ireland including cheeses, meats, and freshly prepared salads. Reflects the growing interest in international cuisine among locals in its interesting selection of imported goods.

Markets

George Street Market Arcade. A cheerful collection of stalls under an old-fashioned arcade, selling trendy fashions, second-hand books and records, collectables, candles, foodstuffs and gifts. You can even have your fortune told. Open daily.

Moore Street. Dublin's main fruit, vegetable and flower market is just off Henry Street. Open daily 10am–6pm.

Mother Redcap's Market, Back Lane. A weekend market (Friday–Sunday 11am–5.30pm) selling second-hand books and records, clothing, bric-a-brac and other goods.

Temple Bar. A small but popular food market selling organic produce and home-made goods sets up in Meeting House Square on Saturdays.

Irish Woollens and Knitwear

Avoca, 11–13 Suffolk Street, tel: 286 7466. The Dublin branch of this famous County Wicklow woollen mill has a beautiful range of scarves, sweaters and other goods in soft contemporary colours and designs.

Dublin Woollen Mills, 41 Lower Ormond Quay, beside Ha'penny Bridge, tel: 677 5014. A good range of traditional and fashionable sweaters, knitwear, shirts, kilts and shawls, at reasonable prices. Also table linen and blankets.

House of Ireland, 37–38 Nassau Street, tel: 677 7949. All the popular brands, from hand-knitted Aran sweaters to tweed jackets. Also Waterford crystal, china, linens, jewellery and crafts.

Kevin & Howlin Ltd, 31 Nassau Street, tel: 677 0257. Specialises in Donegal handwoven tweeds for both men and women. A great range of caps and hats, from the Great Gatsby to Sherlock Holmes to more traditional styles.

The Kilkenny Shop, 6 Nassau Street, tel: 677 7066. Irish woollens and knitwear in a good choice of contemporary styles. This shop also sells an excellent range of fine Irish crafts, from pottery and ceramics to hand-blown glassware and cut crystal, including Waterford and other well-known brands.

The Sweater Shop, 9 Wicklow Street, tel: 671 3270 and **Trinity Sweaters**, 30 Nassau Street, tel: 671 9543. A large selection of sweaters for men, women and children at good prices.

Irish Crafts

The Bridge Art Gallery, 6 Upper Ormond Quay, tel: 872 9702. The work of contemporary Irish artists is on sale here at competitive prices, from paintings and sculpture to hand-blown glass, ceramics and mirrors.

Crafts Centre of Ireland, St. Stephens Green Shopping Centre, Top Floor, tel: 4783122. A tasteful selection of traditional Irish goods and crafts.

DESIGNyard, 12 East Essex Street, Temple Bar, tel: 6778453. A vast collection of unique, contemporary jewellery by Irish and international designers. You can commission individual pieces. On the upper floor, the Craft Council of Ireland has a retail gallery where modern home furnishings and fashions are produced using traditional techniques.

Tower Craft Design Centre, Pearse Street, Dublin 2, tel: 677 5655. Monday–Friday 9.30am–5pm. Beautiful, contemporary crafts from jewellery and leatherwork to ceramics and artworks, purchased directly from the artists in their studios.

Whichcraft, Lord Edward Street, tel: 670 9371. Contemporary Irish crafts, focusing on the work of Irish artists, mostly from rural areas around the country. Ceramics, sculpture, metalwork, glass, wall hangings and jewellery.

Music Shops

The Celtic Note, 12 Nassau Street, tel: 670 4157. Stocks a wide selection of Irish music, from traditional ballads to contemporary artists.

Claddagh Records, 2 Cecilia Street, tel: 677 0262. Specialises in traditional Irish music, folk and ethnic music.

Waltons, 69–70 South Great George Street, tel: 475 0661 and 2–5 North Frederick Street, tel: 874 7805. Everyone from street buskers to rock stars buys their music gear here. Good range of Irish instruments, from whistles and pipes to fiddles, guitars and *bodhráns* (drum). Also CDs, music books and accessories.

Sport

Participant

Adventure Sports

Adventure Activities Ireland Ltd, 5 Tritonville Avenue, Sandymount, Dublin 4, tel: 668 8049. A range of adventure sports within a close range of Dublin, including Hillwalking in the Dublin and Wicklow mountains, canoeing and kayaking in Sandycove Bay and rock climbing in Dalkey Quarry. The Dublin Bay Sea Thrill, Carlisle Terminal Building, East Pier, Dun Laoghaire, tel: 260 0949, is like white-water rafting – only at sea. Wearing weather-proof sailing suits, passengers perch on the buoyancy tubes of marine rescue boats for the maximum wave-riding thrill. Operates from Dun Laoghaire to Dalkey Island and Killiney Bay.

Cycling

Cycling Ireland, 619 North Circular Road, Dublin 1, tel: 8551522. Dublin Bike Tours *(see Walks and Tours)*, tel: 679 0899, also offers bike rental.

Golf

Over 50 golf courses are within an hour's drive of Dublin. The biggest course in the country is Deer Park, Howth, tel: 832 2624. Comprising five courses. Golfing Union of Ireland, Glencar House, 81 Eglinton Road, Donnybrook, Dublin 4, tel: 269 4111. Irish Ladies Golf Union, 1 Clonskeagh Square, Clonskeagh, Dublin 14, tel: 269 6244.

Hill walking

Of the many walks around Dublin, the 132-km (82-mile) Wicklow Way, which runs from the southern suburb of Rathfarnham to County

Carlow, is the most spendid, and accommodation is available at An Oige hostels. An Oige, 61 Mountjoy Street, Dublin 7, tel: 830 4555. They also offer guided hikes of varying difficulty.

Horseriding

Bord Fáilte has a list of horse-riding schools close to Dublin. Try also the Equestrian Federation of Ireland, Ashton House, Castleknock, Dublin 15, tel: 838 7611. The Ashtown Riding Stables, tel: 838 3807 have horses and ponies for trail riding through Phoenix Park and can be reached by public transport. The Paddocks Riding Centre in Sandyford, tel: 295 4278. Has rides through woodland and mountain countryside overlooking Dublin City.

Sailing

Courses are offered year-round by the National Sailing School (tel: 284 4195) in Dun Laoghaire. Yacht clubs at Howth, Dun Laoghaire, Malahide and Clontarf have reciprocal arrangements with clubs in other countries. Contact the Irish Sailing Association, tel: 280 0239 for details.

Surfing

For information on surfing on the east coast contact Irish Surfing Assocation, Murray House, Easkey, Sligo, tel: 096 49428.

Tennis

Tennis Ireland, Dublin City University, Glasnevin, Dublin 9, tel: 668 1841.

Swimming

There are several public swimming pools near the city centre. Try Sean McDermott Street, tel: 872 0752 and Marian Pool, by the Lansdowne Road Rugby Stadium, tel: 668 9539. A variety of beaches, easily accessible by DART train, include the shingle ones at Killiney and Bray and the sandy ones at Sutton, Malahide and Donabate.

Spectator

Gaelic Football

Cumann Luthchleas Gael, Croke Park, Dublin 3, tel: 836 3222. This now houses a museum devoted to the history of this uniquely Irish sport.

Horse-racing

Dublin's Leopardstown racecourse is south of the city centre on Leopardstown Road in Foxrock, tel: 289 3607. Races are held year-round, usually at the weekends. The country's major racecourses are west of the capital in County Kildare, including the Curragh, where the Irish Derby is held, Naas and Punchestown

Rugby

Irish Rugby Football Union, 62 Landsdowne Road, Ballsbridge, Dublin 4, tel: 668 4601.

Soccer

Soccer Football Assocation of Ireland, 80 Merrion Square, Dublin 2, tel: 676 6864.

Further Reading

Non-fiction

Not all the books below are currently in print, but there's a good chance of finding them in one of Dublin's well-stocked second-hand bookshops.

Architecture of Ireland. Maurice Craig. Batsford.
As I Was Going Down Sackville Street. Oliver St John Gogarty. Sphere.
Book of the Liffey from Source to the Sea. Edited by Elizabeth Healy. The Wolfhound Press.
Concise History of Irish Art. Bruce Arnold. Thames & Hudson.
Destruction of Dublin, The. Frank McDonald. Gill & Macmillan.
Dictionary of Irish Biography. Henry Boylan. Gill & Macmillan.
Dublin. Peter Somerville-Large. Hamish Hamilton.
Dublin's Churches. Peter Costello. Gill & MacMillan.
Dublin's Famous People: Where They Lived. John Cowell. O'Brien Press.
Dublin: Portrait of a City. Peter Zöller and John McArdle. Gill & MacMillan.
Dublin 1660–1860. Maurice Craig. Penguin.
Easter Rebellion, The. Max Caulfield. Gill & MacMillan.
Encyclopaedia of Dublin. Douglas Bennett. Gill & MacMillan.
Georgian Dublin, Desmond Guinness. Batsford.
Heritage – a Visitor's Guide. Edited by Eilis Brennan. Office of Public Works.
How the Irish Saved Civilization. Thomas Cahill. Doubleday.
Ireland and the Irish: Portrait of a Changing Society. John Ardagh. Penguin.
Ireland – A History. Robert Kee. Weidenfeld.
Irish, The. Sean O'Faolain. Penguin.
Irish Theatre, The. Christopher

FitzSimon. Thames & Hudson.
James Joyce. Richard Ellman.
Oxford University Press.
James Joyce's Odyssey – A Guide to the Dublin of Ulysses. Frank Delaney. Hodder & Stoughton.
Joyce's Dublin: A Walking Guide to Ulysses. J. McCarthy. Wolfhound Press.
Literary Guide to Dublin. Vivien Igoe. Methuen.
Lost Dublin. Frederick O'Dwyer. Gill & MacMillan.
Making of Modern Ireland. J.C. Beckett. Faber.
Our Musical Heritage. Sean O'Riada. Dolmen.
Penguin Book of Contemporary Irish Poetry. Edited by Derek Mahon and Peter Fallon. Penguin
Traditional Music in Ireland. Tomas O'Canainn. Routledge & Kegan Paul.

Fiction

A Portrait of the Artist as a Young Man. James Joyce. Penguin.
At-Swim-Two-Birds. Flann O'Brien. Penguin.
The Book of Evidence. John Banville. Warner.
The Commitments. Roddy Doyle. Minerva.
Dubliners. James Joyce. Penguin.
The Ginger Man. J.P. Donleavy. Abacus.

The Journey Home. Dermot Bolger. Penguin.
The Leavetaking. John McGahern. Faber.
Mrs Eckdorf in O'Neill's Hotel. William Trevor. Penguin.
Ulysses. James Joyce. Penguin.

Other Insight Guides

Nearly 200 **Insight Guides,** companions to the present title, cover the world, complemented by more than 100 **Insight Pocket Guides**, which highlight a local author's recommendations and contain a full-size map, and more than 100 **Insight Compact Guides**, handy and inexpensive books for use on the spot.

Insight Guide: Ireland covers in detail the history, culture, people, places and attractions of the entire island, both North and South, with superb photography.

For those on a tight schedule, *Insight Pocket Guide: Ireland* sets out 17 timed itineraries designed to make the most of your visit. It contains recommendations from a local expert and has a full-size fold-out map showing the itineraries.

Insight Pocket Guide: Ireland's Southwest takes the same approach to the top tourist region of Cork, Killarney and Kerry.

Insight Compact Guide: Ireland, *Insight Compact Guide: Dublin* and *Insight Compact Guide: The West of Ireland* are the ideal pocket reference works to carry with you as you explore. Text, pictures and maps are all carefully cross-referenced for ease of use. Great value.

ART & PHOTO CREDITS

INSIGHT GUIDE
DUBLIN

Editorial Director **Brian Bell**
Cartographic Editor **Zoë Goodwin**
Design Consultants
Carlotta Junger, Graham Mitchener
Picture Research **Hilary Genin**

Index

Insight Guides Website
www.insightguides.com

Don't travel the planet alone. Keep in step with Insight Guides' walking eye, just a click away

Insight Guides Website

Insight Guide
South Africa

This 370-page book includes a section detailing South Africa's history, 22 features covering aspects of the country's life and culture, ranging from living without Apartheid to spectacular wildlife, a region by region visitor's guide to the sights, and a comprehensive Travel Tips section packed with essential contact addresses and numbers. Plus many quality photographs and 15 maps.

UK: £16.99 ISBN: 981-234-223-0
US: $22.95 ISBN: 0-88729-445-6

(Note: cover shown may differ in some markers.)

Close Window